KU-517-498

KA 0084658 9

WITHDRAWN FROM
THE LIBRARY

UNIVERSITY OF
WINCHESTER

TURNING POINTS IN RELIGIOUS STUDIES

TURNING POINTS IN RELIGIOUS STUDIES

ESSAYS IN HONOUR OF GEOFFREY PARRINDER

Edited by
Ursula King

T&T CLARK
EDINBURGH

T&T CLARK
59 GEORGE STREET
EDINBURGH EH2 2LQ
SCOTLAND

Copyright © T&T Clark, 1990

T&T Clark is an imprint of Harper Collins Publishers

All rights reserved. No part of this publication may be reproduced,
stored in a retrieval system, or transmitted, in any form or by any means
electronic, mechanical, photocopying, recording or otherwise,
without the prior permission of T&T Clark.

First published 1990

ISBN 0 567 09564 9

British Library Cataloguing in Publication Data
Turning points in religious studies.
I. Academic Study of World Religions
II. Christian religious education
III. British higher education
I. King, Ursula
207

KING ALFRED'S COLLEGE
WINCHESTER

207
KIN   00846589

Typeset by Barbers (Highlands) Ltd, Fort William
Printed and bound in Great Britain by Billing & Sons Ltd, Worcester

The essays in this volume are published on the occasion of Professor Geoffrey Parrinder's eightieth birthday and are dedicated to him by his friends, former colleagues and students.

CONTENTS

PART II: TURNING POINTS IN THE DEVELOPMENT OF SOME ACADEMIC SUBJECTS AND THEMES

THE STUDY OF INDIAN RELIGIONS

THE STUDY OF AFRICAN RELIGIONS

THE STUDY OF SIGNIFICANT THEMES

PART III: POINTERS TO NEW DIRECTIONS

APPENDIX:

FOREWORD

Archbishop Desmond Tutu, Cape Town

I was privileged to have Professor Geoffrey Parrinder as one of my teachers when I studied for the BD at King's College, University of London, in the 1960s. He subsequently supervised me for the MTh degree. He impressed me with his warm generosity of spirit, helping his students to have a broad ecumenism that welcomed the insights of those of faiths other than their own. I am grateful for having thus been prepared for the cultural and religious pluralism so characteristic of our times. It is a singular honour to have been asked to write a foreword to this richly deserved publication in his honour.

Archbishop Trevor Huddleston CR, President of the Anti-Apartheid Movement based in London, a few years ago organised a successful Interfaith Colloquium Against Apartheid whose participants were adherents of the major religions. He has suggested to the writer that in the area of justice and human rights issues the different religions should concentrate on their doctrines of creation rather than, for instance, on their soteriology. He contended that they would find that if they did this, they had a remarkable degree of consensus, whereas their different soteriologies proved notoriously divisive. It is not necessary to agree in every detail with his thesis to see that he has an important point, especially when we consider the religious anthropology of the different faiths. The three monotheistic religions (Islam, Christianity and Judaism) have a high doctrine of humankind – that each person is created in the image of God and for that reason has an immeasurable worth. Hinduism and Buddhism regard human persons as aspects of the divine if they would but recognise it, destined in the end to be reabsorbed into a higher, transcendent reality. You cannot be reunited with that from which you are fundamentally alienated a priori, with that with which you are fundamentally at odds.

This high view of human beings found in most of the major religions explains why their adherents are usually strongly motivated to struggle for the observance of human rights and why they usually are so vigorously opposed to injustice and oppression as a matter of religious duty. None of these religions at their best would declare that injustice is praiseworthy nor would inhumanity to our fellow humans be something that they did not condemn out of hand.

Nearly all these religions would claim that their adherents are constrained by religious imperatives to be concerned about their everyday life, that this should in some way be seen as consistent with the tenets of their faith. They are exhorted to engage in the exhilarating enterprise of seeking to transform the world they inhabit so that its conditions of life for those inhabiting it approximated the ideal as nearly as possible, however that ideal was conceived. Any religion that was too otherworldly would be in danger of being jettisoned for seeking to provide pie in the sky when you die – too heavenly minded to be of any earthly good – and would justify the Marxist jibe of being an opiate for the people.

Politicians are usually aware of how potent religion is as a motivating force. It is thus not surprising that many try to coopt religion to sanctify their political solutions and policies, or they try to relegate it to the realm of the nebulous which they call the spiritual in their dichotomising zeal, stridently criticizing anyone who had the audacity to want to mix religion with politics.

We who are engaged in the struggle for justice, peace and equity in places such as South Africa know ourselves to be inspired not by political or any other kind of ideologies. No, we are set on our path and maintained there by our religious beliefs which say human beings count enormously. That this world is not meant to be a hostile environment for God's human and other creatures, that adequate housing, clean water supplies, adequate health and education services, proper sewerage, clean air, and an unpolluted atmosphere and rivers, a just economic order, an end to the arms race, unemployment, sexism, racism and justice and peace – that these are not merely secular concerns. They are fundamentally religious issues and challenge religious women and men precisely because they are religious, to be concerned about them.

TRIBUTES TO
PROFESSOR GEOFFREY PARRINDER

A PERSONAL TRIBUTE TO AN OUTSTANDING CAREER

John R. Hinnells

Born in New Barnet in 1910, Geoffrey Parrinder began his theological studies at Richmond College, London, in 1929. A speaker from the Methodist Mission House inspired him to respond to the call for people to serve in French West Africa. In order to develop French for this work, he studied in Montpellier for a year (1932–33) before moving to the Séminaire Protestant at Porto Novo in Dahomey in September 1933. Four months later he moved to the Séminaire Protestant in Dabou on the Ivory Coast where he remained for a year. In 1935 he worked on the Grand Lahou Circuit of the Ivory Coast for thirteen months. He was ordained in 1936, the year in which he also married Mary. From then until 1940 he again served in the Séminaire at Porto Novo. While he was visiting England, Dahomey was occupied by Vichy France, so that Geoffrey was unable to return there. He worked instead on the Circuit in Redruth in Cornwall from 1940–43. During the 1940s, first in Cornwall and then back in West Africa and from 1946–49 in the French Circuit in Guernsey, Geoffrey pursued his academic studies with vigour. He took London BA and BD degrees externally, proceeded to MA, MTh, PhD, and wrote some of his early books, for example *West African Religion* and *Learning to Pray*, both published in 1949. From 1949–58 he was Lecturer, then Senior Lecturer, in Religious Studies at University College, Ibadan, in Nigeria, the first appointee there in this subject. Similarly, he was the first person to be appointed with a title in the Comparative Study of Religions at Kings College, London, when he was given the post of Reader in 1958. Innovation has, therefore, been an important dimension of his career. While still in Ibadan he completed his work for his DD. The flow of books continued through the 1950s focusing at this stage of his career on African religions and resulting in *West African Psychology* (1951), *Religion in an African City* (1953), *African Traditional Religion* (1954), *Witchcraft* (1958), *The Story of Ketu* (1956).

Before and after his move to Kings College he began to widen his literary horizons, first in the field of Islam, inspired by his contacts with Muslims in West Africa, and then Hinduism for which he studied Sanskrit at the School of Oriental and African Studies, London. Both interests resulted in publications, for example *Jesus in the Koran* (1965) and a translation of the *Bhagavadgita* (1974).

Geoffrey's work is characterised by a firm self discipline, evident both in his vigorous pursuit of academic training through his external degree studies and his sense of responsibility in publishing his studies for a wider readership. In his work he has taken the title of 'The Comparative Study of Religions' seriously, not as in the superficial, generalising approach of earlier generations, but a careful thematic approach as in his *Avatar and Incarnation*, (the Wilde Lectures in Natural and Comparative Religion delivered at Oxford between 1966 and 1969), *Worship in the World's Religions* (1961) and *Sex in the World's Religions* (1980). A further characteristic of his work has been a sensitivity to religious experience. He was active in the Methodist Church until he retired from the ministry in 1972. For some writers such an active commitment to one faith has conditioned their perception of others, but from his earliest writing through to the present he has shown a concern for an empathetic approach which gives value to the serious understanding of another's faith (see for example his first published article on 'The Christian attitude to non-Christian religions' in *The Expository Times*, June 1939, and his more recent book *Encountering World Religions*, 1987).

National and international honours indicate the respect in which he has been held by his peers. He was Secretary for many years and then President of the British branch of the International Association for the History of Religions and President of the London Society of Jews and Christians; he was awarded a DLitt from Lancaster University in 1975. At an international level he was the Charles Strong Lecturer in Sydney in 1964; the Teape Lecturer in Delhi and Madras in 1973, and was Visiting Professor at the International Christian University, Tokyo, in 1977–78.

In his writing and in his lectures Geoffrey has a capacity to convey complex thought forms which are new to his audience in a manner that is at once enlightening and interesting. The elegant grace of his style and courtesy of manner raised the interests of many who were new to the subject. My own experience was typical of many. In the 1960s there was little support for, or interest in, the Comparative Study of Religions, especially in the conventional theological atmosphere as then pervaded Kings College, London. To be frank, my own motivation for studying the subject was no more honourable than timetable convenience. But the quality of the teaching, the evident fascination for the religions, the interest and feelings evinced by the man, his obvious dedication to the subject, proved infectious and resulted in me, like many others, pursuing the subject further, many of us for the rest of our lives. His lectures, like his writing, have a clarity and simplicity which belie the profundity of the thought.

Geoffrey Parrinder has been an inspiration to a wider audience than students at Kings. As a founder member and later Vice President of the Shap Working Party on World Religions in Education he has been an active worker for the spread of the subject at all levels of education. His papers for Shap courses, his wise counsel in deliberation and his encouragement of those new to the subject have had a ripple effect throughout the educational system. His influence has spread wider still. His books have been translated into 12 languages and he, as much as anyone, has been alert to the need to spread understanding of diverse races and religions to the general public. To this end he has written such books as *Asian Religions* (1957 and 1975) and edited the Hamlyn Encyclopaedia, *Man and his Gods* (1971). Through his ministry in the Church he has sought to spread sympathy and understanding to people from many walks of life.

Geoffrey's literary and academic contribution to the Comparative Study of Religions has been manifold. Others better qualified than I have assessed his work on African Religions, particularly Andrew Walls and Harold Turner in the volume of the journal *Religion* (X, 1980) dedicated to Geoffrey. In particular they note his long-term deep involvement in several types of African religion; his concern to identify patterns of similarity and difference and hence to pursue a *comparative* approach based on first hand knowledge and experience; his innovative categorisation of African hierarchy which influenced many who followed him; the formative nature of his work (especially *African Traditional Religion*, 1954) for the study of religion across the African continent, encompassing detailed local studies in a broader scale, as has been done for India, but rarely for Africa. Among the numerous writings which have flown with grace from his pen creative ideas have been generated which have still not been followed. His study *Religion in an African City* (1953) surely points to an important route still needing to be pursued, that is looking at religions not simply as 'isms' in a vacuum, but rather interacting forces in a specific city. His mention of art as a focus for the study of religion merits far more notice than it has yet received. In his writing and in his teaching he has been a significant force for scholarly good.

The 1970s and 1980s have seen a surge of interest in world religions. The foundations for the subject's expansion were laid by a small group of labourers such as E. O. James, G. S. F. Brandon, and not least Geoffrey himself. But unlike the others he continued to be active into the 1980s, so that he has been reponsible for both the foundations and the development of the edifice of the building of Comparative Religion. Few individuals have facilitated the development of the subject as he has, and it is an honour for those of us involved in this volume to pay fulsome tribute to Geoffrey Parrinder as scholar, teacher, friend and guide. To see what a person is really like, it is important to observe what happens around him or her. Around Geoffrey there is a wide circle of warm friendships, active study, a sensitivity to the views of others, a compassion and at all times a lively, invigorationg interest.

SOME PERSONAL RECOLLECTIONS
OF A COLLEAGUE

Maurice Wiles

Good colleagues can make all the difference to the experience of taking up a university position. And when that position is one's first, in a foreign country and in a very small department, their significance is greatly enhanced. So when I began my career as a university teacher in 1955 by becoming the third member of staff in the Religious Studies Department at University College, Ibadan (as it then was), I was remarkably fortunate to find Geoffrey Parrinder as my immediate senior colleague.

Ibadan was the first, and at that time still the only, university institution in Nigeria. It had attracted an interesting staff, made up of many nationalities. Most of us had come with no first-hand knowledge of Africa. There was a handful of exceptions, of whom Geoffrey was one of the most notable. Although only in his mid-forties at that time, he had begun to work in Africa as John Hinnells' account of his career describes, over twenty years earlier. He had come to Ibadan in 1949, the first appointment to the Religious Studies Department, and had already made a notable contribution to building it up into a department with a well thought out syllabus and high standards. But he did not live simply on the laurels of the length of that experience. When the rest of us were taking a well-earned siesta in the hot, steamy Ibadan afternoons after a morning's work which might well (and wisely) have begun with a lecture at 8.00 a.m., Geoffrey was sometimes to be seen setting off, immaculately turned out in white shirt and shorts, with those characteristically long strides, quick but un-hurried, for the city of Ibadan. This was one of the ways in which he built up his wide knowledge of contemporary African religious practice, reflected particularly in his *Religion in an African City*. It is an indication too of the strong sense of dedication and persistence that lies behind the remarkable achievement of working his way through the whole gamut of academic degree from BA to DD while doing full time pastoral or academic work, mostly in West Africa.

But it was not only encouragement of academic endeavour that Geoffrey provided as a colleague by his example; it was also enhancement of the enjoyment of the job by his gift for friendship, his unfailing kindness and good humour. The hospitality of his home, to which Mary contributed so much, was never found waiting. There one could be sure, not only of receiving the long and welcome cool drink, but also of hearing the latest anecdotes about the doings of the country or of colleagues. They would be told with a mischievous sense of amusement, always without trace of malice, and accompanied by the appropriate gradation of laughter, somewhere on the scale from conspiratorial chuckle to loud-ringing laugh.

Perhaps that particular combination of personal traits was well suited to the task that needed doing in building up the work of Religious Studies in West Africa at that time: plenty of hard work and patient observation; indefatigable curiosity about and endless fascination in the behaviour patterns of men and women; a tolerant amusement at the strange forms those behaviour patterns can sometimes take in religious practice. But that tolerant amusement was never dismissive. Religious practice was always to be taken seriously, if not too solemnly. And that was very true of his own religious practice. Our co-operation was not confined to the classroom. As Methodist and Anglican we shared (together with our Presbyterian professor, Allan Galloway) in looking after the splendid interdenominational Chapel of the Resurrection. The religious co-operation was as free from any trace of strain as was the academic. His generous, open and informed investigation of religious practice went hand in hand with an equally generous, open and informed practice of his own religious life and ministry.

We had three years together in Ibadan, and were to become colleagues again nine years later in more serious positions in the much bigger establishment of King's College, London. The setting and the seniority might have changed; and the range of Geoffrey's academic expertise had grown to encompass a much wider range of religious phenomena. But the man himself had changed remarkably little. The same characteristic way of moving, the same characteristic laughter were well in evidence – as they still were more remarkably another twenty years on when we last met a few months ago. His good humour and capacity for harmonious working relationships were not a little tested at that time in the establishment of a distinct department of Religious Studies alongside the existing Faculty of Divinity (with its own peculiar combination of Anglican college and non-confessional university appointments). With a foot in each camp Geoffrey not only kept his characteristic evenness of temper in a sometimes fraught atmosphere, but showed the importance of those personal attributes towards the resolution of academic conflict.

As I have known Geoffrey as a colleague, he has contributed much not only to the substance of the study of religion as his writings bear witness, but also by his person to the spirit in which it has been studied. This volume bears eloquent testimony to the continuing growth in our knowledge about the religions of the world. It is to be hoped that students and practitioners of those religions will have a share also of that spirit which has so consistently informed Geoffrey's study of them and his life.

A PERSONAL TRIBUTE

An unfinished piece by John Ferguson (+ 1989)

It is right to begin from the personal, for Geoffrey Parrinder is a highly personal as well as a highly personable man. At or near 80 with his erect bearing, his noble white hair, his warm smile, his magnetic eyes, he is a handsome and attractive figure. Those who know him only through his books may be awed by the breadth and depth of his learning; yet it is so greatly and easily communicated that something of the man himself shines through. Those who know him personally think of him first as a friend.

I met him first at what was then University College, Ibadan, in Nigeria in 1956. He was one of the early members of staff in Religious Studies, and had swiftly been promoted to Senior Lecturer. With James Welch (previously a notable head of religious broadcasting with the BBC) he had helped to build up a notable department as part of a notable university institution. At the same time they had helped to create one of the most remarkable university chapels in the world, the Chapel of the Resurrection. The material building was designed by Geoffrey Pace, based on a catenary curve, and well symbolizing a cave-tomb, with a disturbing cross casting strange shadows on a curving plain white reredos, a splendid place to worship Sunday after Sunday. Welch and Parrinder, with the support, from 1954, of Allan Galloway (later Professor at Glasgow) who succeeded Welch and whom Parrinder helped immensely, and from 1955 of Maurice Wiles (later Regius Professor at Oxford), succeeded in peopling this chapel with an interdenominational Protestant fellowship of rare quality, to whom faith meant much and denominational differences little.

I was eleven years Geoffrey's junior; more, he had been in West Africa on and off (more on than off) since 1933. I well recall the personal warmth of his welcome, the careful guidance (always sane) which he offered but never imposed, above all the friendship he and Mary gave to us as to many others.

Geoffrey left Ibadan in 1958 to become Reader in the Comparative Study of Religions in the University of London, becoming Professor twelve years later. I was at Ibadan for eight more years, followed by three in the United States. We encountered one another again in 1969 at that remarkable body, the London Society for the Study of Religion, founded in 1904 by Von Hügel and the elder Montefiore to bring together Catholics, Protestants and Jews. I found him unchanged, warm and wise and rich in friendship, and there and elsewhere we have remained in close fellowship. He is a man of firm and eirenic temper. I have never seen him ruffled. He knows where he stands, but he is the least authoritarian of people. I cannot forbear one bonhomous comment. When I joined the LSSR in the 1950s, in the discussions I would be ranged with the nonconformists in friendly debate with the Catholics, but at dinner I quaffed wine with the Catholics while the nonconformists sipped their orange juice: the Jews, I fancy, did all things in moderation. But in the 1970s I found the Catholics sipping their orange juice, and Geoffrey and I rivalled one another for the last glass of claret – strictly under control, it is to be understood.

Geoffrey was on the staff of King's College, and a remarkable staff they were, many of them members of the LSSR. I was delighted reading Shirley de Boulay's *Tutu: Voice of the Voiceless* to find this of Tutu's time at King's in the mid-1960s: 'Being a multi-faculty college where students had contact with other disciplines, it was more alive to the outside world than many universities, becoming a magnet for overseas students and boasting teaching staff of the calibre of Professor Ulrich Simon and Professor Geoffrey Parrinder.' They were indeed outstanding, but there were others too. It was in 1962, the year of Tutu's arrival, that they were joined by Christopher Evans, a New Testament scholar of quicksilver mind, and Eric Mascall, a man of massive learning and great personal grace, author of the influential *He Who Is*. What a team – and how they stimulated one another!

ESSAYS ON
TURNING POINTS IN RELIGIOUS STUDIES

GENERAL INTRODUCTION

Ursula King

A turning point implies a significant breakthrough, a new development or a change in direction. Such breakthroughs and changes occur in many different fields of endeavour, but it is often only possible in retrospect to recognise the most significant changes which have shaped the future course of events. Today, when higher education and so many aspects of academic life are under scrutiny and threat, it is important to take stock and enquire into recent developments in our own area of concern, the study of religion in its widest sense.

Such study has a long history, but at the present moment it seems appropriate to look especially at the last thirty years or so, for the multidisciplinary approaches associated with the field of Religious Studies found wider recognition from the 1960s and 1970s onwards when the term 'Religious Studies' came first into general use. During that time many new departments of Religious Studies were founded in universities and colleges, and old ones were renamed. The study of religion had begun much earlier, but the new interests in Religious Studies brought about a reorientation and created new perspectives which led to some significant institutional and academic developments, to new research, new publications and to wide popular interest. These influenced all sectors of education from schools to colleges and universities.

During most of this period Geoffrey Parrinder was actively engaged in teaching Religious Studies, first in Africa and later at King's College, London. His writings are widely known, and many are his former students and colleagues who have benefited from his teaching and research. At the current moment when so many changes and new developments are occurring, not least the general contraction of higher education, it is important to reflect on the state of Religious Studies and its relationship to religious education and interfaith praxis, especially in the light of the Education Reform Act of 1988 which has led to much heated debate.

We are living at a time which may again prove to be a turning point for Religious Studies in its significance for education and the wider debates of contemporary society. What will the future bring? How important is this rich area of studies for schools, colleges, universities and also for the growing field of adult and continuing education? Looking back we discern past directions and can assess what has been accomplished; looking forward we can ask ourselves which current developments may be of particular significance for the future. It is time to chronicle events as well as to examine ideas about Religious Studies in the British educational scene and relate these to developments elsewhere by setting them within a wider global context.

This volume does not claim to be an exhaustive study of all aspects of Religious Studies, but it attempts to highlight significant historical developments and themes. The following essays are grouped into three parts. The essays in the first part look at historical developments in Britain and chronicle the institutional growth of Religious Studies in the universities of England, Scotland and Wales, including the important developments at the Open University, in polytechnics and colleges of higher education as well as in adult and continuing education. These essays represent pioneering surveys, for such historical accounts are found nowhere else. They show how much the course of Religious Studies and the history of its programmes have been intertwined with, and often curtailed by, earlier institutional developments in the study of theology, so that it has often been difficult to maintain the distinctiveness of Religious Studies.

The essays also indicate how recent cuts have had a proportionally larger detrimental effect on areas of Religious Studies than on traditional theology subjects, yet the four academic journals in Religious Studies, founded during the last twenty five years, have been able to establish themselves firmly and continue to flourish. The wide ramifications of Religious Studies cannot be fully understood without looking at the closely associated developments in religious education and practical issues in interfaith dialogue which several essays address. They also raise the question of how far some recent legal changes which affect the provision of RE teaching in schools may eventually prove to be a backward rather than a forward turning point in the development of Religious Studies.

Whilst the essays in the first part survey the significant points of growth, orientation and changes in Religious Studies which have occurred in different areas of education and interfaith praxis over the last thirty years or so, those in the second part examine turning points in the development of some academic subjects and themes. The principle of selection has been to choose some of the themes and religious traditions where Geoffrey Parrinder's own work is of particular significance, especially the study of Indian and African religions, and the themes of dialogue and mysticism.

The third, concluding part highlights recent developments which point to new directions in Religious Studies. Here some areas of major significance have been selected which promise new insights and orientations for Religious Studies, not only in Britain, but globally. The importance of the arts, of gender, and of the new opportunities of information technology for the future study of religion are discussed at length. No doubt some readers can think of additional aspects not covered here which have promising implications for Religious Studies. Not only is it impossible to be comprehensive but also perhaps less important than to be stimulating and innovative. Whilst the earlier course of Religious Studies was sometimes influenced by a missionary agenda, as several essays in this volume demonstrate, the contemporary geo-political situation has changed so profoundly that the study of religion at all levels can only be carried out satisfactorily if undertaken in a global perspective, given the need for more information, explanation and understanding at all levels of society. This volume concludes with the innovative proposal to form a global umbrella organisation for Religious Studies, a 'World Academy of Religion'. It will have to be seen whether this suggestion will fall on fertile ground and possibly lead to yet another turning point in the future.

Several of the essays are closely interlinked and overlap in some of their concerns. For this reason the arrangement into three different parts may occasionally strike the reader as artificial. All contributors have surveyed particularly significant turning points in their own subject area which also point towards promising developments for the future. Friends, colleagues and former students are offering these essays as a tribute to Professor Geoffrey Parrinder who throughout his long career has been closely involved with the development of Religious Studies. This has been largely at university level, but through his writings and lectures, his wide experience of examining, his active involvement with religious education and interfaith matters, he has also had close contact with and influenced Religious Studies at many other levels of the educational system. The range of his influence is perhaps nowhere more evident than in the large number of his publications, many of which have been translated into other languages. This rich harvest of a long and deeply satisfying scholarly career is documented for the first time in the Bibliography in the Appendix to this volume.

If I may end on a personal note, I first heard Geoffrey Parrinder speak on BBC radio in the mid-sixties, giving a talk on the Bhagavad Gita. However, I did not meet him personally until 1969 when we both attended a Sikh conference in the Punjab and spent a day travelling together with a small band of scholars along many miles of dusty lanes through Punjabi villages to visit Sikh shrines. Little did I know then that he would be the supervisor of my doctoral research on my return to London, a supervisor who gave me much encouragement throughout my work. Nor did I foresee then that one day I would edit this celebratory volume on the occasion of his eightieth birthday, a collaborative effort made possible by all the contributors of this volume. Thanks are due to all of them as well as to the publishers who showed much patience during the gestation period of this work. Last but not least I want to thank Alma Dorndorf and Vicki Jones from the University of Bristol for all their help in the final preparation of the typescript. Without them, and the help of many others, it would have been impossible to complete this book.

PART I

HISTORICAL DEVELOPMENTS IN BRITAIN

1. RELIGIOUS STUDIES IN THE UNIVERSITIES
ENGLAND

Adrian Cunningham

The study of religion in English universities over the past twenty five to thirty years has undergone a transformation. There has been far more change than might have been predicted but, in 1990, the situation is one of stasis. The process of development has been frozen and the outcome is unclear.

In the mid-1950s there were no more than sixteen people in English universities teaching religions other than Christianity. In 1990, all of the sixteen relevant departments include at least an option in another tradition, either taught within the department or drawing upon a cognate department or school of, say, Middle Eastern or oriental studies. Whilst there are only two departments described simply as 'Religious Studies' (Lancaster and Newcastle), another eight now have 'Religious Studies' as part of their title.

The emergence of Religious Studies as a university subject in the mid-1960s was controversial and the relations between it and theology often polemical. The polemical atmosphere is now largely something of the past, but with the university system in an, at best, static state after contraction over the last ten years, older, conservative patterns are still strong. The development of Religious Studies was only possible in a period of expansion of universities. To *add* the study of Hinduism, for example, to a mainly Christian theological syllabus was an exciting possibility, a step towards a fuller study of religion. In a contracting situation such a Hinduism specialist will tend to be professionally isolated, and if they were to move or retire, there is a strong temptation to 'consolidate' the more established fields of study, in other words, revert to the *status quo ante*.

It was not untypical in the 1950s for undergraduates to spend ninety per cent of their time on events, texts, persons and languages up to the fifth century CE. One reason for this restricted emphasis was the heritage of nineteenth century battles over theology as a university subject. What was basically an Anglican-informed subject in both concern and personnel, needed simultaneously to justify itself in a secular university world, and to open itself to non-Anglican (but still Protestant) academics and students. One way of doing this was to emphasise the impeccable linguistic, historical and ancient textual credentials of the subject. The result was paradoxical: the church affiliation of staff and students permeated the departments, but the syllabus was supposed to be neutral. Important and lasting scholarly work was done, the syllabus had coherence and clear definition, but the greater part of Christian history was excluded and contemporary theological debate only part of the syllabus in so far as it could be located in the ancient materials. Some degree of change in this constricting framework occurred with the small but significant increase in philosophy of religion in English universities in the 1950s.

The development of Religious Studies was both fuelled by frustration with the old patterns and, in turn, contributed to their re-thinking. Indeed, it can be argued that only in a multi-religious context can there be wholly open and vital appreciation of contemporary theological issues.

Some of the great changes of the last quarter of a century are irreversible. Only two posts in the country still remain tied to church appointments, and the inclusion of modern (i.e. nineteenth to twentieth century) critical theological and philosophical debate will not be gone back on, but the further extension of specifically Religious Studies has still to be secured.

Institutional Development

Issues of definition and history here are complex. If one is thinking of individuals in universities who helped create the field, then one would obviously look to Friedrich Max Müller as an outstanding example. He was responsible for the 1849–62 Sanskrit text of the *Rig Veda* and the editorship of the fifty volume series of *Sacred Books of the East*. His 1873 *Introduction to the Science of Religion* can be taken as the 'foundation document of comparative religion' (Eric J. Sharpe: *Comparative Religion, a History*, London, 1977: 35). His Oxford post, however, was in modern languages and he was defeated in the contest for the chair of Sanskrit in 1860 partly on the grounds of his religious liberalism.

If one is thinking of courses for students under the actual title of comparative religion, then one would look to Unitarian and Congregationalist theological colleges with John Estlin Carpenter in 1876 at Manchester College (then in London) and A. M. Fairbairn at Mansfield College in Oxford in 1886.

If, however, one is thinking of university departments, then 1904 is the key date with the Manchester Department of Comparative Religion. Once again, a free church influence, in this case Methodist, was significant. The Victoria University had been established in 1880 with constituent colleges in Manchester, Leeds and Liverpool, these becoming separate universities in 1903. Twenty years of opposition to theology in the Victoria University was overcome – Liverpool has never had a department, and that at Leeds was not instituted until 1933. Manchester became the first theological faculty in Europe to require every student to take at least one course in comparative religion, although on the other hand it did not teach history of doctrine or systematic theology. J. G. Frazer declined the offer of the chair and the first incumbent was the Pali scholar T. W. Rhys Davids. When Leeds did establish a chair, it was with E. O. James in History and Philosophy of Religion, the department being called, from 1936, Theological Studies, later Theology, finally becoming Theology and Religious Studies in 1974.

Whilst theological study in the ancient universities had been pursued since their foundation, the first named university posts were the readerships (later chairs) endowed by Lady Margaret Beaufort at Oxford in 1502, and Cambridge in 1503. The Theological Tripos as such at Cambridge dates from only 1879, becoming the Theology and Religious Studies Tripos in 1975. Oxford remains a Faculty of Theology with recognized courses taken in oriental studies. The Spalding Chair of Eastern Religions and Ethics, occupied from 1936 by Radhakrishnan, Zaehner, and Matilal is attached to the Oriental Faculty.

Of the nineteenth century foundations, King's College, London, was an Anglican counterbalance to University College (1827), the only institution of university status to which non-Anglicans could apply but which did not develop theology. King's had a theological department from 1846. With reorganization of the University of London in 1908, the Dean of Theology became Principal of the College. E. O. James took the chair in History and Philosophy of Religion in 1945. Eleven years later some related posts in the Faculty of Arts (including that held by Geoffrey Parrinder) were for the first time funded by the University Grants Committee rather than Anglican sources and by 1969 there was a Faculty of Theology alongside the original department. With reorganization in 1979 there were three wholly UGC funded departments within a renamed Faculty of Theology and Religion. King's represents a whole gamut of changes in university developments, becoming in 1984 a single

Department of Theology and Religious Studies in a newly formed School of Humanities.

Although theology had been taught at Durham since the inauguration of the university college in 1832, a specific faculty of theology dates from 1890. With separation of Newcastle-upon-Tyne as a wholly autonomous university in 1963 Durham retained a faculty containing a single department, until the latter's transfer to the Faculty of Arts in 1985. The department has kept the title Theology, drawing upon courses in Buddhism, Hinduism, and Islam in the university.

Manchester apart, the next significant developments came after the First World War. At Birmingham from the 1920s courses in Hebrew, Theology, and Ecclesiastical History taught in neighbouring theological colleges were recognized within the universities arts faculty. Although theology became a degree, there were no university staff as such until the funding from Quaker sources of a chair in 1940, taken by H. G. Wood, and the subsequent development of a department. Nottingham's department of theology dates from 1930 and Leeds, as indicated, from 1933.

Post World War Two, Exeter had a department of theology from 1945 (the degree being titled Theological Studies from 1984), followed by Hull, and, in 1947, Sheffield with a Department of Biblical History and Literature (since 1968, Department of Biblical Studies) with particular concentration upon Judaism.

Whilst there were a few chairs in the fields variously called comparative/eastern/history of/religions in English universities, in the 1950s the undergraduate subscription was low. Significant change did not come until the latter part of the 1960s. At the new University of Lancaster the department was the first to be established, in 1967, as one of Religious Studies and remains the only one in which all the major historical traditions and social scientific and other approaches are taught within a single department. It is this combination and scale which distinguishes it from comparative religion or history of religions – the terms need not otherwise be all that different. Newcastle-upon-Tyne having been previously Divinity, then Biblical Studies, also became a Department of Religious Studies in 1967. Bristol opened as Theology in 1965, becoming Theology and Religious Studies in 1970. The new University of Kent's Board of Studies in Theology, dating from 1969, became that of Theology and Religious Studies in 1989.

The pattern of 1960s expansion and 1980s contraction is dramatically illustrated in the cases of Southampton and Leicester.

Southampton degrees were until 1963 formally degrees of the University of London and for some twenty or thirty years students had been able to study theology topics within the BA General Degree. From 1963 there was a Southampton degree in Theology, a Board of Theological Studies and one full – time appointment. The Department of Theology and the Study of Religion opened in 1965 with the appointment of Howard Root to a chair in theology. Work in Islam and Judaism was developed, but the hoped for second chair in religion never came and the department was closed on Professor Root's retirement in 1981. The university still validates a flourishing BTheol degree for the associated colleges, but the continuing work in Theology and Religious Studies as an ancillary BA subject will cease with the retirement of the remaining member of staff. At Leicester work started as a programme of studies within the Department of Philosophy from the appointment of Harold Turner in 1966, and Peter McKenzie in 1970. This was the only one of the English departments to take the simple title, Religion. It ran from 1977 until Dr McKenzie's retirement in 1989. This was not only a loss to the diversity of activities that make any university worthy of the name, at the practical level Leicester's distinctive work in phenomenology of religion and on Australian and North American materials will not be covered elsewhere.

The variety of terms and changes of titles baldly summarized here point to the extreme difficulty with which attempts at an open and full study of religion in English universities developed in this century.

Institutionalization

The formation of a new academic area of study is enormously exciting and creative. In this context to consider the *institutionalization* of Religious Studies as a serious issue may sound a little deadening, but it bears upon the seriousness with which teachers, students, and the wider world take a subject. An example may help here. Religious Studies has more intellectual coherence than psychology often has in the university, for it can be hard to see what connects the study of rodent brains and that of inter-personal relations, except that these are the kinds of things that departments of psychology actually do and are generally expected to do. The loose intellectual coherence of university psychology to the innocent outsider is acceptable largely because it has a good seventy years of history behind it, fairly obvious career paths for its students, and well-organised professional affiliations for its practitioners. Religious Studies, by contrast, is still a relatively young subject. It has to maintain both contact with and distance from theology or oriental studies. It has to be a bit careful, as well as constructive and inventive, in its involvement with particular religious bodies, in say, clergy education, or in its connection with specifically English questions of religious education in schools.

The creation of the subject drew upon people with diverse specialisms, and this has given it a great deal of energy. It is, however, only when enough people with an education in Religious Studies are employed in the university teaching of it that the subject starts to get a clear autonomous profile and leaves behind the vestiges of negative definitions – 'not just philosophy of religion', etc. It is good, indispensible indeed, that people with a background in, for instance, oriental languages, come to work in departments of Religious Studies. It is even better when people with a first degree in Religious Studies go on to do research degrees involving oriental languages, and then take university teaching posts. The same is true of biblical and theological, or any other division, of enquiry into religion. The next turning point will only come when the preponderant influence in university departments is exercised by a generation that has, even to a limited degree, experienced work of a Religious Studies kind as part of their own undergraduate education.

On students themselves there is no useful data for the English universities as a whole which would enable one to identify, for instance, demand for specifically Religious Studies courses within predominantly theological departments. One can only say that applications for both Religious Studies and theology remain buoyant. More impressionistically, there used to be some distinct clusters discernible in Religious Studies applications of which two might be rather crudely called 'world travellers' and 'monoglot evangelicals'. On the one hand there were applicants in their mid- to late-twenties who had spent some time in Asian (and to a less extent Middle Eastern) countries before coming to university. On the other hand there were more standard eighteen or nineteen year old applicants who might, initially at least, have preferred to take a more wholly biblical or theological degree, but lacked the aptitude for languages that was more frequently required fifteen or twenty years ago than it is now. The mixture of these two constituencies was highly educational for all concerned. The former might often be quite ignorant of even those broad features of Christian belief which could be thought to be part of the general culture of an English university student, but brought with them a lively experience of Asian contexts and not just texts. The latter might have considerable difficulty in facing problems for their own position posed by the study of traditions other than Christian, or indeed other Christian ones than theirs. In the last few years, with the growth of a more conservative or even fundamentalist caste among many young Christians, the picture has changed somewhat. The more fundamentalist-inclined student might well keep clear of Religious Studies or theology altogether as problematic subjects permeated by disturbing if not false modes of thought. If such a student does take up studies of this kind they may actually show a *preference* for Religious Studies courses, trying to keep the potential threat of uncongenial biblical or directly cognate work to a minimum, and feel far more at ease studying non-Christian traditions. The complexity of the subject matter is reflected in those who pursue it! Postgraduate Religious Studies work generally has been prolific in this period, and remarkably so in the study of Indian religions. Although numbers are small as yet, the presence of indigenous Islamic, and to a much lesser extent Hindu, students, more women perhaps than men, is starting to become apparent both as graduates and undergraduates.

In terms of career, which can be another index of the institutionalization of a subject, the data are again both limited and scattered. Not surprisingly, those entering church or other ministry are a smaller percentage than they would be in a traditional theology department. Approximately fifty per cent go into education of primary, secondary and tertiary kinds. A further fifteen to twenty per cent go into 'caring professions', quite often working with the physically or mentally handicapped, and a roughly comparable number go into management, the Civil Service, or commercial careers. The generally increased flexibility of the fit between specific university qualifications and future career has definitely benefited continuing recruitment to Religious Studies as a university subject.

The Situation in 1990

A significant development of recent years has been the formation of an Association of University Departments of Theology and Religious Studies (AUDTRS). This built upon informal contacts between Northern universities in the first round of government cuts in university funding in 1981, and all departments in mainland Britain are, in 1990, directly or indirectly represented. There was already in existence the Institute for Religion and Theology, which covered both Britain and Ireland, but it was felt that a more active and clearly university-based association was needed for the specific task of responding to and resisting the erosion of academic posts which was particularly severe in the humanities. The Department of Theology at Southampton had already been closed and the Religious Studies programme at Sussex discontinued some years earlier. The loss of the Leicester department and contraction at Hull means that, despite some relevant work at Warwick, Religious Studies in English universities is very weak in the middle and central areas of the country, areas which have large Hindu and Muslim constituencies, and significant Sikh and Jain ones. (Birmingham's Selly Oak colleges fall outside the brief of this survey). The situation in other English universities is not, at present at least, so dire, but the distortion of syllabuses following the freezing or deletion of appointments will be with us for some time to come. The activities of an association of this kind are obviously limited, but the pooling of information and expertise has for the first time built up a reasonably detailed profile of the various subject specializations and, as importantly, brought departments of very different complexions into a common forum.

In the period of UGC subject reviews and reorganizations in the late 1980s there was considerable discussion in AUDTRS about the desirability of some regrouping of dispersed Religious Studies specialists within 'mixed' departments into stronger regional centres. The transfer of staff between universities can obviously involve considerable family strain and the combination of theological and Religious Studies is often very fruitful but, from the point of view of the vitality and strength of the area as a whole, this missed 'opportunity' under severe pressure is something we may very well come to regret.

Fairly detailed information exists on the work of fourteen of the English university departments of Theology and/or Religious Studies. This gives a useful index of the growth of Religious Studies. In terms of courses offered, either within the department itself or by arrangement with a cognate department, traditional areas not unexpectedly predominate: Christian theology, biblical studies, church history, and philosophy of religion. Judaism also comes towards the top of the list but this may be misleading, for it is sometimes taken as equivalent to the study of Christian Old

Testament, and in only a very few and recent instances is it studied as a living tradition. In the second rank of undergraduate coverage, and this is the major change, now come Islam, followed by Hinduism and Buddhism. In the third rank come areas like ethics, liturgy and, of more relevance for the general health or otherwise of Religious Studies, work in anthropology, psychology (represented in only four universities) and sociology of religion. I shall return to this point.

The inclusion of at least minimal opportunity to study aspects of traditions other than Christian in most university departments is a major advance. As noted at the outset, however, the development has been uneven and enormous areas like Africa, and 'gaps' the size of the Orthodox churches in Christianity, or Catholic theology, are not much better represented than they were thirty years ago. Judged against the minimal requirements for a well-rounded study of religion, there is still a daunting way to go.

Criteria for Religious Studies

What are the basic minima for a decent university programme in the study of religion? I would suggest that there are three. There are many more desirable, indeed necessary things, but without these connected three we are certainly engaged in patchwork. First, such a programme is concerned with an aspect of human experience and in that respect is more like the study of economics or politics than it is like the study of German literature or Greek history. Religious institutions, texts, practices, beliefs, and experiences are the core preoccupation of our study. Secondly, because it is aspectual, the study of religion in the university cannot be bound to one tradition alone. The absolute minimum in a department is acquaintance with more than one tradition to generate reflexion upon the extreme differences and occasional similarities between religious systems which are today in perhaps more visibly extensive contact and conflict than at any time in the past. Thirdly, because it is aspectual and concerned with many traditions, the study of religion is multi-disciplinary, drawing upon a variety of methods. Linguistic, historical, and philosophical skills have always been used, within and between traditions, but in the contemporary world these have to be supplemented by methods taken from anthropology, psychology and sociology, to name the most obvious lines of enquiry, if we to start making sense of the data with which we are presented.

It may seem odd not to have included the term 'comparative

religion' in the minimal requirements for the study of religion. Comparative religion, as we have seen, has an honourable history in England and is the term many people would use conversationally for Religious Studies. This title too has an honourable, if brief, history, although perhaps 'religious' may still carry hints of its earlier usage to describe adherents, and of the ambiguities of 'religious education', and it would be better for the university area to be simply called 'religion'. In practice, very little work of a properly comparative kind was actually done in the past – the label often meant simply that something other than Christianity was being studied, in which case 'history of religions' might have been more accurate. It is still true that specifically comparative work is very underdeveloped. The mere juxtaposition of teaching in Buddhism and Judaism, say, is in no way a comparative exercise, especially when the diversity of periods and topics studied in each is more than likely to make any effort at comparison meaningless in practice.

Of classic English themes for comparative study, sacral kingship and sacrifice are less in evidence these days, but work on issues of suffering and death in religions, and the general issue of myth, remain steady. New areas, with a significant contempoary emphasis, are emerging in the study of spirituality, of fundamentalism, and of new religious movements in the West. In the convenient hindsight of 1990, the most striking gap in the Religious Studies agenda of the mid 1960s is the very topic of 'Women and Religion'. The issues involved here cut across most of the previously accepted teaching curricula and research fields, and may eventually turn out to be the greatest turning point of all in the study of religion.

Being female is, of course, not a prerequisite for engagement in these issues, but they would have got on to the agenda, to the very small degree that they have, sooner if there were more women professionally engaged in the university teaching of religion, or religions. Amelioration, let alone progress, in this respect will probably take us beyond the millennium.

From what has gone before it is clear that Religious Studies has so far been something between a fundamentally transforming agent and a useful irritant in academic work on religion in England. In the immediate future it is improbable that any further major change can come, as it did before, from the expansion of the university system as a whole. Any further expansion is likely to be governed by short-term pragmatic interests blind to the long, medium and short-term influence of religious factors in the shaping of the contemporary world. The scope for development of the Religious Studies approach over the next five to ten years will probably depend upon debate within what is roughly the present constituency of university teachers.

Regardless of the people available to do the job, which is a pretty crucial factor, the greatest need for a well-rounded, or more than adequate, study of religion, lies in the direction of the social sciences. We should not necessarily expect any major single development in sociology of religion, to take one case, of the kind that produced the fruitful, if faulty, secularisation hypotheses of the 1960s. Nor should one expect, desirable although it might be, that anthropological and psychological work on religion would transform the understanding of what it is to understand a society, as was the case with Durkheim and Freud early in this century. Changes of that scale are not a subject for prediction. Instances of a different kind of study, internationally, would include the work of William A. Christian Jr. and of Victor and Edith Turner on pilgrimage, of Peter Brown or Wayne Meeks on early Christianity, and of Richard Gombrich on Buddhism.

In pointing to anthropology, psychology and sociology (and the increasing emphasis upon contemporary issues by people teaching in Religious Studies confirms this) I suggest that it will become more and more difficult to follow standard modes of enquiry inherited from the past to deal with our subject matter adequately. The past strengths of the university study of religion have primarily been textual and philosophical; to some extent they have been historical but often in what now seems a rather narrow history of ideas way. Over the last two decades it has become more difficult to sustain the idea that what we are dealing with are intellectual or credal systems to which there is *also* a social dimension. What we are dealing with, surely, in the first instance, are the interactions between religion and other practices and beliefs in particular social contexts. The social study of religion, in narrow or wide senses, is the locus of our work and not an optional extra. The time in which we can convincingly speak of 'a religion' as if it were an entity primarily located in doctrines and texts is starting to run out. The next turning point in matters of intellectual integrity, coherence and excitement should occur under the different pressures coming from the social sciences and the diverse energies engaged in the issues of women and religion.

SCOTLAND

Andrew F. Walls

The Study of Religion as an Export Industry

Until the 1960s the production of Religious Studies in Scotland was rather like that of Harris tweed: a small-scale industry, soundly based, distinctively local, and essentially for export.

These features are seen in those Scots who were among the pioneers and builders of the discipline. William Robertson Smith would never have become a founding father in anthropology and the comparative study of religion but for the learned demands of the Free Church ministry; yet the process brought about his ejection from his Church chair at Aberdeen, and a life of exile in Cambridge. It was the friendship of an Edinburgh lawyer, J. F. McLennan, that had awakened the young Aberdonian Hebraist to the wider implications of his study of the religion of Israel. McLennan integrated the study of kinship and marriage, and of totemism, into the history of religion, but then spent his later years drafting Parliamentary legislation. Robertson Smith in turn infected a young friend of his own, J. G. Frazer, the son of a blameless Glasgow chemist; but it was in Cambridge that the Golden Bough sprouted.

Healthy academic disciplines need demolishers as well as builders, and Scotland produced the most accomplished wrecker of the earlier period of the autonomous discipline of Religious Studies. Andrew Lang's prickly independence, his preparedness to experiment on new frontiers, his insistence on facing inconvenient evidence, make him the great iconoclast of his generation. He lashed evolutionism in a period when it appeared to have achieved the status of 'assured results', while lacerating also the constituency to whom his conclusions were most welcome ('mostly idiots', he decided cheerfully). And he could satirize fashionable transcendentalism with these lines, headed simply 'Brahma':

> *I* am the batsman and the bat,
> *I* am the bowler and the ball,
> The umpire, the pavilion cat,
> The roller, pitch, and stumps and all.

But the imagery gives away the provenance. Lang was soaked in the atmosphere of the Scottish Borders where he grew up; but his literary career was in Oxford ('a dismal ante-room') and Kensington.

One might have expected some effects in Scotland from the special status of the missionary movement there. Perhaps Scotland's most important contribution to the missionary movement was its lack of inhibitions about learning. That fact had the potential to transform the whole of Scottish scholarship, sacred and profane, by opening to systematic plunder the quarries of non-western religion and literature which the missionary movement had uncovered to westerners. In the event, the impact was muted. Alexander Duff's vision of a chair of missions provided for study of 'the mythological systems, superstitions and distinguishing characteristics of the leading branches of the family of man', but his presentation of such topics as professor at New College, Edinburgh, was not such as to create mass enthusiasm for the subject. The University of Aberdeen and the London Missionary Society combined to produce James Legge, the greatest sinologist of the nineteenth century, and John Nicol Farquhar, the most comprehensive western historian and commentator in the field of Indian religious literature. Neither returned to Scotland; when the long years in China and India were over, Oxford and Manchester provided the scholarly sustenance. A. G. Hogg, one of the most interesting of all the missionary explorers of inter-religious relations, certainly spent his last years in Scotland, but the ecumenical jet age had hardly dawned by the time of his death, and the full significance of his work was not by then recognized. There was no shortage of scholarly missionaries. Duff MacDonald's *Africana, or the heart of heathen Africa* might be claimed as the first systematic and sympathetic account of the religion of an African people; and there was an abundance of interpreters, of varying quality, of Indian religion, philosophy and devotion. Where such names were widely known in Scotland, however, as in the case of Nicol MacNicol, it was usually on the ground of their popular works about the contemporary scene. And it may be significant that the Scottish theologians most interested in other faiths, such as A. M. Fairbairn and A. E. Garvie, belonged to minority churches and devoted their teaching careers to England.

The large secular Scottish diaspora also seems to have had a rather limited reflex effect on Scottish intellectual life. The major exceptions came from the enterprise of the learned Indian civilians John and William Muir. John founded a chair in Sanskrit at Edinburgh. His brother, already the author of the standard study of Muhammad in English and of the history of the early caliphate, was Principal of that University from 1885 to 1905. Although since the 1960s the various 'oriental studies' components, all small in themselves, that arose in

Edinburgh (where 'The Muir Institute' still exists) have contributed significantly in the development of Religious Studies, this seems to have been a rather late growth. Arabic has often appeared in the syllabuses of the four older Scottish universities; yet it was commonly an adjunct of the Hebrew chair, the central concerns of which lay in divinity teaching. At Edinburgh, where Arabic had an independent existence, the work of Richard Bell furnished new materials for the serious study of the Qur'an and extended the study of early Islamic history, foreshadowing the contributions which were to come from his successor, W. Montgomery Watt. But in the period before the second world war, even in the Arabic field, Scotland's most important contribution to the study of the religious aspects of the topic was exported. Duncan Black MacDonald (1863–1943) went to teach in America when not yet thirty. That was to lead to influential works on Muslim theology, fine contributions to the *Encyclopaedia of Islam*, above all the Kennedy School at Hartford Seminary Foundation in the days of its glory. It needed New England to provide the conditions for the germination of Glasgow seed.

Thus the best early Scottish work in Religious Studies, whether in building, demolition or roadmaking, went out of Scotland. Only in the academic equivalent of town-planning was there a major Scottish indigenous achievement. A Free Church of Scotland minister, James Hastings, backed by a Scottish publisher, T. and T. Clark, conceived and brought to birth the *Encyclopaedia of Religion and Ethics*. Hastings never held an academic post.

Conditioning Factors in Scotland

There are often structural reasons for stoning the prophets. How far this was the case in Scotland is hard to determine. It is easy to blame the divinity faculties. Each of the four ancient universities – St Andrews, Glasgow, Aberdeen and Edinburgh – provided for the teaching of divinity; and (a situation rather different from England) the universities undertook the entire training of the ministry of the national church. The division of that church in the middle of the nineteenth century produced duplicate theological faculties in Edinburgh, Glasgow and Aberdeen, to serve the Free Church. At the reunion of the churches in 1929 these colleges were absorbed into the university faculties which were consequently somewhat enlarged. The faculties were viewed as providing a professional ministerial training for candidates who had already received a liberal university education.

Similar conditions on the continent did not inhibit the development of *Religionswissenschaft* in the universities, and, even in Scotland, the exclusion was never total. Where the professor was so minded, the courses of apologetics or philosophy might be turned in this direction; and Allan Menzies, Professor of Biblical Criticism at St Andrews, produced a *History of Religion* (dependent on Tiele, Chantepie and others) which had thirty years of life in four editions. But the subject never became a firmly entrenched part of a regular curriculum, nor one likely to be taught by a specialist. As the patterns of study in the humanities changed, divinity professors sometimes saw their role as closer to that of their medical colleagues than to those in the humanities.

Occasionally someone sought to promote an alternative framework for the study of religion. The best known is the foundation of the Scottish judge, Adam Gifford (died 1887), who established a lecture series, open to the public, on 'Natural Theology' to be given at all four universities. He desired the subject to be taught like chemistry or mathematics, which presumably meant, *not* like divinity. Lord Gifford's stated desires, however, have always been hard to translate into academic discourse, and have been subject to generous interpretation. While, therefore, lecturers have included Max Müller and Andrew Lang in earlier days, and Åke Hultkrantz and Raimundo Panikkar in our own, there was room in between even for Karl Barth. Another attempt to break new ground was made by William Riddoch, who left the residue of his estate to found a lectureship, and ultimately a chair, in comparative religion at Aberdeen. Riddoch indicated his desire (he did not make it a condition) that the resultant comparative religion course should both be available to arts students, and required for all divinity students. The bequest was notified in the middle of the Second World War, and then seems to have dropped out of sight; at any rate, no one held a regular appointment as Riddoch Lecturer until the Department of Religious Studies was independently created in 1970.

Even after the second world war, therefore, the Scottish academic scene presented a single institutional approach to the study of religion. The divinity faculties were confessional, professional and post-graduate; essentially preparing men for entry to one of the learned professions; belonging fully to the university and yet closely related to the church. The four faculties offered very similar patterns of study; the Plan of Union of 1929 had indicated that there were five principal branches of divinity – viz., Old Testament, New Testament, church history, systematic theology and practical theology. In a less

institutionalized form, certain types of religious question might figure
largely in the logic and moral philosophy courses that were part of
the staple diet of the average arts student; in the presence of an A. E.
Taylor or a D. M. Mackinnon they could hardly be ignored.

Scotland up to this time simply had not known the conditions that
produced the firmly secular tone of those English universities which
embargoed the teaching of theology or defused it of any dogmatic
content. Nor had it known that separation of university and church
which in England and Wales produced degree courses in theology
not directly related to ministerial preparation. In England and Wales,
dogmatic or ecclesiastical issues could be thought divisive, and
church-related matters could be left to the theological college. The
desire to demonstrate the validity of the subject as a liberal and
academic discipline led to the development of the theological degree
as a sort of 'Sacred Greats', stressing biblical languages and literature,
and historical and philosophical studies. It was in this context that
what was the commonly called comparative religion first developed.
In Scotland there was no obvious space for it to take root.

In the decade after the war some of the universities did institute
lectureships in biblical studies (not in the divinity faculties), offering
courses to undergraduates. The reason for this had little to do with
any idea of 'Sacred Greats', but rather with the needs of the teaching
profession. Since this question was to have a bearing on the later
development of Religious Studies, it is worth some reference here.

Scotland, unlike England, had a history of schism within the
national church but (if one leaves aside the Catholic minority) little
dissent from it. The Education Act of 1872, the statutory basis for
national education, made religious education a compulsory – indeed,
the only compulsory – subject in state schools; but (since no-one
could foresee dispute over content) there was no equivalent of the
'Cowper-Temple' clause in the parallel English Education Act. For
the same reason, religious education was put outside the system of
examination and of government inspection, and these positions were
reaffirmed in legislation as late as 1962. There could thus be no
agreed syllabus for religious education, no recognized and enforceable
standards, and no requirement of a specialist training for RE teachers.
The colleges of education supplied courses in RE, but until the 1970s
secondary teachers had to obtain specialist status in another subject;
RE was an 'extra' in the course of a teacher's training. It was to give
academic substance to such intending teachers (other than those with
degrees in divinity) that the biblical studies lectureships were

instituted; the assumption at the time was that RE in schools would be essentially biblical in content. The courses always attracted a wider student following, but only at Aberdeen did a lectureship blossom into a full (though always small) department with a four year course.

Currents of Change

After such a long period of structural immobility, the last thirty years have seen unprecedented currents of change. The social and educational changes of the 1960s gave Religious Studies as a discipline a base in the Scottish universities for the first time, and provided the opportunity for an indigenous Scottish approach to the subject. The icy political and economic winds of the 1980s seemed set to destroy most of what had been achieved. More has survived the blast than for a time seemed likely, and new shoots are beginning to feel towards the light; but it is not yet clear what the pattern for the 90s will be.

Religious Studies in Scotland is indebted to the period of university expansion in more than one respect. The number of Scottish universities grew from four to eight, and the new ones followed different patterns from the old. None of them had a divinity faculty; Stirling, indeed, the most unconventional in form, did not have faculties at all. And the older universities expanded too, in students, staff and subject fields. The Scottish university system has always favoured breadth. The traditional 'ordinary' degree has permitted multiple combinations of quite diverse subjects, and even in the honours degree, subject specialization did not usually begin until the third year of a four year course. It was structurally simple, therefore, to introduce new fields of study as first year subjects, allowing them to proceed to second year and then to honours status if the incidence of student choice seemed to justify this. The 1960s saw a burgeoning of such new subjects, especially in the social sciences; philosophy, once the lynchpin of the arts programme, suffered somewhat.

The climate of the time favoured interest in international concerns, in other cultures, in the wider world in general. The professor of Islamic Studies at the University of Edinburgh said in his inaugural lecture in 1965: 'It seems probable that by the year 2000 no man will be considered truly educated unless he has engaged at university level in some study of a non-European culture.' Some of the new subject fields introduced these, and quite a number of the newly recruited staff had served overseas, often in the Commonwealth universities. Area studies developed; the Hayter and Parry funds gave impetus to

African, Asian and Latin American studies. Edinburgh became a 'Hayter centre' in African Studies and Aberdeen also had a small Hayter African grant. The students of the period shared in this interest in the non-western world. For some, the focus was the growing world poverty and world development movement; others were attracted by the possibility of alternative sources of knowledge in eastern cultures.

The student religious picture reflected an immense change from the Scotland assumed by the 1872 Education Act. True, in some areas, especially in the north, something like the old pattern of religious assumptions and practices remained. But a large proportion of students, from Scotland or from England, had known no more than a tenuous connection with active religion. University teachers of English literature complained that students could no longer understand Milton, teachers of history that the issues of the sixteenth century were unintelligible to their students. The old landmarks had gone, the most elementary knowledge could not be taken for granted. And yet much of this student generation was patently interested in religion, if not always in conventional church-related terms. Unlike their predecessors, they were not rebelling against the church; they had never been an active part of it. The idealism and rejection of materialism that were so noticeable also found religious echoes, though these were as likely to resound from India or the American civil rights movement as from the parish church.

The church, however, was undergoing its own revolution, which were soon at work in the divinity faculties. New interests, new concerns with the wider world and with the nature of society set up pressure for new subject fields there. The composition of ministerial recruits changed; so many were of mature years, with experience of another career, that the traditional postgraduate character of the faculties could not be maintained. Once divinity could be studied as a first degree, the professional character of the divinity faculties was also eroded. Increasing numbers of men and women who were not ministerial candidates entered the course. The divinity faculties became, actually or potentially, part of a sort of 'single market' with the humanities and social sciences.

Meanwhile the anomalous framework and thoroughly unsatisfactory condition of religious education in schools became more and more obvious. In 1968 the Secretary of State for Scotland appointed a committee under a Professor Malcolm Millar (a mental health specialist) 'to review the current practice of Scottish schools (other than Roman Catholic schools) with regard to moral and religious education and to make recommendations for its improvement'. The Millar report appeared in 1971. It stressed the importance of religious education in its own right, on educational grounds, and a corps of trained religious education specialists. It recommended alternative routes for the academic part of that training; a divinity degree or an arts degree with not less than two years of Religious Studies. It pointed, rather tentatively, towards bringing religious education, like other subjects, under the aegis of the Consultative Committee on the Curriculum. These recommendations were adopted, and educational opinion swept on where Millar had feared to tread (or at least to urge). Religious Studies became a subject available in the Scottish Certificate of Education. Not only did those examinations, at the higher grade, provide for study of different religious traditions; the option dealing with Christianity required some reference to its manifestations in Africa.

Looking at the Millar Report again almost twenty years after its publication, it seems extraordinary that it hardly mentions religions other than Christianity, nor deals with any of the arguments about religion and culture. The issue of religious pluralism had not yet impinged on the Scottish consciousness, and few schools had significant numbers of pupils from ethnic or religious minorities. For the Millar committee the urgent issues were how far religious education could or should involve explicit Christian commitment, and the implications for religious teaching of current knowledge about the stages of mental development.

On the first issue the report was cautious, granting the 'possibility in the senior school of both a more traditional' approach and one which found 'much more radical and sweeping' implications in the 'secularization of present day society' while recognizing ominous features in that society which 'may well spring from spiritual deprivation'. Likewise, the Committee saw a place for both the committed Christian and 'the teacher whose views are different from those of traditional Christianity'.

In fact the developments which produced and which flowed from the Millar report also produced in the Scottish Colleges of Education and in the schools a much more comprehensive and multi-cultural approach to religions than the report itself reflected. That this is the case was probably the fruit of the work of a small group of enthusiastic members of the profession. The influence of the Shap Working Party was felt amongst the relatively small number of Scottish specialists; indeed, a small-scale Scottish version gradually emerged as the Scottish Working Party on the Religions of the World in Education (sometimes known as MacShap). The working party published a journal and occasional papers, organized conferences and produced materials to assist in teaching on Hinduism. In this and many other projects, it is worth noting the efforts of the late John Langdon, Head of Religious Education at Moray House College of Education, Edinburgh. A member of the Millar committee, his influence was brought to bear in many ways in the Scottish educational scene, and he did much to bring about the interest in eastern religions and a world vision of Christianity.

Without proposing any direct chronological link between the influences just mentioned and the new pattern of Religious Studies (it is clear, for instance, that developments in the universities and the schools fed off each other), all these things form the background of a transformation of the academic teaching of religion in Scotland between 1960 and 1975. During that period Religious Studies appeared, with new structures to sustain it, in the curriculum of Glasgow, Aberdeen, Edinburgh and Stirling universities, and peripherally at Dundee, while St Andrews produced a new forum and format for divinity teaching and all the divinity faculties underwent more fundamental modification than even the 1929 union had brought them. The independent biblical studies lectureships quietly disappeared, crushed between the upper millstone of the new concern for Religious Studies and the lower of the wider availability of divinity courses. In no two places were the circumstances that brought about change the same; nor were the structures that emerged the same, nor the approach to the subject reflected in them.

Comings and Goings

The honour of primogeniture belongs to Glasgow, whose programme for the academic year 1961–62 announces a new arts course in Principles of Religion. In searching for a lecturer to direct and develop the course, the University invited applications from candidates to teach at least two out of four subject areas: biblical studies, comparative religion, philosophy of religion and psychology of religion. The appointment went to Allan Galloway who had been Professor of Religious Studies at the University of Ibadan, Nigeria. This was very appropriate; I have argued elsewhere that Ibadan, where Geoffrey Parrinder held his first academic post, was the first department of Religious Studies as the subject is currently understood.

Galloway had gone to that department as a theologian, the author of a major work called *The Cosmic Christ*. At Glasgow, the new department announced a course in 'some of the major problems of the interpretation and evaluation of religion, with particular reference to the Christian tradition'. The course was divided into two sections, 'The general phenomenology of religion', and 'Biblical Studies'. Scotland's first Religious Studies course thus began with a phenomenological approach. Over the years the dialectical relationship with Christian (and indeed western Christian) studies remained, sharpened by the presence of a strong Faculty of Divinity. Galloway indeed, moved over to become first Senior Lecturer and then Professor of Divinity; and in later years the department had other innovative, philosophically minded theologians in A. J. Cumpsty, Joseph Houston, Alastair Kee. As a second year course developed, a new appointee, Nicholas Wyatt, undertook teaching in Indian and Ancient Near Eastern Studies, and thereafter the department maintained these areas of study alongside 'Religion in the West' and comparative studies of such topics as God and human freedom, or the problem of evil, with reference to the main religious traditions and to Marxist and humanist positions. When the department closed in 1988, its listed honours courses (in programmes shared with other departments such as drama, Hebrew, history and sociology) included the life of Jesus, Judaism, Egyptian religion, Canaanite religion, Hinduism, Buddhism, Islam, modern Judaism, theology and culture, phenomenology of religion, philosophy of religion.

The Aberdeen department began in 1970. The occasion was the impending retirement of both members of the Department of Biblical Study and of the Professor of Divinity who had been concerned with the philosophical and social (as distinct from the dogmatic) aspects of theology. The university debated various options: maintaining the status quo, converting the biblical posts to posts in the philosophy of religion, or giving them to one of the hungry new subjects; even transferring the chair from divinity to arts to give status to a new 'open' approach to religion. The example of Lancaster (under Ninian Smart, another expatriate Scot), had caught various people's imagination and, in the event, a new Department of Religious Studies was created to inherit and extend the work of the Department of Biblical Study. The dormant Riddoch Lectureship in Comparative Religion was brought to life and attached to the departmental headship. The department was set up in the Faculty of Arts and Social Studies, but with a Board of

Studies of its own which included members of the Faculty of Divinity. Throughout its existence, the department both used the courses available in that faculty and supplied to it teaching in the history of religion. The new department described its concerns as 'The study of religion, in its own terms and in its social, phenomenological and historical aspects'. It was able to proceed smoothly to a full four year honours programme, but in the nature of things could never expect to have a large staff. It therefore developed its own specializations at honours level, to follow two years of general consideration of the forms and history of religion.

Once again the key came from Africa. Glasgow's first head of department had come, as we have seen, from Ibadan; his immediate successor, Eric Pyle, was from the University of Ghana; his final successor, Alastair Kee, from the University of Rhodesia. (Nicholas Wyatt had also served briefly at Ibadan). At Aberdeen the African link was still more marked; the first two members of staff were Andrew Walls, who had worked in Sierra Leone and Nigeria, and James Thrower, who had been at the University of Ghana. A core programme in phenomenology and history of religion was maintained along with a range of options and two areas of particular strength: the primal religions and non-western expressions of Christianity, to which were added iconography and Thrower's developing concerns in non-religious interpretations of reality (always considered *in relation* to religion) and in eastern European studies. Over the years the staff of the department included H. W. Turner (who had followed his service in Sierra Leone and Nigeria, and his pioneer work on independent churches' new religious movements in primal societies by pioneering the Religious Studies enterprise at the University of Leicester), Adrian Hastings (with wide experience in East Africa and interests and publications covering aspects of African and Western Christianity), Lamin Sanneh, a Gambian scholar who had done original work in African Islam, for a short time Kwame Bediako, a Ghanaian exponent of African theology, and Rosalind Shaw who had done research in Sierra Leone and taught in Nigeria. An active research link was established with the University of Calabar, Nigeria, through Rosalind Hackett. The department had a one year postgraduate course in Religion in Primal Societies and a steady international succession of PhD students in the primal religions and non-western Christianity. It provided the editors of the *Journal of Religion in Africa* and of the quarterly bibliography of the *International Review of Mission*. Turner's ground-breaking project and collection on New Religious Movements in Primal Societies was based in the department until his move to Birmingham; another documentation project brought together quantities of material on Christianity in the Non-Western World.

The troubles which beset British universities after 1981 hit Aberdeen with particular severity. After a period of uncertainty, the decision not to fill vacant posts brought about the loss of departmental status, and the attachment of the surviving elements to the Faculty of Divinity. With an eye on the coming storm, a Centre for the Study of Christianity in the Non-Western World was independently constituted in 1982. For a brief period from 1985 this centre carried on much of the postgraduate programme of the department, until the decisions about the latter's future brought the centre, with Andrew Walls as director, to Edinburgh. A sustained rearguard action has maintained in Aberdeen a small Centre for the Study of Religions under James Thrower.

Religious Studies at Edinburgh followed a different pattern. There the initiative for development came from within the Divinity Faculty itself, especially from the Professor of Divinity, John McIntyre. Edinburgh was early in modifying the concept of a postgraduate and essentially professional faculty; further, it had always offered some of its courses in the Faculty of Arts. A course in Religious Studies was announced for the academic year 1974–75. No department was originally projected; the intention from the beginning was to make use of resources already available in the University. The originating course offered an introduction to religion by means of various methods of study – psychological, historical, anthropological, philosophical – and involved members of different departments of the Faculties of Divinity and Arts. Elizabeth Maclaren, a new young lecturer in philosophy of religion, provided linking seminars. The appointment of a full-time member of staff, Frank Whaling, made possible the development of a second year and then an honours course. Whaling provided courses in phenomenology and history of religion, as well as in his specialist area of Indian religion, and co-ordinated a programme which was able to draw in specialists from the departments of Islamic and Middle Eastern Studies, Sanskrit, Chinese and East Asian Studies and Social Anthropology besides the whole range of theological disciplines available in Scotland's largest Divinity Faculty. The interest of these specialists in the study of religion was not a merely contingent one, as witness the regular involvement of W. Montgomery Watt and later Carole Hillenbrand to deal with Islamic Studies and John Brockington with Hindu texts.

Later rearrangements in the faculty have resulted in the creation within the faculty of a Department of Theology and Religious Studies responsible for systematic theology and philosophical theology, as well as Religious Studies. The latter has been strengthened by the transfer to it of the members of the former Glasgow Department of Religious Studies. The transfer of the Centre for the Study of Christianity in the Non-Western World from Aberdeen as a postgraduate teaching and research centre makes another set of resources open to it, including some of the teaching in primal religions formerly available at Aberdeen.

Edinburgh has also been the scene of an enterprising campaign by Emily Lyle of the School of Scottish Studies. The Traditional Cosmology Society, with lectures, conferences, journal and even a fellowship programme, has been the fruit of her activity, often entering fields neglected in this country, such as arctic and native American religions, and drawing on a wider range of expertise, local and distant.

Stirling University was not originally intended to provide teaching in the field of religion at all; but a course begun within the philosophy programme by Stewart Sutherland dealing with religious issues proved attractive to numbers of students in its early years. So successful was it that it became possible to expand, with new appointments in biblical studies (John Drane) and Indian religions (Glyn Richards). By the time Sutherland went to King's College, London, as professor and eventually principal, there was a flourishing department. Stirling, small and late founded, looked particularly vulnerable in the university contraction of the eighties; but both university and department, though buffeted and bruised, have survived. It is interesting that Stirling, which has no divinity faculty, has developed a substantial programme in Christian studies. The interest in Japanese religions introduced by Brian Bocking has been maintained since his departure by co-operation with the new and substantial Centre for Japanese Studies.

The University of Dundee has as one of its most substantial benefactors Mrs Margaret Harris, who endowed a chapel and other facilities. Since 1965 an annual series of public lectures on religion have been given by invited scholars, and are now designated the Margaret Harris Lectures. They are similar in scope to the Gifford Lectures, and have covered many aspects of Religious Studies. Philosophy at Dundee has given a place to eastern philosophy, which has enabled David Bastow to maintain courses in Hindu and Buddhist thought; and before the amalgamation of Dundee College of Education with that at Aberdeen, the University had a BEd with papers in Religious Studies.

In 1980 Religious Studies in Scotland appeared to be thriving. Ten years later all its bases except Edinburgh had contracted, the Glasgow presence had ceased, and Aberdeen had lost departmental status. The College of Education departments suffered equally, or more. Yet all the university courses had proved attractive to students. At the time of their demise the Aberdeen and Glasgow departments had enrolments that were the envy of many other departments, and Aberdeen had a substantial postgraduate element and the only chair (albeit a personal one) in the subject in Scotland. There was a substantial record of publication – a topic not covered in this article – in every department.

L'Envoi

There is no need to assume any conspiracy against Religious Studies; all small departments came into question after 1981, and a retirement, a resignation or an illness could bring about a crisis. We may be grateful that so much has in fact survived, and that such potential remains for the future. And Geoffrey Parrinder is part of the story too. He was crucial to that first Department of Religious Studies at University College Ibadan; and Scottish Religious Studies owes more than is commonly realized to the experiences of West Africa.

WALES

Cyril Williams

The Background

An account of the development of 'Religious Studies' in Wales, however brief, would be deficient without recalling the role of its precursor 'History of Religions'. Since that subject was born within theology and never quite severed the umbilical cord which tied it to the theological faculty some mention must be made of their relationship and of the circumstances which led to a situation where biblical studies flourished within the Arts faculties while the study of religions was confined to optional divinity courses.

The teaching of theology had been precluded by the charters of the university colleges, which anteceded the university, due in measure to the fear of sectarianism but even more of dependence on Treasury funding, and theology therefore was restricted to the denominational colleges. However, when the University of Wales was founded in 1893, its charter empowered it to give degrees in theology. A Theology Board was established in 1895 and a year later the degree of *Baccalaureus in Divinitate* was launched, but the university colleges still fought shy of theology. However, on more than one occasion, in the early part of this century, plans were considered for its inclusion, but they did not materialise. Some progress in that direction came about when both the University College of North Wales, Bangor, and what was then called the University College of South Wales and Monmouthshire, established lectureships in Hebrew, a language which could be read for both the BA and the BD degrees. It was from these lectureships that departments of Semitic Languages came into being at the two centres. When the Faculty of Theology replaced the Theological Board in 1921, the ties between the theological colleges and the university colleges became firmer, particularly at Bangor where a Joint School of Theological Studies had been established and some teachers from the theological colleges were appointed 'special lecturers' to teach certain subjects such as Hebrew, Greek, philosophical theism and church history within the university college, but other 'theological' subjects were still considered to be inappropriate for inclusion. Further co-operation came about when a number of the members of the academic staff of the University College participated in the work of the new Faculty of Theology.

This was the heyday of *Religionsgeschichte* and liberal theology, and no one strove more to develop it within the university than Sir Harry Reichel, Principal at Bangor, who was imbued with the ecumenical spirit and sought to establish chairs of theology in the university colleges. He also championed the case for establishing a chair in the history of religions at Bangor, a subject which he envisaged as part of the arts degree. Moreover he believed that the study of theology and religion had practical relevance in what he described as the intellectual crisis resulting from the experience of the 1914–18 war. The vision remained but a dream in spite of much support, and the nearest it came to fulfilment was when the 'Council authorised the Senate to organise a course in the History of Religions on condition that it did not cost more than £280'.[1]

In 1912 the Theological Board of the university had received a proposal from its Committee of Studies that the scheme of study for the BD should be amended to enable specialisation in selected subjects. While it was accepted in principle, the syllabus drafted by Dr A. E. Garvie was at first rejected. It entailed three parts:

1. The Philosophy of Religion.
   Definition of the nature of religion and theories of its origin.
   The relation of religion to morality, society and history.
   The development of religion.
   The history of the philosophy of religion.

2. The Comparative Study of Religions of
   India, China, Japan, Egypt, Assyria, Babylon, Judaism
   and Islam as regards doctrine, worship and moral code.

3. The Historical Study of one religion, as prescribed each year,
   in the following rotation: –
   Brahmanism and Hinduism;
   Buddhism and Lamaism;
   Confucianism;
   Islam;
   including a study of prescribed portions of the literature translated.

It was a programme of encyclopaedic range which would overwhelm the staunchest of polymaths, but for good measure at a later stage Zoroastrianism was added to the rotation circuit!

When the Board eventually put forward amendments to the BD

regulations in 1913, the general title of the subject appeared as 'History of Religions' but later it is also designated 'History of Religion' in some records. However, the plural form prevailed until it was substituted by the present title 'The Study of Religions'.

The subject was never a core subject for the degree in divinity and its career has been somewhat chequered. Records show that from 1925–1934 only two candidates were presented for examination in the subject at subsidiary (second year) level and one only at the principal (third year) stage, but there was a marked change thereafter since from 1935–1953 one hundred were presented at subsidiary level and thirteen at the principal grade. Tribute can be paid to the theological colleges for their promotion of the subject in this period, made all the more remarkable considering their meagre resources. But for some reason this upsurge was not maintained in the second half of the century while other areas of theology more than held their own. It has remained at the periphery of theological interest ever since, even at the very time when society became increasingly conscious of its multicultural and multi-faith constituency.

The University of Wales had to wait until 1944 for its first full time appointment in the history of religions when the Reverend D. W. Gundry joined the staff at Bangor. A year later Dr Christopher R. North was appointed Professor of Hebrew at the same college to succeed Professor H. H.Rowley and both have publications of special interest to the student of religions. North had published *An Outline of Islam* in 1934, and Rowley, who at one time had lectured in Shantung, includes among his voluminous works his *Prophecy and Religion in Ancient China and Israel*, published in 1952. While at Bangor, Gundry wrote his useful introductory study *Religions* (1958). He was succeeded in 1962 by a former student, the Reverend Islwyn Blythin, who was at the time on the staff of 'Didsbury' Theological College, Bristol. Changes in departmental nomenclature at Bangor reflect an awareness of the changing milieu and attitudes to the role of religion as a subject in university education. The Chair of Hebrew had been established in 1905, but the department, while retaining its preoccupation with Hebrew and semitic languages, extended its courses in biblical history and literature even before the 1944 Education Act which highlighted the need for trained teachers in the subject, due to changes in school curricula. Subsequently the department was known as Department of Hebrew and Biblical Studies, truncated to simply Biblical Studies in 1972, to be changed yet again in 1988 to Department of Religious Studies. It has made a substantial contribution to biblical understanding but is now poised to meet the challenge of a new era under the leadership of Professor G. H. Jones.

Meanwhile at Cardiff there had been similar developments. The lectureship in Hebrew had paved the way for a Department of Semitic Languages under Professor T. H. Robinson who was on the staff from 1915 until 1944. He had taught at Serampore and his period in India had enabled him to see 'both Hinduism and Islam at work'. It also provided insights for his book *An Outline Introduction to the History of Religions* (Oxford, 1926), where he expresses the opinion that 'Christianity itself can only be rightly appreciated when it is set alongside of the world's other faiths'. After the Second World War the department at Cardiff became known as the Department of Semitic Languages and Biblical Studies, under the distinguished chairmanship of Professor A. R. Johnson, but it was not until 1958 that an appointment was made in history of religions to coincide with the forming of the Joint School of Theology. The Reverend C. G. Williams, a former student of the department, who had sat at the feet of both Professors Robinson and Johnson, was appointed Assistant Lecturer in History of Religions, but the subject remained firmly within the faculty of theology and was not offered to students reading for an arts degree.

The Introduction of Religious Studies

The next significant development in the history of Religious Studies in the University of Wales was the introduction of the subject at the University College of Wales, Aberystwyth, in 1973 when C. G. Williams was appointed with a view to developing it. He, meanwhile, had benefited from his experience as Professor of Religion and chairman of a vigorous department of religion of Carleton University, Ottawa, in a period of rapid expansion and a lively interest in eastern religions. This experience proved to be invaluable to face the task ahead, different though the situations were. It was a novel venture at Aberystwyth in more than one sense. Not only was Religious Studies for the first time ever to be offered as a subject in its own right in an arts degree scheme in Wales, but lectures were to be given in it through the medium of Welsh as well as in English. In addition there was the task of demonstrating the distinctiveness of Religious Studies in its aims and methodology, its educative value as a proper academic pursuit and the right of each religion to be studied for its own sake in an empathetic manner. Some objections had been raised to its introduction for good reasons, mainly, that it should not be undertaken without full funding and adequate staff resources. One had to share such apprehensions and, in retrospect, it may have been foolhardy to grasp the opportunity without proper provision, but optimism prevailed over discretion, in the hope that conditions would allow expansion, and had that foothold not been taken, the course of Religious Studies in Wales would have been halted at a crucial period. The response was encouraging in terms of student enrolment and assistance was given by supportive members of other departments, particularly Professor T. A. Roberts of the philosophy department, a department, incidentally, where Roderick Ninian Smart had his first academic appointment in 1952. It is sad to think that such a department has now been eliminated due to the ravages of financial dictates.

For two years Religious Studies remained a first year subject only, but in 1975, with the appointment of the Reverend Islwyn Blythin from Bangor, and with further assistance from the theological colleges, it became possible to launch a balanced joint honours scheme which meant that the subject would be taught over the three years of an undergraduate programme. It included courses in methodology, philosophy of religion, Judeo-Christian tradition, Indian tradition, Islam and Zoroastrianism.

Religious Studies attained full departmental status in 1977 and the stage was set for further development and a full single honours programme. Student demand remained reasonably high and, significantly, a high proportion of first year students were electing to pursue the subject in part two of the degree scheme. In 1980 Religious Studies was also one of the subjects offered in a pilot scheme for an external initial degree through the medium of Welsh introduced at the University College of Wales, Aberystwyth. That scheme has turned out to be a success, but in that very session the University Grants Committee recommended that the University of Wales should consider concentrating provision within the university as a whole in Theology/Religious Studies (sic) and the writing on the wall was clear.

A Successful 'Merger'

With the deteriorating economic conditions in the universities it became obvious that there would be no expansion and no increase in resources. Survival became an urgent concern, particularly for small departments which were exceedingly vulnerable. It was then that negotiations took place with the Department of Theology, Saint David's University College, Lampeter, with a view to implementing the call for rationalisation. The result was the transfer of Professor C. G. Williams and Mr. Blythin to Lampeter and the successful merger of the two departments in 1983 to form the 'Department of Theology and Religious Studies'.

Saint David's is the smallest of the Welsh university colleges, but also the oldest university institution in England and Wales apart from Oxford and Cambridge. It was founded in 1822 and opened in 1827, and from the very first and throughout its history, theology has been given prominence as an area of study in the college. Thus when Saint David's became part of the University of Wales in 1971, a full programme in theology was offered for the first time as an arts subject and read for a BA degree in the University of Wales.

Some intriguing coincidences emerge from the historical background which are of interest now that Religious Studies and Theology are juxtaposed at Lampeter. In 1856, the Reverend Rowland Williams, one of its most distinguished professors, whose rationalist views alienated the orthodox, published a remarkable book of nearly six-hundred pages which still merits thorough study. His name does not appear anywhere in the book itself but it is given a full title: *Parameswara-jnyana-goshthi A Dialogue of the Knowledge of the Supreme Lord, in which are compared the claims of Christianity and Hinduism and various questions of Indian Religion and Literature Fairly discussed.* (Cambridge: Deighton Bell)

It is worth recording that some seven miles or so from Lampeter is the little village of Ffald-y-brenin often visited by Rowland Williams to converse with the village smithy who was none other than the father of Timothy Richard (1845–1919), Baptist missionary in China and founder of Shansi University. Richard was given the highest possible honours by the Chinese for his services and his devotion to the people. One can but speculate as to early influences which may have derived from Rowland Williams's visits to the home. What has not been sufficiently recognised has been Timothy Richard's contribution as a pioneer in comparative studies prompted by his discovery of and respect for Chinese Mahayana Buddhist texts. He published extensively, including a translation of the *Lotus Sutra* and Ashvagosha's *Awakening of Faith*. It is a further coincidence that another exponent of Buddhism, the eminent Pali expert, T. W. Rhys Davids, had a remote connection with the village, from which hailed his paternal grandfather.

Recent Developments

In the immediate past, the way had been prepared for the advent of Religious Studies to Lampeter in that the philosophy department already offered a course in 'Oriental Philosophy' which had been taught by Professor A. Cavendish. There was also a full honours programme, run by members drawn from several departments, under the title 'Religion and Ethics in Western Thought'. This scheme covered many areas of contemporary relevance for Religious Studies. Any apprehensions regarding the merger therefore were quickly dispelled for the general ethos of the department and the leadership of Professor D. P. Davies were such as to encourage the full development of Religious Studies and a sensitivity to its methodological principles to the mutual enrichment of both Religious Studies and Theology.

New appointments were made: Dr Deirdre Green in 1985 to teach Indian religions (who met an early, tragic death in a car accident in March 1990), and a year later, as a result of the beneficence of the Emir of Qatar, Mr Mashuq Ally to a sponsored post in Islamic Studies. A further munificient gift from the Crown Prince of Bahrain made it possible to appoint Dr Moel Izzidien lecturer in Islamic Studies with Arabic. Dr Sheikh Anas Al-Sheikh Ali became Visiting Research Fellow and the University appointed Professor Ninian Smart Honorary Professor to the department. By 1987, there had been launched a full honours programme in Religious Studies, a joint honours scheme in Islamic studies, as well as the structured MA programmes in 'Death and Immortality', organised by Dr Paul Badham, and 'Inter-Faith Studies'. In addition a number of graduates are pursuing research for higher degrees on a wide range of related topics. The department is now one of the largest in the college and entering a period of consolidation. Also, subsequent to Professor Williams's retirement in 1988, Dr C. Arthur has been appointed to a lectureship and hopefully, before long, the resources of the department will be further strengthened, particularly in Judaism.

In Cardiff, in the early eighties, the department, which had contributed so much throughout its history, suffered severe depletion through retirements, and the degrees in Biblical Studies and Near Eastern Studies were withdrawn, but postgraduate work in the latter continued under Professor H. W. Saggs until his retirement in 1986. Religious Studies had been re-constituted under a Board of Studies, providing a full honours programme with elements from several departments. Two new appointments were made in biblical areas (Drs J. Watt and Christine Trevett) and the Board soon attained departmental status with Professor Humphrey Palmer of the philosophy department as chairman. The situation seemed precarious when University College, Cardiff, was faced with the merger with the University of Wales Institute of Science and Technology to form the new University of Wales College of Cardiff. However, the department has retained its position and the value and relevance of Religious Studies should become increasingly evident in a university college in a cosmopolitan, capital city, and an institution in which twelve per cent of the students are from overseas.

Such in barest outline is an account of Religious Studies in the University, but the story of its development in Wales would not be complete without a least referring to the work of the institutes of higher education which have offered degrees of the University of Wales in Religious Studies, and the valuable work of the Welsh National Centre for Religious Education at Bangor and its counterpart at Trinity College, Carmarthen, not to mention the efforts of dedicated religious education teachers in schools and the support of the Welsh Joint Education Committee.

In Wales on the whole the prevailing attitude in schools towards the study of religions other than Christianity has been conservative, but one now detects a change in the traditional reluctance to enter non-biblical areas. The Welsh Joint Education Committee had introduced wider options in its curricula for 'A' level and the new GCSE courses, but these syllabi will need to be constantly reviewed to encourage participation by larger numbers in studies relevant to the contemporary scene. The need for trained teachers remains paramount for a recent survey showed that 38 percent of those who had taught 'O' level courses and more than half of those who taught religious education as a statutory requirement were without qualifications to teach the subject.

Scholars and Published Work

In terms of academic publications in the study of religions, Wales cannot claim to be prolific for its most productive authors have been attracted in other directions, notably poetry, hymnology, devotional writing, and literature. Yet, as already suggested, it is not without the inspiration of links with past luminaries, not least of whom were the eminent orientalists, Sir William Jones (1746–94) and David Price (1762–1835) whose best known work *Chronological Retrospect . . . of Mahommedan History* was highly regarded in its day. A more recent polymath who, it is claimed, had scholarly competence in twenty-four languages, was J. J. Jones, an employee at the National Library of Wales who translated the *Mahavastu* in two volumes for the Pali Text Society from Hybrid Sanskrit. He also contributed important articles on Buddhist philosophy to *Efrydiau Athronyddol.* One would expect investigations in Celtic mythology and religion in Wales, and in fact it is an area in which there is growing interest. One of the earliest scholarly publications is that of Sir John Rhys whose Hibbert Lectures of 1888 appeared under the title *On the Origin and Growth of Religion as illustrated by Celtic Heathendom.* Interest in the subject was promoted with the establishing of the Board of Celtic Studies in 1920, and since then there have been a number of articles and scholarly publications of relevance to students of religion including Alwyn and Brinley Rees, *Celtic Heritage* (London, 1961) and Pennar Davies, *Rhwng Chwedl a Chredo* (Cardiff, 1966).

Public lectures at the various colleges on several occasions had examined topics in Religious Studies or ancillary fields before it became a recognised subject in an arts course. These have included, for example, the Sir D. Owen Evans Memorial lectures at Aberystwyth incorporated in E. E. Evans-Pritchard, *Theories of Primitive Religion* (Oxford, 1965) and Charles Davis, *Christ and the World Religions* (London, 1970). Of recent lectures, the 1988 Sir D. J. James Lecture by Islwyn Blythin, *Religion and Methodology: Past and Present* examines important issues for current studies.

Space prevents us from mentioning other publications and it would take us too far afield to offer even brief reference to works in philosophy of religion where names such as Professors H. D. Lewis and D. Z. Phillips come readily to mind. Similarly one has to forego other relevant, albeit specialized areas such as ancient Babylonian and Egyptian studies by Professors H. W. Saggs and J. Gwyn Griffiths respectively, while the subject of advances in Hebraic and Biblical studies by professorial staff and lecturers at Bangor and Cardiff, not to mention a distinguished alumnus such as Professor W. D. Davies, would need at least a whole chapter to itself. All these, broadly speaking, could be said to fall within the purview of Religious Studies and serve to demonstrate the vastness of range and multiple approaches involved.

What cannot be ignored in reviewing developments in Wales is the special situation occasioned by the Welsh language, particularly in view of the efforts being made by those for whom it is an important issue to make it a medium at all levels of education from nursery school to university. I have recalled elsewhere[2] what seems to have been the very earliest attempt to write of a non-Christian religion in the Welsh tongue, namely that of Charles Edwards in *Y Ffydd Ddiffuant* in 1667 where he presents a chapter on Islam and a rendering of passages from some Qur'anic Suras. In the following century Wales's most famous hymn writer, William Williams of Pantycelyn, produced over a period of two decades, but not without protest, a series of booklets, at threepence a copy, forming a *Pantheologia* which outlined the beliefs and customs of 'All the religions of the world'. His main source seems to have been Thomas Salmon, *Modern History*. In this century, the first proper landmark was the appearance of D. Miall Edwards, *Cristnogaeth a Chrefyddau Eraill* (Dolgellau, 1923) but the field remained fallow until the appearance of C. G. Williams *Crefyddau'r Dwyrain* (Cardiff, 1968). Subsequently, grant aided by the Welsh Office, handbooks on Hinduism, Buddism and Islam, have been produced for class use by the University College of Wales, Aberystwyth. Some attempt has been made to meet the need of schools, but all too little. The Welsh Joint Education Committee has published a glossary of terms in religious studies and J. G. Harries, the editor, has also written introductory works on three of the world religions. The situation will not improve until teachers, at school, college and university, are seconded for substantial periods to the specific task of the preparation of texts.

The Future?

What then of the future? It would be a bold person who would forecast the future of the subject, particularly in the University in the present cash-saving climate. But now that we have three departments of Religious Studies within the University of Wales, at Bangor, Cardiff and Lampeter, hopefully, they will be allowed to develop as fully as possible by availing themselves of the opportunities which a federal structure can provide. Already lecturers in Religious Studies occasionally give lectures in colleges other than their own, and all three departments join together annually for a colloquium of staff and students at Gregynog Hall which is in idyllic surroundings in the heart of Wales. It provides an opportunity for discussion and the exchange of views. The call for the more effective use of resources may lead in the future to closer co-operation between the centres involving video-links and the mobility and exchange of staff and students, enabling each department to develop its own specialisation. In the past, each seems to have forged ahead regardless and anxious to preserve its autonomy with the result that the advantages of federalism have not been realized. In my view, the future will demand a greater degree of interdependence if departments are to survive, but this can be an advantage to a subject like Religious Studies which ranges over so many areas, calling for specialised knowledge as well as the means to correlate different approaches.

An encouraging feature is the increase in the number of mature students and the provisions for adult external students. Saint David's University College, for example has a thriving programme for a College certificate in which the study of religions is one option. Classes are held at a number of different centres throughout the country and some students progress to pursue a full degree course and, in the case of those who are already graduates, a Licentiate in Religious Studies. Closer co-operation is also envisaged with the colleges of education to provide in-service training for teachers.

In conclusion: in Wales, as elsewhere, 'the religious drive cuts across all phases of human life'[3] and demands proper study, not least as a factor in personal, social and international relations.

NOTES

[1] R. Tudor Jones, *Theology in Bangor*, University of Wales Press, 1972, p. 136. I should like to record my indebtedness to this little volume for much of my information.

[2] 'The Unfeigned Faith and an Eighteenth Century Pantheologia', *Numen* xv (1968), pp. 208–17.

[3] M. Novak, *Ascent of the Mountain Flight of the Dove*, New York: Harper and Row, 1971, p. 5.

THE OPEN UNIVERSITY

Terence Thomas

The Open University

The Open University received its Royal Charter in 1969 and in 1971 it opened its doors, metaphorically, to the first students. The university was designed as an adult, off-campus institution, to cater for the higher educational needs of those who had never had the opportunity to go to a conventional university, or who wished to upgrade their academic qualifications, or who wished to qualify for a change in career. Originally billed as 'The University of the Air', from the beginning radio and television played only minor roles in what was a distance teaching and learning institution. The main core of the teaching was in the form of printed course units, allied to already existing or specially produced textbooks. In addition there was created a network of local tutors and counsellors giving personal teaching and support to each student through local study centres.

The Faculty of Arts

The Open University began with a big rush. In less than two years four faculties had produced four foundation courses, complete with printed units, set books, radio and television. Of the four faculties one was the Faculty of Arts.

The university was the product of a certain ideology and some of that influence was seen to be at work early on. In the light of this the Faculty of Arts was fortunate to have as its first Dean John Ferguson, a Christian gentleman to be sure, but also one of the truly humanistic academics of his time. He insisted that the study of religion should be included in the faculty's offerings, alongside the other humanities, against opposition from within the university and from at least one Labour peer outside. Those who opposed him thought that the teaching of the history of religion in a secular university was a contradiction and that such a step would open the door to proselytization or worse. It is strange how otherwise liberal people cannot see that the history of religion can be taught as objectively as, or at least not less objectively than, any other history.

Many years later the fact that Religious Studies was taught in the university was used as a counter to allegations that certain courses manifested a Marxist bias. This was hardly a compliment to the teaching of religion since it was at all times taught without any bias, at least no conscious bias.

The History of Religion

The first attempt to teach the history of religion, (in the first few years the discipline was part of the history discipline), was a couple of units in the arts foundation course entitled *What is a Gospel*. The material was written by John Ferguson and was a rather pedestrian offering which did not fit in well with the other material in this interdisciplinary course divided broadly as it was into two periods of history, European Renaissance and British Industrialization

By the time it was in the hands of the students in February 1971, two second level courses were far advanced in production and this is where the history of religion began to take off. One of these courses was *Renaissance and Reformation*, another inter-disciplinary course. Recruitment of academic staff in those days was partly based on the general needs of such a faculty, and the first wave included academics of outstanding ability, and partly on the plans for courses which would follow the foundation course. Having decided on a course which included a study of the Protestant Reformation, a scholar of standing in that field was looked for.

The faculty was fortunate in recruiting such a scholar, Francis Clark. A former Jesuit, he had major publications behind him, including a substantial work on eucharistic theology in the Reformation period. Francis Clark approached the subject on the basis that there had been two primary Reformations, the Protestant and the Catholic. His study made up a quarter of the whole course and established the study of religion in the Open University on a strong foundation.

The study has been recognized as a major contribution to the teaching of the subject at university level. Students thought the work demanding, but extremely rewarding. When *Renaissance and Reformation*, introduced in 1972, came to the end of its natural life, after eight years, Francis Clark successfully conceived of the

Reformations section continuing as what was then called a post-experience course. It was taught in the associate student programme as a self-standing study, and for about five years it continued to attract a steady clientele of over one hundred students a year. He likes to relate that students would write to him accusing him of bias, some accusing him of bias in favour of Catholicism, others in favour of Protestantism, but his impartiality was firmly established when someone said that from his writing on the Reformation he was obviously a Jew.

Such was the tempo in those days that by the time *Renaissance and Reformation* was on offer, a course which combined classics and the history of religion was in production. In 1973 another second level course was introduced, *The Early Roman Empire and the Rise of Christianity*. A number of classicists within the university, including John Ferguson, wrote the major portion of the course, but a quarter of it, on the New Testament and sub-apostolic period, was again written by Francis Clark. The study itself tended towards the conservative position, though gospel criticism was included. An interesting television programme presented by Francis Clark took the students under St Peter's in Rome to the *scavi*. It was an example of the versatility of the Open University's study material and was a pointer to much that was to follow when the history of religion gave way to Religious Studies. Later the section of the course dealing with the rise of Christianity also appeared as a post-foundation course and again carried on for many years attracting well over a hundred students each year.

Religious Studies

I joined the Open University as a staff tutor in the history of religion based in the Welsh region in May 1971. I was lucky to find myself, within a couple of days of landing in this country from India, where I had worked with a missionary society for the previous eight years, working in an institution which expressed many of my own views on what education should be. If it had been in existence twenty years earlier, I would have been one of its first students. During my interview for the job the possibility of making a contribution to a course on world religions was mentioned, but it took a few years before anything tangible materialized. In 1974 a working group consisting mainly of Open University staff, but including Ninian Smart, agreed on an outline of a course which would be half methodological and half a study of one or two eastern religions in depth. The plan lapsed due to inadequate staffing resources. By this time the name History of Religion had been dropped and the discipline was known as Religious Studies.

The discipline, so-called since faculties did not have departments in those days, was small in size, just two of us. At this time and over the next few years much discussion took place concerning the status of the discipline. The Faculty of Arts as a whole was determined that we should not be allowed to grow to parity with the main disciplines, history, music, art history, literature and philosophy. Various nomenclatures were suggested, minor discipline, quasi discipline and non-discipline. By this time there were two other areas of study in the same position, classics and history of science. Eventually in the early 80s a departmental structure emerged for the whole faculty, and Religious Studies found itself in tandem with classics with the Dean of the Faculty as the departmental head.

All this has happened against a background of the considerable popularity of the study of religions among the students, and the same could be said for classics and the history of science. In the early years of the faculty's existence other smaller disciplines had engaged in vigorous politicking and had grown to be major disciplines and later departments, in spite of the fact that they did not draw students in the same numbers. Whether a campaign by Religious Studies in the early days would have made any difference it is difficult to judge. It could be said that John Ferguson's own position and standpoint appeared at times to stand in the way of the expansion of the discipline as such. It seemed as if he was aware that there were those who were not happy with his insistence on the presence of Religious Studies and that he was afraid of antagonizing them further by advocating an expansion of the discipline. The result has been a chronic shortage of staff and a limitation of studies to one full credit apart from any contributions to inter-disciplinary courses.

The Teaching of World Religions

In 1975 the idea of a course in world religions again surfaced and this time we were able to proceed to concrete planning. The course was now to be the study of a number of world religions with a methodological introduction. It was to be called *Man's Religious*

Quest, a title which drew, quite reasonably, ire from feminist quarters. After a struggle to acquire adequate staffing resources and finance, the course planning and production got under way in 1975/6. According to Open University practice a course team was set up.

A course team is a marvellous idea. Ideally it is an arrangement whereby a number of academics and broadcasting staff join together to pool their knowledge and expertise. It is the course team that agrees on the components of the course and on the composition of the authors. Course material is produced in draft form, circulated to all members for comment, and, ideally, is redrafted on the basis of comments received. I remember well a discussion of a radio script on mysticism written by John Ferguson. Francis Clark was very unhappy about some of the sexual analogies introduced by John, especially a reference to semen being emitted during a particular ecstatic mystical experience. It was very difficult to maintain a straight face while these two men discussed the topic in a most gentlemanly and dispassionate way not sparing any of the intricate details nor sparing the sensibilities of female members of the course team.

Many, perhaps most, course teams in the Open University operate in a less than ideal way and ours was no exception. It consisted of permanent Open University staff drawn from the Arts Faculty and the Faculty of Social Sciences, a temporary appointment, John Hinnells from Manchester University, a visiting Fulbright professor, Robert McDermott of City University, New York, someone from the Institute of Educational Technology, one or two editors and a full team of Open University BBC production staff. The course material was to be produced by a mixture of in-house staff and external consultants. Among the external consultants were leading names in their own fields, Kenneth Cragg, David Goldstein, Ninian Smart, Simon Weightman and Joseph Masson.

The course was planned as a full credit at second level, the equivalent of Part I in conventional degrees. This amounted to thirty two units, each unit a one week study. In addition there was to be a specially published 'Reader' of articles and excerpts from sacred texts. This was eventually very successfully edited by Whitfield Foy and published under the title *Man's Religious Quest*. Three other books already published were part of the whole package, Zaehner's *Encyclopaedia of Living Faiths*, Ling's *History of Religion East and West* and Stevenson's *Seven Theories of Human Nature*. On the broadcasting side there were sixteen radio programmes, including a number of 'testimonies', individuals talking about their own religious beliefs, and a series of twelve television programmes, some of them filmed in the original habitat of the religions concerned.

Working with external consultants presented certain hazards. We failed with one distinguished consultant to get the quality of material we were looking for, with another the kind of material we were looking for. Yet another presented us with material which had to be considerably editorialized to conform to the methods employed in our teaching units. John Ferguson used to say that in the Open University designing courses was a matter of cutting the suit to fit the tailors, not the cloth. Because of the staff and consultants engaged or available the treatment of the individual religions was sometimes in inverse proportion to their world importance. Hinduism got five units, Buddhism and Zoroastrianism three, while Judaism, Christianity and Islam got two each, the same as African religions and secular alternatives to religion. One religion, Sikhism, chosen on account of its growing importance in Britain, originally did not have a tailor. I was given two years to study it and write two units. An example of the course team working at its best was the criticism of my first attempt to write two units on inter-religious encounter and dialogue. The second attempt was accepted and I was happy to acknowledge that my colleagues had been right to reject the original.

The course was to be a joint production of the arts and social sciences with the latter contributing in the areas of anthropology and sociology of religion. In the end these contributions were minimal, one unit on African religion and one of a general nature on sociology of religion. Attempts to integrate sociology in the studies of some of the religions were firmly resisted by the course team chairman. Small concessions were made, notably in the treatment of institutionalization in the study of Sikhism, but this was offset by the insistence that an article on institutionalization in the Reader, which was used in the study of Sikhism, but was not written with Sikhism in mind, was confined by the course team chairman to the Sikhism section of the Reader rather than be included among the more general, methodological entries. This eccentric decision has been remarked on by puzzled reviewers of the volume.

Much time was spent in planning the way in which the package of material should be taught. We were in the business of teaching, on the whole, about living religions. The main exception was Graeco-Roman religions which could not be excluded with John Ferguson on the course team. The television programmes showed religions at work, as far as possible on their native heath. Radio programmes dealt with people's experience of religion and other aspects such as the music of religions. An important part of the tutor's role was to take students to places of worship as part of their tuition. Temple, mosque, synagogue, gurudwara and church authorities collaborated with us in many cities throughout Britain and the course team was always grateful for this collaboration.

'Man's Religious Quest'

The course was eventually launched on the students in 1978. By the beginning of 1978 we had everything more or less ready but there were still elements of the course being produced, as is usual for a course in its first year of presentation. We did have a good corps of course tutors scattered across the thirteen regions of the Open University. Much of the success of the course is due to their efforts, including the time they spent, often for inadequate remuneration, in taking their students to various places of worship. We had been fortunate in recruiting as external examiners scholars and teachers such as John Bowker, Geoffrey Parrinder and Joan Hazelden Walker who brought her experience as a senior administrator in the CNAA. This team served us very well for the next six years, giving us confidence in what we were doing, encouraging us when we needed encouraging, and helping us to improve the quality of the teaching as we all gained experience of the course.

We waited for public reaction. The students found the going tough, but rewarding. We had discussed endlessly the order of religions to be studied. Following the introductory, methodological units which, apart from the sociology of religion, were a bit of a disaster, we decided to plunge the students into a study of Hinduism. The decision was based on a number of assumptions. We did not want to begin the study with western religions and run the risk of setting an ethnocentric stamp on the course. We thought that the students would find Hinduism and Buddhism difficult and that the sooner they were introduced, the fresher they would be. Open University courses have a reputation of inducing exhaustion half way through. The study of Hinduism in the villages did get us off to a good start. Students enjoyed the study from the first year and continued that way. Classical, philosophical Hinduism did prove more difficult than we had anticipated, and this in spite of the fact that the units were written in a user friendly way. And so on through the course. Some units worked well, others not so well. Some were more popular than others. Buddhism and Judaism persisted as the most popular religions over the years.

We knew that our peers had been invited to judge us through a major review of the course in the journal *Religion*. There were many criticisms, not unexpectedly. The reviewer of the Christianity material, through some oversight, did not receive the printed material, the most important element, when promised. He rushed to review the television and radio elements totally out of context and the review turned out to be a crotchety bit of writing. On the whole the content of the course material was well received. The overall structure was severely criticized. The anomalies were highlighted, especially the relative weighting given to the different sections. They didn't know about the limitations imposed by our dependence on tailors! Some of the criticisms and the likely reception of the material by students was not well founded. For instance, the judgement of the reviewer of Hinduism was not borne out by student performance. The students found the anthropological treatment of Hinduism relatively easier and the classical and philosophical studies relatively more difficult.

It became apparent as the course became known over the years that we had made a significant contribution to the study of religions at university level. Francis Clark was the architect of a course of which we could be proud. The importance of the course only became really evident when it became known that it was coming to an end. Courses in the Faculty of Arts generally have an eight year life. *Man's Religious Quest* was due to end in 1985 and to be replaced by another. Many voices were raised in protest, not least by such persons as Kenneth Cracknell of the British Council of Churches. The course had become important for a few thousand students by now. These students included some hundreds of teachers, especially teachers of RE. None of them wanted to see the course end and it was a course which by its very nature had not aged very much. The course was also considered important in the general climate of improving community relations.

At this point fate, in the guise of a government determined to cut back on public spending, including spending on the Open University, took a hand. The university did not have the resources to fund a replacement course. The faculty was having to economise in any case. The course team was asked one morning to produce a plan to cut the course in half by lunchtime on the understanding that we would continue teaching the truncated course for a further two years. That was in 1984. In 1989 the course still continues as a half credit, with improvements introduced in 1988.

This 1988 extension gave us an opportunity to introduce some amendments to the original course. The original units on Christianity had always been criticized, by students, tutors and external users, not for the quality of the material, but for the type of material they contained. In a course which was, on the whole, designed along phenomenological lines, these units were heavily doctrinally based and did not fit in with their companions. Arrangements with members of a department in another university to provide alternative material only partially succeeded, so much of the new material had to be generated internally. This provided an opportunity to experiment in writing a phenomenological study of Christianity.

When we looked for models to work on we found that there was nothing which exactly suited our needs. The nearest was Ninian Smart's *The Phenomenon of Christianity* (London, 1979) but this was too much of a survey of world-wide Christianity than a study of the phenomena which make up the Christian religion. American works which claim to offer a phenomenological study were also found wanting, being still too confessionally oriented. A recent example, Sandra S. Frankiel's *Christianity* (San Francisco, 1985) persists as predominantly ecclesiastical history. Peter McKenzie's *The Christians* (London, 1988) would have been more useful, but it had not yet appeared.

The new units are divided between a fairly conventional study of the history of the Christian religion from its origins in the life of Jesus the Christ and a study of the phenomena of the religion, under such sections as 'sacred space', 'sacred persons', and ending with a discussion of some contemporary ethical issues. After one year of use the new units have been well received by both tutors and students with minor reservations.

Since visits to places of worship had to be formally discontinued due to financial cuts in tutors' fees, an alternative strategy for 'earthing' the study of the religions more firmly in Britain had to be found. In 1988 John Bowker's *Worlds of Faith* (London, 1983) was introduced as part of the study package. Its introduction met a twofold need, to earth the study in Britain as has been said, but also to introduce an element which was missing from the original course. Originally the course had been designed deliberately as a study of the 'mainstream' in religions, hence the opposition to the introduction of too much sociology. With the introduction of *Worlds of Faith* the study of 'popular religion' was introduced. Both tutors and students have welcomed the addition and from reading student essays it is clear that the additional material has become an important resource for them. We believe that this continues the innovctive nature of Religious Studies in the Open University.

The course in its amended form will continue until 1992. By that time some six to seven thousand students will have successfully completed the course. By that time too the faculty will cease to teach Religious Studies as understood in this volume. In 1989 the faculty introduced what looks like being an extremely successful course on *Religion in Victorian Britain*. First reviews suggest that this course is as ground-breaking today as *Man's Religious Quest* was in 1978. In 1993 it will be joined by a course titled *Religion and Society in Britain from 1945 Onwards*. This course will include studies of the newly domiciled religions, but like the Victorian course the emphasis will be on religion as part of social history. Other times bring other priorities.

By 1992 *The Religious Quest* (the sexist title eventually disappeared in 1988) will have performed a valuable service. In 1983 Ursula King suggested that the consequences of 'introducing historical and systematic thinking about the religious traditions of mankind within a comparative and scholarly context to society at large cannot be fully assessed at present but should not be underestimated' (in F. Whaling, ed., *Contemporary Approaches to the Study of Religion*, Berlin, 1984, p. 62) A true assessment is probably not possible. We who were associated with it from its inception hope that its contribution to academic progress as well as to society at large will be valued for years to come.

'RELIGIOUS STUDIES'

Stewart R. Sutherland

In the early 1960s several areas within or proximate to the study of religions were well served by academic journals. Journals which paid special attention to theology, biblical studies, Near Eastern studies and ecclesiastical history were all well established. Specialist papers in the philosophy of religion and the history of religions could find various outlets, but there was no journal forum within Britain to aid the academic development of Religious Studies.

Religious Studies was created to meet that need and Cambridge University Press published the first part of the first volume in October 1965. Within four years the Press was sufficiently impressed to move to a quarterly rather than bi-annual format and in 1970 the present pattern of four issues per calendar year was established.

The first editor, H. D. Lewis, presided over an editorial board and international panel of editorial advisers which included philosophers and specialists in the history of religions, as well as those who had pioneered work in comparative religion. Geoffrey Parrinder is one of the founding members of the editorial board and one of the three members of that board who is still active as a contributor to the journal.

A significant focus of much of the best work published in the journal has been in the philosophy of religion and the tone and quality of many of the early contributors in this field was set by the first article featured in vol. I, pp. 5–27, H. H. Price's seminal 'Belief "In" and Belief "That"'. However, early indication of the refusal to be constrained by over-narrow horizons was given in vol. 1/2, which opened with R. W. Hepburn's excellently probing exploration of 'Questions about the Meaning of Life' (April 1966).

To the first issue Parrinder contributed 'Recent Views of Indian Religion and Philosophy' which set a pattern of using the close study of specific traditions to raise broader questions about religion and religions, continued to the present day. (See for example David B. Burrell's first class 'The Unknowability of God in Al-Ghazali' published in vol. 23/2, June 1985 or John Clayton's 'Religions, Reasons and Gods' in vol. 23/1, published in March 1987.)

The emphasis throughout the 25 volumes published to date has been to provide a forum for debating questions about the nature and truth of religious beliefs and practices; for examining important issues of the appropriate methods to be used; and for allowing the further development of the contribution to be made to these issues from other established fields. Thus for example from time to time papers are published which might equally find outlets in journals devoted to sociology, anthropology or psychology, although the number of such papers of high quality submitted is fairly low. Most recently there has been an encouraging and encouraged development of papers of interest which draw upon and apply to religious issues themes and techniques from the study of literature.

'THE SCOTTISH JOURNAL OF RELIGIOUS STUDIES'

Glyn Richards

The *Scottish Journal of Religious Studies* was established in 1980 and has appeared in the Spring and Autumn each year. It was launched to reflect the increasing interest felt in Scotland in the academic study of religion, as distinct from Christian theology, and in the development of Religious Studies as an academic discipline in its own right. It was envisaged that the journal would have a Scottish flavour, but it was not designed to be parochial in any way nor simply to present a Scottish outlook. The editorial board has a Scottish aspect, it is true, but the international editorial advisory board ensures the world-wide scope of the journal which has been borne out by the articles and reviews that have been submitted over the years. The primary aim of the journal is to promote a critical investigation of all aspects of the study of religion through the use of different methodologies which have included anthropological, sociological, philosophical, phenomenological, historical and comparative approaches. It also seeks to encourage enquiry into the cultural background of the major world religious traditions and the significance and importance of their interelationship in the context of what has been described in modern times as a global village and a planetary culture.

Articles over the past ten years have dealt with a variety of different topics and with all the major world religions. Philosophy, education, morality, mysticism, truth, nationalism, ecology, nuclear warfare, humanism, fundamentalism, art and literature are among the subjects that have been dealt with from time to time, and apart from papers dealing with different aspects of the study of religion there have been articles on Islam, Buddhism, Hinduism, Shinto, Confucianism as well as Christianity. Should the journal continue for another decade, it can do no better than to cater for the wide spectrum of subjects raised by the study of religion and at the same time provide a forum for the examination of issues raised by the diverse religious traditions of the world.

'THE JOURNAL OF RELIGION IN AFRICA'

Adrian Hastings

The *Journal of Religion in Africa*, published by Brill, Leiden, the Netherlands, was begun in 1967 by Andrew Walls in Aberdeen and continued to be edited by him until I took over in 1985 when the editorship moved from Aberdeen to Leeds. Since 1985 Rosalind Shaw (Edinburgh and now Boston, Massachusetts) has been deputy editor with responsibility for reviews. As both Rosalind and I were formerly members of the Department of Religious Studies in Aberdeen (now destroyed by vandals), it may well be claimed that the journal maintains in exile the Aberdeen spirit and its pioneering approach to the interdisciplinary study of African religion. It consists at present of three issues a year and a little over 300 pages, but it has grown in size of late and will continue to do so, to become a quarterly in the quite near future.

The journal is concerned with all aspects of religion in Africa, traditional, Christian and Islamic. It is open to historical, anthropological, sociological and phenomenological approaches of all types. It has no theological or ideological commitment other than one to serving its subject as imaginatively and openly as can be, but it does try to limit itself to the publication of genuinely innovative work. While articles on many aspects of religion in Africa do, of course, appear in *Africa*, *African Affairs* and many other journals, ours is the sole internationally recognised scholarly journal, without theological commitment, wholly devoted to African religion. Its contributors include scholars from almost every continent. Issues are usually thematic and are generally planned about a year in advance. They include both commissioned and uncommissioned articles. The review section is growing, but we still find it difficult to cope adequately with the range of books in our field published in many different countries and are continually looking for a wider reserve of competent Africanist reviewers.

The *Journal of Religion in Africa* endeavours to provide an exciting forum in which specific themes are explored and advanced and in which anthropologists, historians, students of literature and even theologians can mix easily and in ways fully intelligible to one another. A number of senior African scholars are on the editorial board and every issue includes work written by Africans, but the journal remains very much an international and intercontinental venture with the majority of its subscribers in the United States, but its base in Britain.

The final, October, issue of 1989 is devoted to the 1940s, for much of Africa a fairly quiet and under-studied decade. Geoffrey Parrinder has contributed to this issue an account of his own work and experience in Dahomey which led to the publication in 1949 of his first book, *West African Religion*. The scholarly, tolerant, genial character of his several works on religion in Africa provides one of the early formative influences upon the journal, and it is pleasant forty years later to contribute our own *Oriki*, or hymn of praise, for this living ancestor of the study of religion in Africa.

'RELIGION': ITS ORIGINS AND RENEWAL

Stuart Mews

'I have been in touch with Dr Parrinder only to discover that he is not planning anything in parallel/rivalry with us'.[1] In June 1969 the writer of that letter, Ian Calvert, a clergyman from Dudley, was one of a number of people who were in contact with Ninian Smart about the need for a new academic journal. They were mainly based in the north, but the eminence of Geoffrey Parrinder was such that it was deemed prudent for him to be consulted. In 1969, Smart was in his second year at Lancaster, where he had brought into existence the first Department of Religious Studies in Britain, and as part of his cultural revolution, was determined to create a new academic journal where his approach could be demonstrated and discussed. That concept, however, only emerged gradually; his first thoughts had been for a periodical devoted to Buddhist studies which had suffered from the demise of the journal of the Pali Text Society, and to a lesser extent, from the closure of the *Hibbert Journal*. However a journal restricted solely to Buddhist studies would be unlikely to generate a large enough circulation. So the answer seemed to lie in a journal appearing three or four times a year with one number devoted exclusively to Buddhist topics. The remaining numbers were to carry articles in the history of religion, but in such a way as not to overlap substantially with the philosophical approach which had become characteristic of *Religious Studies*. In particular the interdisciplinary approach pioneered at Lancaster, and especially the insights of the then new discipline of sociology of religion, were to be encouraged. Also considered was the possibility of providing an abstracting service on the model of the *Sociology of Education Bulletin*, an idea put forward by Kenneth Jones, who had been interviewed in the previous year at Lancaster, and was subsequently to obtain a PhD degree there. With no shortage of ideas, Smart now felt that the time had come to approach publishers, only to be shot down in flames by Basil Blackwell: 'on the whole, our advisors are against it because they feel that its ideas are strangely assorted'.[2] Undaunted, enquiries began for a multilith in-house production to be printed in the university library and called *Lancaster Religious Studies*: 'but where are we to get £400?'

The key link in the chain which produced *Religion* was provided by John Hinnells, then a lecturer in Newcastle, where he had begun a collaboration with Bruce Allsop, who taught the history of architecture in the same institution and had set up the Oriel Press in 1962. Hinnells had already discussed the idea of a British journal of comparative religion with Eric Sharpe, with whom he overlapped for a short time in Manchester before the latter moved to Lancaster in 1970. Both of them now joined forces with Smart's team of three young Lancaster lecturers: Michael Pye, Adrian Cunningham, and Stuart Mews, together with Ian Calvert. To make the team more representative, they soon added Trevor Ling, then at Leeds, and Eric Pyle from Glasgow. Ling had been supervised as a doctoral student by Smart at King's, London, and had in turn taught Mews, while Pyle had visited Lancaster for colloquia and was known to be sympathetic to the Religious Studies approach. On 3 December 1969, Hinnells secured Allsop's backing for the venture. At this stage, the proposed title was *The Journal of Religion and Religions*, but by March 1970, it had become *Religion: Journal of Religion and Religions*. The journal was to be directed not by an editor, but by the board who elected Ninian Smart as chairman, John Hinnells as editorial secretary, and Ian Calvert as administrative secretary.

Religion first hit the streets in the spring of 1971. Its first number was meant to be a shopwindow and included two articles from social scientists, the psychologist Gustav Jahoda and sociologist Bryan Turner, as well as contributions on methodology by Eric Sharpe and a pioneering study of new religious movements by Harold Turner. Some continuity with Smart's original dream was provided by a survey article on the present state of Pali studies in the west by Miss I. B. Horner, President of the Pali Text Society. After the first flurry of the launch, subscriptions rose sluggishly. The January 1972 board meeting noted with disappointment that reviews in the *Times Literary Supplement* and *The Journal of Teachers in R.E.* had been both off beam and unhelpful. Clearly in 1972, the non-confessional, multi-disciplinary approach to the study of religion was still viewed with suspicion and incomprehension by some professionals in the field. It was felt that a better reception could be expected in the USA and John Wilson of Princeton and Ed Perry of Northwestern were co-opted to promote the journal in America.

In 1972 Oriel Press went into liquidation. Routledge & Kegan Paul, having first refused to take on *Religion*, eventually acquired it. The mid-seventies were a difficult time for publishers and in a bid to avoid continual price increases, the new publishers proposed that *Religion* should lead the way by going into what they called 'direct edition', which effectively meant photographing a typescript. The board tried to hold out against this development. Smart was sent to negotiate with RKP chairman, Norman Franklin. He reported back: 'I asked for a stay of execution for a further year regarding the style of printing. Norman Franklin laughed in his iron manner. As we appear to be no more than growling chickens, I surrendered. The moral is, those who have no cards to play growl like chickens.'[3]

On this occasion, the board was right and the publisher wrong. The unattractive character of the journal deterred authors and put off potential subscribers. Circulation figures, which had been ever so slightly rising, flattened out. The editorial board found the situation depressing. Then in the midst of Britain's 'winter of discontent', in January 1979, came a promise of spring from America. Ninian Smart was now teaching for the winter semester in California. He reported that former Lancaster graduate student Ivan Strenski of Connecticut College and Hans Penner of Dartmouth College had been discussing the idea of a study-of-religion oriented journal in the USA, 'somewhat like *Religion* in fact, but with more in the way of lively feedback'.[4] Strenski and Penner with Smart's encouragement now suggested that *Religion* should expand from two numbers per year to four with two of the numbers to be edited from, and the whole journal published and printed in, the USA. This last idea was unacceptable to the board, but discussions continued. Adrian Cunningham, now the editor, had recently contributed a chapter to a book published by Academic Press, and discussed the journal's future with one of the directors, Anthony Watkinson, who had been working in a similar area as Mews when they were both graduate students in Cambridge. Academic Press were interested, particularly in the idea of an Anglo-American editorial team. They already published the *Journal of Historical Geography*, edited jointly from both sides of the Atlantic. Cunningham sought the advice of the British editor of that journal. This was John Patten, who was preparing to abandon academic life for the House of Commons (he is now minister of state at the Home Office) and was an enthusiast for the Atlantic alliance. Academic Press were willing to spend money promoting the journal, providing they could be assured of its worth. They canvassed the opinions of twenty-five senior academics. One of them, inevitably, was Geoffrey Parrinder. Although the publishers removed the names of their respondents, internal evidence such as the reference to a report on the governance of London University, suggests that he gave the journal a glowing recommendation. Quite independent from these considerations, the board was delighted in 1980 to devote an issue of the journal to a collection of essays in honour of Geoffrey Parrinder's seventieth birthday.

Religion was now relaunched with an attractive type-face, four numbers per year, and British and American editors. Though there have inevitably been some cross-wires, the arrangement has served the academic community well. This account has concentrated on the harsh realities of creating, sustaining, and renewing an academic journal in a cold economic climate. Though grateful for his support, those who have been associated with the journal from its beginnings, might sometimes wonder whether Geoffrey Parrinder was not wise in 'not planning anything in parallel/rivalry with us'.

NOTES

[1] Ian Calvert – Ninian Smart, 20 June 1969.
[2] John Cutforth – Ian Calvert, 13 March 1969.
[3] Ninian Smart – Eric Pyle, 4 February 1976.
[4] Ninian Smart – Colleagues on the Board, 5 January 1979
[5] John Patten – Adrian Cunningham, 30 May 1979.

2. RELIGIOUS STUDIES IN POLYTECHNICS AND COLLEGES OF HIGHER EDUCATION

Brian E. Gates

It is a source of both potential strength and weakness that provision for the study of religion in higher education outside the university sector takes its size, shape and colour from the needs and interests of children. This is principally because in origins and present opportunities it has an intrinsic association with teacher education. The truth of this assertion is immediately apparent from an historical review of the institutional settings involved. It is confirmed by subsequent inspection of course content and approaches.

Institutional Evolution and the Size of Provision

Higher education outside the university sector has been rigorously controlled by central government. Apart from universities, the institutions engaged in aspects of it for much of the last century have been teacher training colleges. Their role and status in this regard was made explicit only within the last twenty years, when re-designated by government as colleges or institutes of higher education. Alongside them are the polytechnics, dating back to the 1880s, but more substantially creatures of the 1960s. Each in its own distinctive setting has had a part in the present level of provision.

There are several important turning points in the development of this provision. Since it is difficult to understand the present distribution, let alone the strains for its future, without an appreciation of its past, it is worth identifying these for the whole sector from its inception:

1839   Chester College founded: first of many church-related teacher training institutions
1870   Forster Education Act: inauguration of Dual System – joint funding by church and state of public elementary schools for all
1880   Regent Street Polytechnic founded by Quentin Hogg
1902   Education Act introduces LEA teacher training colleges and universal secondary schools
1911   University education departments provide degree and professional certification for secondary teachers

1925   Minimum 18+ entry stage established for teacher-training, primary and secondary; end of pupil-monitor system

1944   Education Act endorsing RE provision for all pupils in school; expansion of teacher training colleges

1956   Designation of 8 colleges of advanced technology

1960   Teacher training for non-graduates extended from 2 to 3 years

1963   Robbins Report: further expansion of teacher training colleges, now re-designated as colleges of education, and of regional polytechnics

1965   Formation of Council for National Academic Awards (CNAA)

1971   James Report: diversification of colleges of education into Dip HE and BA teaching; emergence of colleges and institutes of higher education

1978   All graduate entry to teaching profession takes effect, i.e. BEd, BA (Ed), or degree plus PGCE.

1988   Education Reform Act (ERA): creation of Polytechnics and Colleges Funding Council (PCFC) and of Universities Funding Council (UFC). Re-iteration of requirement of RE for all school pupils including sixth formers.

1. Teacher Training Colleges

Teacher training colleges were either voluntary foundations sponsored by one or other of the Christian churches or they were established by LEAs. Initially, most were of the first kind, but following World War II the others came to predominate. Thus, in 1945 54 were church-related and only 29 from LEAs, whereas by 1951 there were 56 in the first category and as many as 76 in the latter.

The partnership of church and state, in jointly providing public education for the nation's children, itself ensured that religion had an institutional presence, not only in church foundations, but also in most LEA ones as well. This was reflected first in the general exposure of every elementary school teacher to basic aspects of the Christian tradition. Thus, in 1839, at Chester Diocesan College all students were expected to study 'Scripture Knowledge, Evidences of Christianity and Church History', as well as English, history, maths, geography, science, art and music. A century later, this would be still recognisable in both church and LEA colleges. Secondly, the teacher training colleges also came to contribute, in addition to the university provision for this, to the training of secondary school RE specialists.

The quality of learning in teacher training colleges was certainly mixed, but for many students it provided the only available form of full-time higher education affordable to them. In this context, the study of religion, though modest in proportion, was universally guaranteed, whether the college was church-related, non-denominational voluntary, or LEA based. Until 1960, certification was achieved after two years; thereafter, the course was lengthened by a year. It was a further decade before the 4 year Honours BEd became the normative alternative to the university BA plus PGCE as a degree based route into teaching.

2. Colleges and Institutes of Higher Education

In the wake of the Robbins Report, there was expansion of the training colleges comparable to that of the universities on other fronts. Thus, in 1958 of 18,000 student teachers 14,500 were college based, 3,500 in university departments. Ten years later, there were over $2\frac{1}{2}$ times as many student teachers, of whom 41,500 were college based and only 5,000 in universities. Of these, there was the expectation that all primary students would study religion sufficiently to enable them to fulfil their primary teaching role and there was a substantial secondary specialist contingent.

Significantly, Robbins was sensitive to the pejorative implications of the existing system. Colleges were seen to be for the *education* of teachers; henceforth, instead of being called teacher training colleges, they would be called colleges of education. Many student teachers working in this context rather than in a university were recognised as having the capacity for honours degree achievement. Similarly, many tutors in colleges were judged capable of that level of teaching. In many instances the route to effecting this change of emphasis included the extension of university links to set a college in the orbit of a university school of education.

A further dimension to those changes was provided by the James Report. Given the principle of higher education experience as intrinsic to teacher education programmes and the ability of colleges to deliver this, there were seen to be advantages in making some of these same elements available to non-teacher students in the form of liberal arts and humanities degrees. Economy of resource was seen to combine with greater opportunity for student choice of course components and even course outcomes – routing in or out of the teaching degree after one or two years.

This in turn was achieved by two concomitant changes. Firstly, in staff appointments, in the case of some tutors academic prowess was sought in subject studies as much as, or even more than, in education and primary/secondary teaching experience. And secondly, some of the smaller colleges were amalgamated to form Institutes of Higher Education. Thus, the Liverpool Institute of Higher Education combined three colleges: St Katherine's (CE), Christ's and Notre Dame (RC). West London IHE was formed from Borough Road and Maria Grey (RC) and the West Sussex IHE from Bishop Otter College (CE) and Bognor Regis (LEA).

Remarkably, as a result of all these developments opportunity for degree level study of religion was massively increased in the space of a very few years. New BEd and BA programmes with common elements on religion, ranging from a single 'module' to two years of full-time study became available throughout England and Wales.

Unfortunately, the opportunity was not always exploited to best advantage by the particular institution. Moreover, further changes were afoot. 'Rationalisation' brought more amalgamations/absorptions in which the religion interests of a small institution were sometimes ingested by a larger one, with success in terms only of completing an effective disappearing trick. This was the fate of St Gabriel's in relation to Goldsmiths' and Keswick Hall with the University of East Anglia. Manpower planning to correlate teacher supply with school age cohorts also led to cuts in quotas of BEd students given to particular institutions. Since one year PGCE numbers are much easier to increase/decrease at short notice, there was a corresponding switch in DES thinking in favour of providing more primary PGCE places in university departments of education and accordingly less BEds in colleges and institutes of higher education. This last move, coupled with changes in the funding arrangements for teacher in-service courses, has weakened the ground in at least some institutions for what otherwise would have been a strong staffing base for the continuing study of religion in a college or institute of higher education.

3. Polytechnics

The early polytechnics emerged in the 1880s, led by Quentin Hogg's Regent Street Polytechnic. They were principally concerned with technical education, often part-time. Where they led to degrees, it was usually by the extra-mural route of a local university. There is little evidence of religion being studied in this early polytechnic context.

In the mid-fifties, building on the earlier Percy Report (1945), the government announced a National Council for Technical Awards and 8 colleges of advanced technology. They were to concentrate on science and technology, but provide also for courses in industrial organisation and liberal studies. This policy was endorsed by the Robbins Report and in its subsequent implementation, the humanities dimension of polytechnics as they now came to be called, was deliberately reinforced. The creation of the CNAA for Britain as a whole provided the complementary agency to that of the universities for the validation of degrees. Though initially polytechnic-related, after several years increasing numbers of colleges and institutes of higher education looked to and found in the CNAA the means of combining institutional autonomy with academic authentication. CNAA's role in facilitating the study of religion should not be underestimated.

So far as the polytechnics themselves are concerned, however, such provision as has existed there for the study of religion has once again been related to a simultaneous involvement in teacher education. This is true both of basic courses as part of a primary BEd/PGCE programme, or of more substantial components for secondary specialists, or on a BA. Only in a minority of instances has the opportunity been sensed for BA development in the study of religion parallel to that which is teacher related. Moreover, except in polytechnics with involvement in teacher education, religion does not usually figure on the polytechnic curriculum.

4. The Current Position

Provision for the study of religion in a non-university based HE context is most substantial in the colleges and institutes of HE. The position is patchy, however. Institutions which once offered main subject study in religion are fewer than they were 15 years ago. This is inevitable since there used to be over a 100 colleges involved in teacher education, and some study of religion within it. Now there are 38. Of these, if it figures at all, it is only in a basic curriculum course in 7: Anglia, Bedford, Bretton Hall, Bulmershe, Nene, West Glamorgan and Worcester. In the rest, it is relatively alive and well either in the BEd alone or also in the BA.

It may not be altogether surprising that opportunities are greatest in the church-related institutions. Of those church colleges offering a BA programme, only King Alfred's, Winchester, provides no opportunity to study religion in that context. In most, religion is a major component in the Combined Studies BA programme. In three, the degree is actually in Theology (Southampton's BTh) or Theology and Religious Studies (Leeds, Liverpool and Westminster). Of the former LEA colleges, there are substantial BA components on religion at Bath and at Crewe & Alsager; by contrast, it is being phased out at Humberside.

The position in polytechnics is much poorer. In no case is there any programme in religion except where a merger with a college of education has occurred. Sometimes, a flourishing college tradition for studying religion has been run down, as at Brighton, Bristol, Leeds, Newcastle and latterly Trent. Even the incorporation of a church college as at the first two, has been no guarantee of religion's survival beyond a basic curriculum course. Of the 30 polytechnics of England and Wales only 5 or 6 have any major offering in the study of religion: Middlesex, Sunderland (both RS) Thames (Theological Studies) BA and BEd; Hatfield, Manchester and Wolverhampton BEd only.

Since the Education Reform Act, all colleges and institutes of HE and polytechnics are managed jointly by the newly created PCFC. LEA sponsorship is gone, though established church links remain. What priority will be given to religion in BA programmes by PCFC remains to be seen; in principle there is no bar to additional bids being made to the Council for funding. Priority in BEd and PGCE is guaranteed at a basic level for all primary student teachers and secondary specialists by the ERA requirements and further specification from the Council for the Accreditation of Teacher Education. Those institutions presently without any specialist tutors in religion will find it more difficult to evade their responsibility to appoint such if they are to remain in good professional standing. As for main subject studies of religion in the BEd, PGCE and in-service named awards, the need from schools to implement the ERA should guarantee at least the continuation of the present range of offerings and even, recruitment permitting, invite expansion.

The Shape and Colour of Religious Studies in the PCFC Sector

The story of how religion is studied in colleges and polytechnics has a similar plot to that of the universities, but it is not identical. The chief difference lies in the effects and opportunities arising from the professional context to which the study is commonly related.

1. The Name of the Game

Like its namesake in schools, the study of religion by student teachers was until the 1960s known principally as scripture, or divinity. The former title reflected the fact that RE in county schools from 1870 onwards should not by law be denominationally distinctive, or doctrinally specific. Given the religious diversity and squabbles, which Agreed Syllabus Conferences were instituted to address, the Bible was taken as the common ground on which Christians of all complexions, as well as others, could meet. Divinity had a potentially broader reference, as was made plain in an annual lecture at the London Institute by Geoffrey Parrinder (1971), but common usage had given it a narrower Christian focus. Thus, student teachers in both church-related and LEA colleges met religion in a predominantly biblical form. In Roman Catholic colleges, teaching from within the faith, to students and for schools also within the faith, made rather more of catechetical doctrine and sacraments.

The major shift of name had taken almost universal effect by the early 1970s. In 1971 the subject section of the Association of Teachers in Colleges and Departments of Education (subsequently NATFHE) voted to change from divinity to Religious Studies. Most colleges conformed. The exceptions which remain are all church related. Divinity is still used at Liverpool and theology at Southampton; the others prefer a conflate of theology (taken as Christian) and RS – so Leeds All Saints, Newman-Westhill, Ripon St John, Westminster and, sometimes, Liverpool.

The lead undoubtedly was taken from the Lancaster model, as described by Adrian Cunningham. Though critics might see it as fad-following, the rationale was keenly felt in colleges, attuned as they are to the changes in religious sensibility shown by children in school. Christian belonging could not be taken for granted amidst the sea of secularisation, and faiths other than Christianity were now more physically noticeable than when their main representation had been Jewish. RS was perceived as a declaration of impartiality.

To the traditional elements of biblical studies it became usual to add both introductory and advanced courses in other religious traditions. The chief obstacles to this were generally not ideological so much as constraints of time and competence. It was also more common to give greater attention than hitherto to other aspects of Christianity – social, cultural, ethical. One such example of this trend was set out as follows:

Year 1: The religious phenomenon
       (a) Major communities and their traditions: Buddhists, Hindus and Sikhs, Jews, and Muslims
       (b) Sociological perspective on religion in human history.
Year 2: The Christian tradition
       (a) NT credentials   (b)Theology: creeds and systematics
       (c) Liturgy and culture: faith expressed in arts, social action and worship.
Year 3: Theological insights into human existence
       (a) Twentieth century atheism   (b) Comparative ethics
       (c) Field work – hospital, prison, theatre visits.

This is the revised content of a three year teachers' certificate course introduced in 1968. The shape of the subject was becoming different!

Curiously, the distinctiveness of this Goldsmiths' College course lay as much in the title of the department: Religion. Since we do not usually speak of historical/geographical/scientific studies, but of history, geography and science, arguably 'religion' is a better name than RS. Perhaps it is a mark of defensiveness that the subject has persisted in using the supporting 'Studies' label to 'prove' its intellectual respectability?

2. Religion as Comprehended by BEd and BA Degrees

Time constraints inevitably sharpened thinking about how religion is to be defined and delivered. As in a university so in a college or polytechnic – on a BA course in RS, a student might reasonably be expected to have anything from a third to most of his/her study time on the subject. But with the BEd (all graduate entry to the profession after 1978) the time available ranges from as little in some instances as 20 hours for a basic course for all primary students to a maximum of a third of a student's time over 4 years, the rest being given to education theory, curriculum applications and school experience.

Within this time a student engages with religion, as it were, bifocally. Alternating in the foreground and background is the subject matter of religion and the subjective potential of individual boys and girls to make sense of it. There is even a third focus. In addition to the starting points of children and the substance of religion that may appropriately be shared by them, there is the personal interest and intellectual satisfaction of the students in their own right.

At worst, this is an impossible condition. One or other of the targets is not met. Thus, the course is too academic and removed from the school classroom, or it is over-simple to the point of being superficial. In the interests of connecting personal experience around the triangular circuit of tutor, student and child, hermeneutical fuses can easily be blown!

At best, however, personal and professional sympathies combine to achieve understanding of real depth. There is recognition of the range of Christian experience and tradition, as of any religion, and of the need to select to comprehend. There is appreciation of the likely assistance available from different disciplines in interpreting the experience, including linguistic, sociological, philosophical, artistic. And there is a sense that in boys and girls, or peers, or even adults, there is a potential for human resonance in meeting round the picture language and imagery, the body language and ritual, the story line and myth through which religion commonly finds expression.

In practice, it is usual for BEd related approaches to religion to draw on the very disciplines that are important to both religious and educational studies. Psychology figures therefore, but not as dead men's remains. The diagnoses of Freud and Piaget are actually tried out and tested against the classroom pulse. How do children think and feel and learn? What sense do they make of the wonderings of others in songs and other emblems of faith? What wondering do they themselves engage in? Psychology of religion may not be widely taught in university departments, but in the colleges it has been no accident to find tutors with well developed research expertise in this field.

Similarly, philosophy looms large. How could it not when daily tutors and students are called upon to justify, without special pleading, the place of religion in any curriculum? Its focus is more likely to be on conceptual analysis and the explication of religious language than as an historical discipline, but recurrent issues such as theistic evidences, the nature of revelation and the autonomy of ethics are frequently treated.

In related ways, there is expertise in phenomenological analysis and methodology, interpreting the nature of religious artefacts and actions. Typically, this includes notions of sacred persons, places and times, and examples are commonly drawn from across the history and anthropology of religions. The invitation, to disengage from private conviction and to make sense of what may be treasured by strangers, plays the double role of contributing to academic self-understanding and prospective professional involvement.

The substance of the Christian tradition is thoroughly addressed. In biblical terms, study of the interpretation of the gospels and Pauline literature is widely offered, just occasionally with Greek. Much rarer, sadly, is opportunity to study the OT. This is not a Marcionite conspiracy, more a consequence of the enormous dimensions of religion in the world and even of deference to Judaism as a living religion. Christian theology is taught, both historically and thematically, as is also its expression in the visual and performing arts. Relatively little attention has been given to Christianity outside western Europe, but this may be changing under the combined influence of Afro-Caribbean settlement and contemporary world events.

Attention to other individual religions is a consistent feature of college and polytechnic departments. Sikhism may even have received more attention here then in university departments. Islam, Hinduism and Judaism are extensively taught; more fleetingly, the faith of the Jains and Parsees. It is, however, Buddhism which is perhaps best served in terms of academic excellence.

Religion is well served by this range of scholarship in the PCFC world. It is not solely the content of the scholarship, but how it is shared, of which the sector has much to boast. Perhaps again because of the sensitivity to the skills needed for work in schools, there is ample evidence of active learning methods being employed by college tutors. Similarly, it is in the colleges that the three major resource centres for the study of religion are housed – at Ripon St John in York, at Westhill in Birmingham and at West London IHE.

The precise shape and shade of colour given to the study of religion varies from department to department, but there is much that is simultaneously stimulating and weighty that is available to support both BA and BEd degrees outside the universities.

3. Three Degrees

By way of illustrating the capacity of the sector for relative distinctiveness or new departures, fuller summaries of three degree schemes are now included. The first is the S. Martin's BA in Religion and Social Ethics of Lancaster. It is a much heard criticism that Moral

Education has suffered from being a poor relation of RE; similarly, ethics and religion can be hurt by mutual capsize or polarisation. The S. Martin's venture offsets this by ensuring that the groundwork for ethics is simultaneously laid in moral philosophy, social science and comparative ethics. Separate course areas of application are health and medicine, discrimination, economics, war and peace, and social policy. The range of options permits a student to keep the religious ingredient to a minimum, or to make it into the co-ordinating thread. In the latter case, following introductory courses in the first year, s/he may set alongside 3 'straight' religion courses (NT, Related themes in Buddhism and Christianity, and Islam *or* Christianity and the Arts) 6 in Social Ethics. These are chosen from the available 11, including 2 in comparative ethics (Buddhist, Christian, Hindu, Marxist, Muslim and Secular Humanist, plus thematic applications), philosophical issues, psychology of moral behaviour, western ethical traditions and the 5 areas of applied ethics, along with a dissertation. After more than 10 years of teaching and resourcing, there is something here of more than passing interest.

The second example is that of the Westminster BA in Theology newly launched on the Oxford scene in the early 1980s. It has been designed to approach both the study and practice of theology in the modern world. The emphasis is on doing theology by developing theological skills in the contemporary context. It begins with courses on biblical studies, the development of doctrine (early fathers and Reformation), exploring religious phenomena and an introduction to philosophy. These are followed in year 2 by further biblical studies and doctrine (Enlightenment and contemporary theology), plus ethics and philosophical theology. In year 3 there are courses in hermeneutics, social context of theology, and an option chosen from: political theology, Christian response to other religions, Christian ethics, belief and problem of evil, or Christian and Marxist views of man. Although this degree will draw on at least some of the well treasured resources of the Oxford tradition of theological study, it is complementary to, rather than duplicating, its neighbouring degree in the university.

Thirdly, we turn to the Roehampton Institute, where with the combined resources of 4 colleges (Digby Stuart – RC, Froebel – undenominational, Southlands – Methodist, and Whitelands – CE) there is a 'two track' approach to Theology and RS, variously available to BEd and BA students. The foundation year comprises both tracks: A – anthropology, phenomenology and philosophy of religion, plus a non–Christian faith; B – biblical and Christian texts and background. Thereafter the tracks diverge. Track A takes in Buddhism, Hinduism, Islam and Judaism, including textual study; plus philosophy of religious language, political theology and contemporary RE. Track B covers Old Testament text and theology, revelation *or* ethics; New Testament texts and theology, early Christian tradition, medieval theology, Christian tradition in contemporary society, Barth and Rahner, and Christian ethics. Although the institutional diversity of the Greater London area has vastly diminished since the 1960s, when there were as many as 25 colleges outside the university sector offering opportunities to study religion, this Roehampton scheme, alongside those of Strawberry Hill, WLIHE and the London Bible College, ensures that the tradition thrives.

Turning up or Turning Down?

There are various possible scenarios for the future of RS in polytechnics and colleges of higher education. One of them fears the worst, and for several reasons. Too many of the best advocates of RS, those responsible for its consolidation in the last 25 years, have left, or are leaving their institutions. Nor will their posts necessarily be maintained for others to fill. The effects of the ERA will be further to alienate pupils and parental faith communities from RE, so that no appetite will be aroused in schools for its pursuit into higher education. Finally, the PCFC regime is itself a threat to RS. As a humanities subject, it is given the lowest funding base of all, and little sign of research and encouragement. It would therefore be no surprise were HE institutions to be attracted to give priority attention to more generously endowed alternatives. On this scenario RS will be another victim to a 1990s wasting disease.

More optimistically, these same factors could be the occasion of both encouragement and expansion. Senior colleagues may be taking early retirement, but many of them are relatively youthful and may still deploy their energies on behalf of RS. At the same time, they have created space for a new generation of appointments. As for the ERA, instead of reducing momentum for RS, it may actually increase it. For there should now be more provision in school, including the sixth forms. Moreover, it has established Standing Advisory Councils for RE in each LEA, whose job it is to monitor delivery in schools, as also in HE institutions locally involved with teacher education. Even the PCFC may work to the advantage of RS, and for at least two reasons. Firstly, RS is not a costly programme. Therefore, provided it can continue to recruit as well as it is doing at the moment, the risk factor to an institution to go on offering it is limited, especially if the staff base can be used to help meet CATE (Council for the Accreditation of Teachers) criteria for professional courses (BEd or PGCE) in RE. Secondly, the differential funding for subjects and professionally oriented degrees may provide the incentive to RS departments to forge partnerships beyond the humanities, and additional to the teaching profession, that will be both economically attractive to institutional self-interest and revealing of dimensions long hidden within the scattered terrain of HE.

In sum, it is worth remembering that the college part of what is now the PCFC sector had a religious foundation. In this respect at least it shares some common ground with the early university tradition. Although things have changed, such that exclusive Christian sponsorship for HE is almost unthinkable, so they have with regard to a secularised norm. The idea either that the world at large, or HE in particular is not shot through with full-blooded religious concerns flies in the face of experience as blindly as church has never done with science. RS colleagues may perhaps find an opportunity to be as modest as Galileo as their institutions meet yet another turning point.

NOTE: Since this essay was written, the CNAA has published a report on 'Theology and Religious Studies in Polytechnics and Colleges' which also includes details about Religious Studies in Humanities courses. The report is available from the Publications Division, CNAA, 344–354 Gray's Inn Road, London WC1X 8BP.

SUGGESTED READING

J. R. Garnett, ed., *NATFHE Handbook of Initial Teacher Training, Other Degree and Advanced Courses in Institutes/Colleges of Higher Education Polytechnics and University Departments of Education in England and Wales 1990*, London: Linneys ESL, 1989.

B. E. Gates, *RE Directory for England and Wales*, Lancaster: RE Council, 1990.

F. H. Hilliard, 'Divinity Studies in Teacher Training' in *Theology* LXVII, p. 532, October 1964, pp. 438–42.

D. Naylor, *Religious Education: Preparing the Teachers*, Unpublished MA thesis, Lancaster University, 1970.

E. J. Sharpe, 'The Comparative Study of Religion in Colleges of Education' in
. J. R. Hinnells, ed., *Comparative Religion in Education*, Newcastle: Oriel Press, 1970, pp. 103–8.

N. Smart, *Secular Education and the Logic of Religion*, London: Faber, 1968.

3. RELIGIOUS STUDIES IN ADULT AND CONTINUING EDUCATION

Michael Combermere

There are 50 departments of Adult and Continuing Education at British universities listed in the Universities Council for Adult and Continuing Education Year Book 1986/87. All departments were written to requesting information, but only approximately two-thirds replied. I therefore propose in this chapter to illustrate developing trends and the current state of studies, firstly from programmes offered in London, which has the largest provision, and secondly from Manchester and Birmingham. All three of these universities have a full time lecturer in Biblical and/or Religious Studies at their Extra-Mural Departments or Departments of Adult and Continuing Education. Thirdly, provision for Religious Studies at other university departments of Adult and Continuing Education will then be referred to.

The term Religious Studies is usually understood to refer to such subjects as philosophy of religion, the study of world religions or comparative religion and sociology of religion, while theological studies usually include biblical studies, Christian doctrine and church history. The terms have often been confused and this confusion also occurred when inquiring specifically about Religious Studies. In more than one case I was provided with details of courses which would normally come under the heading of theology, as distinct from Religious Studies. However, this has in fact proved useful as it has enabled me to set Religious Studies within the context of a broader picture, for the overall predominant provision in Adult and Continuing Education has been in terms of biblical and theological studies rather than in Religious Studies as such.

London

The developments in the teaching of Religious Studies over the last thirty years or so can only be understood if one knows something of its earlier history and background within adult education. University extension lectures were first held in London during the autumn of 1876 under the auspices of the London Society for the Extension of University Education (LSEUT). This society was succeeded by a board to promote the extension of university teaching (BPEUT) in 1900. Both bodies provided lectures and examinations from 1876 to 1928, while in 1909 BPEUT first organised a series of tutorial classes in conjunction with the Workers' Educational Association (WEA) to supplement the work done in extension courses.

In 1928 a University Extension Committee and a Tutorial Classes Council were set up with separate committees to deal with their respective work. In 1952 the two committees came together with the creation of the Council of Extra-Mural Studies. The most recent re-organisation came in 1988 when the Department of Extra-Mural Studies was integrated with Birkbeck College as a major resource centre.

It has not been possible to discover when the first course or series of lectures was offered in either Biblical or Religious Studies by LSEUT or BPEUT, but a three year tutorial class in religion was taken by a Miss West starting with the 1925–26 session. The subject was 'The Scientific and Comparative Study of Religion' and the syllabus was an interesting amalgam of biblical studies, Greek philosophy, ancient religions of the past, and modern world religions. In the first year, for example, primitive and tribal religions were studied as well as the religions of ancient Egypt, Babylon and Assyria, but the main emphasis was on Old Testament studies from 'Primitive Israel' to 'The Return from Exile'. In the second year attention focussed initially on Hinduism, Buddhism and Zoroastrianism; then, after the last of the Hebrew prophets were discussed, students were taken through Greek drama, religion and philosophy. Attention then turned to the Old Testament again, to Jewish apocalyptic literature and to the Book of Daniel, for example, before considering the origin of Christianity, and then on to Islam. The third and final year was concerned exclusively with the New Testament. This three year course on the scientific and comparative study of religion concentrated largely on biblical studies while the study of ancient religions and philosophies and world religions appear to have been used largely as background material and regarded as of secondary importance.

A milestone was reached on 1 February 1928 when it was agreed that a sub-committee be established to report as to how far the existing Diploma in Theology and the Certificate in Religious Knowledge are 'suited to or can be adapted for University Extension students attending courses organised by the Divinity Lecturers

Committee'.[1] This resolution followed an earlier proposal for the institution of a Diploma in Divinity intended primarily for students attending courses under the auspices of the Board.

At this time university extension lectures were organised in London by the Divinity Lectures Committee. The programme included full sessional courses on the Literary and Historical Study of the Old Testament, and the Literary and Historical Study of the New Testament. The Senate took note of the report of the sub-committee that neither the existing Diploma in Theology nor the existing Certificate in Religious Knowledge was suitable for students attending courses organised by the Divinity Lectures Committee. The Diploma in Theology was regarded as being too wide, while the standard of the Certificate was considered to be too low. The sub-committee therefore recommended that a new Diploma be established for students attending courses under the auspices of the Divinity Lectures Committee.

Accordingly, it was resolved that a Diploma in the Literary, Historical and Comparative Study of the Bible be instituted and that it should offer a general course of study consisting of three sessional courses which 'shall include a study – literary, historical and comparative – of the Old Testament and the New Testament and Apocalyptic literature so as to afford a suitable groundwork for further study.' This further course of study, which was to be pursued by the students after the general course, could have reference to *either* the History of the Bible in the Christian Church to 611 *or* The Philosophical Study of Religion and Ethics *or* The Comparative Study of the Religions of the World *or* a detailed study of selected books of the Bible to be approved. The Committee resolved that students 'shall attend such courses of lectures on the special subject of study as the University may require.'[2]

The first examinations for this new diploma were held in 1929 on the Old Testament and the Gospels, then in the following year (1930) as well as two papers, one on the Old Testament, and one on the Gospels, two final examination papers were set – one on the Philosophical Study of Religion and Ethics and one on the Comparative Study of Religion and History of Religion. In the latter paper candidates were required to attempt not fewer than 7 and not more than 9 questions while the paper itself was divided into Part 1, Comparative Study, and Part 2, History. It is apparent from the examination paper that the syllabus covered aspects of primal religion, including magic and totemism, Sikhism, Hinduism, Buddhism – both

Theravada and Mahayana, – Shintoism, Confucianism, and the religions of Greece and Rome. This is interesting because this pattern, established in 1928, survived until 1973 when it was changed. In other words, world religions and other subjects coming under the heading of 'Religious Studies' were only taken *after* students had passed examinations in biblical subjects. Secondly, the examination syllabus for the world religions paper continued to cover all the major world religions. The last time an examination paper was set under this syllabus was in 1972.

Between 1928 and 1968 the diploma was reviewed six times and various changes were made, but none were of a really radical nature. Consequently one finds that in 1967 candidates were still required to do both the Old Testament and the New Testament first (part I), and then they could select two of the following subjects: Religious and Social Life and Thought in England from 1800 to the present day, Church History to 451 AD, the Philosophy and Psychology of Religion, the Living Religions, Biblical Theology, and Sociology of Religion (part II). Alternatively, if an introductory course on The Ancient World: Religions and Civilisations to the Birth of Christ was taken in Part I, then only one subject needed to be selected for Part II.

The Religious Studies programme as a whole will now be considered and in doing this, illustrations will be taken first from the 1951–52 programme which is the earliest available from the Senate House Archives. The programmes for 1956–57, 1960–61, 1967–68, and 1972–73 will then be considered because at these times the diploma syllabuses were re-examined. Finally, the programme for 1988–89 will be noted. The most recent revision of the Diploma was in 1986.

The 1951–52 programme for Biblical and Religious Studies concentrated primarily on diploma courses. Ten diploma courses were offered, five in central London and five in various centres located in Middlesex, Surrey, Essex and Southend, and all were on biblical studies. In addition, a further course, An Introduction to Bible Studies, was also offered, but as it appeared in the programme under diploma courses, one must assume that it was an introductory course for candidates who intended to take the Diploma in Biblical and Religious Studies. Five non-diploma sessional courses were offered in central London as follows: The Old Testament, Christianity and Society, Christian Institutions and Social Life, The Christian Concept of God, The New Testament, the The Thought of

Cardinal Newman. One residential weekend course on Religion and Science in the Modern World was offered, and this appears to have been the only course offered in 1951–52 that could broadly be classified under the heading of Religious Studies.

By the 1956–57 session the programme had expanded somewhat. Twelve Diploma classes were offered, 11 on biblical subjects and one on the ancient world. One of the 12 diploma classes was offered as a final year course for students who had completed Part I. This course was on Genesis and on St John's Gospel. A further 10 sessional and three terminal (one term) courses were also offered, but only one sessional course was offered which could be termed Religious Studies. This was on Metaphysics and Natural Theology.

In 1960–61 seventeen diploma courses were offered; five were introductory courses on the ancient world, ten were biblical subjects, one was on the world's living religions, and one on the philosophy and psychology of religion. Twenty non-diploma sessional and terminal courses were now being offered, and of these eight could now be classified as being courses in Religious Studies. These included courses on Primitive Religions, The History of the Hassidim, Religion and Humanism, and Comparative Religion. One course in particular should be mentioned, The Confrontation of Religions Today, which was given by Geoffrey Parrinder. Two weekend courses were offered, one on St Luke's Gospel and one on Christianity and Psychiatry.

By 1967–68 the programme of the University Extension Committee now included courses offered by the Tutorial Classes Committee. On the extension side 15 diploma classes were offered. Nine compulsory biblical courses and 2 optional classes on the ancient world were offered under part I of the diploma regulations, while under part II, one course was offered on the world's living religions, one on biblical theology and two on church history. On the non-Diploma side, under extension courses, six sessional courses were offered: Psychological and Philosophical Aspects of the Christian Faith, Christian Ethics, The Church and the Modern World, Christian Doctrine, Anthropological Studies of Isaiah, and finally one course on comparative religion which was cancelled owing to inadequate numbers. There was also a weekend course offered on St Mark's Gospel.

However, while interest in Religious Studies as such remained at a disappointingly low level in the extension programme, the WEA courses sponsored by the Tutorial Classes Council and included in the extension programme, revealed the reverse. Seven courses in world religions or comparative religion were offered in the TCC programme and none in biblical and theological subjects. All these courses were given in the suburbs, none in Inner London.

A full time lecturer in Biblical and Religious Studies was appointed on 1 April 1972. Work began almost immediately on establishing a working party with a view to undertaking a complete revision of the Diploma in Biblical and Religious Studies. All syllabuses for the nine options were completely revised. The syllabus for the world religions option was confined to the choice of two, and not more than three, religions selected from: Islam, Hinduism, Buddhism and Judaism from 70 AD, while the course on the philosophy and psychology of religion was renamed 'Philosophy of Religion' and the psychology syllabus was dropped. Two radical changes to the regulations were made. Firstly, candidates in their fourth and final year, instead of being required to take a second examination paper on the subject of their choice in Part II in the Scheme of Study, were required instead to write an essay of 3,000 to 4,000 words on a subject agreed between lecturer and student and related to their fourth year of study. Secondly, the division between Part I and Part II of the syllabus was abolished. This meant that students could select any four of the nine options available in any order. In practice, in subsequent years this meant that while the biblical subjects were still as popular as ever, Religious Studies subjects such as the philosophy of religion and world religions were offered regularly every year. Usually one, but sometimes two courses in each of these subjects were now offered in the programme, whereas before they were offered only infrequently.

The Religious Studies programme for 1973–74 reflected the new regulations for the Scheme of Study for the Diploma, now retitled Diploma in Religious Studies. In that year, one course was offered on the ancient world, five on the Old Testament, three on the New Testament, two on world religions, two on sociology of religion, three on philosophy of religion, one, a new course, on pastoral studies, which was later to prove extremely popular, and two on church history. Twenty-two other extension courses were offered, six on world religions, of which one, 'Islam in its Turkish Context', was intended for members of a party travelling to Istanbul on a study tour arranged for January 1974. Five classes were WEA courses sponsored by the Tutorial Classes Committee, four of which were on comparative religion, and one on philosophy of religion. Three courses were residential weekend courses, of which two were on aspects of world religions, while one on Hinduism was a University Summer School Course at Wye College in Kent. In the previous year at Wye College an Introduction to World Religions had been offered for the first time.

The Scheme of Study for the Diploma in Religious Studies was last revised in 1986. One option, the Ancient World, was dropped and two new options were added, Christian Ethics, and Christian Theology in Modern Times. Three changes were made, however, in the regulations. Firstly, students who passed three of the examinations in the subject options were awarded a Certificate. Secondly, students were required to submit a unit of course work for examination and this carried 20 per cent of the marks for the relevant examination. Thirdly, the final essay was extended to 5,000 words. These regulations took effect in the 1986–87 session.

For the 1988–89 session five courses were offered in the Old Testament, eight courses in the New Testament, three courses were offered on early church history, three on nineteenth century church history to the present day, one on philosophy of religion, two on Christian ethics, two on pastoral studies, three on Christian theology in modern times and one on world religions. There was no course on sociology of religion. A total of 27 non-diploma courses were also offered, i.e. public lecture series and courses of one and two terms' duration; nine of these courses were on aspects of world religions. In addition eight day or weekend courses were offered, and two of these were on world religions. One of these courses in particular deserves to be mentioned. This was a weekend course on Christianity and the World Religions organised in co-operation with King's College London and the World Congress of Faiths. In this course Professor Hans Küng responded to distinguished Hindu, Buddhist and Muslim scholars who had critically examined his book *Christianity and the World Religions* (London, 1987).

To summarise trends in Religious Studies in the London University extra-mural area is not easy, but one can say that of the three subjects that could broadly come under this heading i.e. world religions, philosophy of religion, and sociology of religion, the first subject has been most in demand. But now demand for the subject comes from a very different constituency. Until the early 70s most of the demand came from WEA branches who required mainly a general introduction to world religions. However, demand from this particular quarter has diminished significantly in the last decade and it is now virtually non-existent. When a course is required by a WEA branch, then, unless that branch is particularly strong, the course will not attract enough students and it will fail. However, while interest in world religions declined in the WEA, new specialist centres emerged which were rooted in the various ethnic communities. Centres and Institutes of Christian Study had in any case already developed over many years, but more recently, Centres of Jewish Study, Islamic Study and Buddhist Study have come into being. All of these provide courses in conjunction with the Centre for Extra-Mural Studies, Birkbeck College, University of London.

Firstly, the Islamic Cultural Centre at Regent's Park offered a course of public lectures in 1981, then the West London Synagogue did likewise in 1982. The Islamic Cultural Centre dropped out, but the newly-established Muslim College at Ealing under Dr Zaki Badawi started offering courses in 1984. This latter centre gradually expanded its provision, and from the 1989–90 session it will be offering three courses: Quranic Exegesis, The Sufi Orders of Islam, and Classical Arabic. In 1987 the London Buddhist Vihara was established as a University Extra-Mural Centre and for 1988–89 offered three courses on Theravada Buddhism. Finally in 1988–89 the Indian Cultural Centre was established, offering a course on Indian religions. Future plans include provision for a Bahai Studies Centre in 1989–90.

These centres attract mainly students who belong to the particular faith concerned, but not exclusively so by any means, and overall provision in this connection is a relatively small part of the Religious Studies programme as a whole, which still reflects an overwhelming demand for biblical subjects, mainly at specialised centres of Christian study. This demand is likely to continue.

Manchester

The Department of Extra-Mural Studies at Manchester University has a large programme in Biblical and Religious Studies and, like London and Birmingham, a full-time staff lecturer in the subject. For 1987–88 the Department arranged 49 courses in Religious Studies for 1,230 students, and it is the fifth largest subject-area within Manchester Extra-Mural Department after literature and language, history, art and architecture and archeology. The Department offers a Certificate in Religious Studies, and all courses organised by it count towards the certificate. The main subject areas are biblical studies, doctrine, ethics, pastoral studies and 'Understanding Christianity Today' which includes liberation theology. World religions is a difficult subject to recruit for, but provision is made for teachers in multi-cultural schools by offering a course on world religions, e.g. Sikhism, as represented in the Manchester community.

An important element of the programme is arranged in collaboration with the Manchester Christian Institute for students, which includes ordinands on their Christian Leadership course. In this connection eight concurrent courses are held over 10 weekends. All except one or two students on these weekend courses normally aim to acquire the Certificate in Religious Studies. Elsewhere the programmes provide for the needs of Anglican lay readers who are doing further study for the Archbishop's Diploma. Special provision is made for students who have little formal education, while there is a small WEA programme which this year amounts to one sessional course. In general about one-third of the students attending Manchester extra-mural courses are lay readers, ordinands, and others who have a professional interest in the Christian ministry.

The general trend at Manchester in recent years has been towards students who pursue Biblical and Religious Studies with a particular ministry in mind. Other than this the main developing areas of interest seem to be in spiritual and pastoral theology. Interest in philosophy of religion and sociology of religion remains marginal. As mentioned above, provision for world religions is made for teachers in multi-cultural schools. In addition a course on world religions is offered for Baptist College students once every two years although the main focus here is on Christian theology. A course on Islam aimed at adult students in general is planned for next year and it is hoped that this trend will develop.

Birmingham

Birmingham University's School of Continuing Studies offered 18 Religious Studies courses in Birmingham and some additional courses outside for 1988–89. Seven of these courses were Saturday schools and topics ranged from History in the Old Testament, The Authority of the Bible, and the Creeds, to Religion and Science Today. These courses are very popular, normally drawing over 100 people; they give students the chance to hear two speakers, sometimes with opposing views on the subject.

Some courses, each of 24 weeks' duration, are for part-time divinity students. Subjects include: Religion in the Modern Context, Classical Christian Theology, and New Testament Greek. This is a two-year introductory course for students who wish to take a degree. They then go on to do full-time study at the university.

Two courses are run over linked weekends: Introduction to Christian Doctrine is linked with Introduction to the Old Testament. They are part of a two year Certificate in Theology, in association with the Centre for Black and White Christian Partnership at Selly Oak Colleges.

Other courses on a variety of topics are regularly offered and include subjects like St Luke's Gospel, From Genesis to Deuteronomy, and Leaders of Christian Thought. Some courses on aspects of world religions are held periodically, but very seldom have enough support to warrant continuation into the second year. For 1988–89 subjects offered in this connection were: Introduction to Indian Religions, Hinduism in History and Today, and Zen Buddhism and other forms of Enlightenment.

Generally most courses are run on the university campus. Outside the campus evening courses are difficult to run and are declining. Very little is done through WEA branches, but some courses are held at the Selly Oak Colleges; for example a regular course on Judaism is taught there every year under the supervision of Dr Norman Solomon.

It is difficult to see any trend in the future which would diverge in any significant way from the pattern indicated above.

Courses arranged at other University Departments of Extra-Mural Studies and Departments of Continuing Education

The remaining universities other than London, Manchester and Birmingham, which have been discussed in some detail, offer a very wide range of courses, but in the space available it is not possible to refer to all of these. In very general terms, the pattern noticed at London, Manchester and Birmingham is repeated elsewhere, i.e. the great majority of courses offered are on biblical and theological studies with relatively few courses on world religions, philosophy of religion and sociology of religion.

Provision for courses in general ranges very widely from, for example, Reading which offers courses only occasionally and has none in this year's programme, and Lancaster, which offers only one summer school course, to, for example, Nottingham which offers Certificates in Theological and Pastoral Studies and Church History as well as a wide range of other courses, while Southampton offers 24 courses in Biblical and Religious Studies including a course on Buddhism and two courses on liberation theology. Hull also has a relatively large programme with the help of a lecturer in New Testament Studies, half of whose duties are with the Department of Adult Education. The main emphasis here is on biblical and theological studies and recently two new courses, A Certificate in Theology, and a Bachelor of Theology course have been set up, and both include courses in Religious Studies. The former course includes in one year an overview of post-biblical Judaism, Islam, Zoroastrianism, Buddhism, Sikhism and Hinduism.

Other universities offering certificates and diplomas in Biblical and Religious Studies, or whose courses are intended to lead on to a degree, include Belfast, Edinburgh, Exeter, Kent, Oxford, Leicester and Leeds. Two universities, the University of Wales at Cardiff and Glasgow, are hoping to offer some courses in the future.

University syllabuses for the above courses vary in emphasis, but are primarily centred on biblical and theological topics. Hull, however, offers a wider range of courses in Religious Studies, including philosophy of religion as well as world religions, while Kent's part-time Diploma in Theology includes options on comparative religion, the Church and society, and psychology of religion.

Some universities offer courses for the clergy and lay readers of the churches. This sort of provision has already been referred to in connection with London and Manchester. Outside these areas Hull specifically aims to attract lay readers under its 'The University of Parish Programme' whereas University College of Swansea's School of Theological Study, while open to the general public, is mainly for the clergy. The University of St Andrews runs an eight-week course on A Christian Creed for Today and attracts mainly ministers, while Leicester concentrates primarily on pastoral counselling and provides courses for the East Midlands Ministry Training course. Liverpool runs a three-year course on Christian theology (which includes an element of philosophy of religion) in collaboration with the Carlisle Diocesan Training Centre. Other universities, while not specifying that their courses are primarily intended for clergy and lay readers, organise those courses at institutes or centres of Christian study.

As already indicated, most university departments find that the overwhelming demand is for courses in biblical studies, theology and to some extent church history. Apart from London, Manchester and Birmingham, universities which have specifically referred to this or whose programmes indicate this pattern include Nottingham, Hull, Southampton, Edinburgh, Oxford, Glasgow, Bristol, Newcastle-upon-Tyne, Exeter, St Andrews, and Leicester. Some universities offer *only* biblical studies or theology or church history; for example Oxford, Exeter and St Andrews. Others have a significant provision for Religious Studies, i.e. up to half the total programme. These include Sheffield, Warwick, and Leeds. Leeds in particular believes that this area could expand in the future. Only one university, the City University, offered courses predominantly in Religious Studies, but all but one of the five courses on offer failed to attract a sufficient number of students.

Overall, the very wide range of courses offered in Biblical and Religious Studies is very impressive. Essex, for example, in their Centre for the Study of Theology, offers 27 one-day seminars under the heading Theology and Society. This covers courses ranging from Para-Psychology and Religious Experience to The Justice of God. Elsewhere, countrywide, the range of courses planned is very impressive. It would be impossible to list them all, but among topics offered one could mention: Stained Glass Windows, Great Gothic Cathedrals, Liberal Christianity in the Parish, Faith in the Inner City, Illuminated Manuscripts and Gospel Codices, and Christianity in Africa.

In conclusion, it should be stressed that this survey is neither comprehensive nor systematic. Some universities have given me much information while others provided very few details of their programmes. This has inevitably meant that the main emphasis has been on London, Manchester and Birmingham where full-time staff are involved and where the largest programmes exist.

With this important qualification in mind the overall impression in this area of university education is that biblical and theological studies are flourishing. This is particularly the case if courses of this nature are arranged in co-operation with the churches. Some universities offer courses in Religious Studies (world religions, philosophy of religion and sociology of religion) which amount to between a quarter and half of their total programme in biblical and theological studies, but generally these overall programmes are small, i.e. less than 10 sessional courses per annum. More than one university has commented that far more could be done if they had a full-time member of staff.

Looking into the future it is very difficult to see a different pattern emerging which would significantly change the present provision. In most cases programmes are arranged on the basis of demands from the various partners involved, i.e. the churches, the WEA and LEA's.

Turning specifically to world religions, the demand for this subject from WEA branches has collapsed in London and probably elsewhere as well. One strong field of growth for this subject, at least in the London area, is in the provision of specialist centres which are linked to the various religious communities. In London, centres like the London Buddhist Vihara, the West London Synagogue and the Muslim College at Ealing are flourishing, while new centres like the Indian Cultural Centre and the Bahai Community Centre are being established.

NOTES

[1] Minutes of the Board to promote the Extension of University Teaching 1927–28 (ref: EM1/4/30). The Diploma in Theology and the Certificate in Religious Knowledge were both external awards.

[2] Minutes of the Senate House 1927–28, number 3596.

4. RELIGIOUS STUDIES AND DEVELOPMENTS IN RELIGIOUS EDUCATION IN ENGLAND AND WALES

Robert Jackson

A consideration of the development of religious education in England and Wales must take account of a number of factors such as the legislative setting, the changing social climate, empirical research relevant to RE, critical discussions about nature of religious education and a bundle of issues concerned with the delivery of RE in schools, including the provision of resources in the form of teachers and funding to support RE teaching and in-service training (INSET).

The Legal Framework

Religious Education has been an ingredient of English and Welsh state education since the first Education Act of 1870 which set up the first entirely state-funded Board Schools. School Boards could opt for Bible teaching without denominational instruction, in accordance with the so-called Cowper-Temple clause which stated: 'No religious catechism or religious formulary which is distinctive of any particular denomination shall be taught in the school'. This clause influences the legislation to this day. The Act also included a conscience clause by means of which parents could withdraw their children from religious instruction. The 1902 Education Act confirmed the 1870 settlement on religious instruction, adding a further conscience clause for teachers and establishing the dual system of partnership between the state and the churches in providing a national system of education.

The 1944 Act clarified the dual system, by distinguishing different types of maintained (as opposed to privately funded) schools. County schools were entirely publicly funded. Voluntary schools (partly funded by religious bodies) were of three types: Aided, Controlled and Special Agreement. Aided schools (Anglican, Roman Catholic, some other Christian schools and a few Jewish schools) had a majority of governors appointed by the sponsoring religious body and the character of religious instruction was determined by the governors of each school. RI in Special Agreement schools usually followed the pattern of Aided schools. Unless parents opted to have denominational religious instruction taught by 'reserved teachers', RI in Controlled schools was identical to that in County schools.

The 1944 Act made mandatory the use by County Schools (and, normally, Controlled Schools) of Agreed Syllabuses for Religious Instruction. Early versions of these – aimed at finding agreement at the local level between Christian denominations over the content of RI – had been in use in some local authorities since the early 1920s. Under the terms of the 1944 Act English LEAs had to convene a Syllabus Conference consisting of four committees representing i. the Church of England ii. other denominations iii. the local authority iv. teachers' organisations. In Wales there were three committees, with Anglican representation confined to the committee made up of religious denominations.

In practice 'other denominations' meant 'other Protestant Christian denominations', since the Roman Catholics confined their energies to their voluntary (aided and special agreement) schools and no other religion was envisaged. It was not until the 1970s that some LEAs liberally interpreted the Act as allowing representatives of non-Christian religions on to the 'other denominations' panel. Since the publication of the City of Birmingham Agreed Syllabus in 1975, many new Syllabuses have included a significant amount of work on religions other than Christianity in addition to studies of the Christian tradition.

The 1988 Education Reform Act has retained many of features of the 1944 Act (provision, withdrawal and Agreed Syllabuses), but has introduced changes which strengthen RE's place in the curriculum and acknowledge some recent developments in the subject. A significant change is the use of 'religious education' to replace the term 'religious instruction' with its suggestion of deliberate transmission of religious beliefs. The subject must be fully educational with its aims and processes justifiable on educational grounds. Recognising the need for different interest groups to have a say in the production of syllabuses, and for local circumstances to be considered, the arrangements for producing Agreed Syllabuses have been retained in a modified form. For the first time in law, representatives of faiths other than Christianity are given a place on Agreed Syllabus Conferences where they are among the principal religions represented in a Local Education Authority, on what used to be the 'other denominations' committee. Also Standing Advisory Councils on Religious Education (SACREs) now *have* to be set up (post 1944 they were optional) with functions that include monitoring the use of Agreed Syllabuses and the power to *require* an LEA to set up a Conference to review the locally agreed syllabus. SACREs have a composition which parallels that of Agreed Syllabus Conferences, and they can co-opt extra members.

The importance of RE is emphasised by its being part of the 'Basic Curriculum'. Religious education and the National Curriculum together form the Basic Curriculum which is the entitlement of all pupils. RE stays out of nationally agreed assessment arrangements and does not become a Foundation subject, in order to ensure that Agreed Syllabuses reflect local circumstances and the contributions of the different interest groups which constitute local Syllabus Conferences. DES Circular 3/89 (*The Education Reform Act 1988: Religious Education and Collective Worship*) states that Agreed Syllabus Conferences may decide to include assessment arrangements in syllabuses that parallel those established in National Curriculum subjects. Several projects have already emerged which are exploring issues concerned with the assessment of RE (see M. Hayward 'Planning Religious Education' in R. Jackson and D. Starkings, eds, *The Junior RE Handbook*, Cheltenham, 1990, for references).

The Reform Act requires that any new Agreed Syllabus 'must reflect the fact that religious traditions in Great Britain are in the main Christian, whilst taking account of the teaching and practices of the other principal religions represented in Great Britain'. This says nothing about instruction *in* Christianity. *New* agreed syllabuses need to give proper attention to the study of Christianity and, regardless of their location in the country, should also give attention to the other major religions represented in Britain.

The Act also sets religious education in the context of the whole curriculum of maintained schools which 'must be balanced and broadly based' and must promote 'the spiritual, moral, cultural, mental and physical development of pupils at the school and of society . . .' (*ERA* 1, 2 para 2). Religious education then, as well as being broad, balanced and open should not simply be a study of religions but, like the rest of the curriculum, should relate to the experience of pupils in such a way that it contributes to their personal development.

Social Change

The process of secularisation that has characterised post-war Britain is reflected in research on young people's attitudes towards religion. Psychometric research conducted by Leslie Francis and others shows a decline in positive attitude towards traditional Christian religion, associated with increasing age (beginning during the primary years, continuing through the first four years of secondary schooling and markedly accelerating around the ages of fifteen and sixteen). One piece of sociological research concludes that most young people are indifferent to traditional religious beliefs (B. Martin and R. Pluck, *Young People's Beliefs*, London, General Synod Board of Education, 1977), though research on young people from within religious traditions reveals a more complex state of affairs (e.g. L. Francis, *Teenagers and the Church*, London, 1984).

There has also been a trend towards religious pluralism evident since the 1950s when Britain's labour shortage attracted many immigrants from South Asia and the Caribbean, but increasing dramatically in the late 1960s and early 1970s when many ethnically South Asian migrants arrived in Britain from recently independent East African states, following policies of 'Africanisation'.

The issue of race relations was treated in some Agreed Syllabuses of the late 1960s, and issues of secularisation and pluralism were discussed seriously in some of the theoretical RE literature of the period. It was not until the mid 1970s, however, that Agreed Syllabuses acknowledged both trends, with the 1975 City of Birmingham Syllabus rejecting any evangelical or faith-forming aim while promoting an objective study of world religions represented in Britain. A major report on the education of children from ethnic minority communities reached similar conclusions (M. Swann (ed.), *Education for All*, London, 1985).

Such developments have not been sufficient for members of some communities (notably some Muslim and 'fundamental' Christian groups) which have established independent schools and are lobbying for their own (mainly state-funded) Voluntary Aided schools. Their objection is not specifically to RE, but to a perceived bias towards secularism in County schools in which the faith of minorities is allegedly not taken seriously.

Empirical Research

Research on the development of children's thinking about religion has tended to follow general trends in educational psychology. Ronald Goldman's work (*Religious Thinking from Childhood to Adolescence*, London, 1964) was very influential, partly because in the early sixties he was virtually a lone voice in British RE research. The work, heavily influenced by Piaget's research on cognitive development, was based on interviews with a small sample of pupils using three Bible Stories. Goldman's findings indicated that religious thinking went through a series of stages of increasing complexity (intuitive; pre-operational; concrete; abstract) and developed in ways similar to all other thinking. His conclusion that abstract religious concepts should be excluded from RE until children had attained a mental age of thirteen led over-zealous followers to excise much explicitly religious material from primary school RE. Later Piagetian work by the American researcher John Peatling overcame some of Goldman's methodological weaknesses and supported a stage-development view of religious thinking, though Peatling's findings suggested a long intermediate stage between the concrete operational stage (mental age 10) and abstract thinking (mental age 16). This genre of work has attracted critics from several quarters. For example, Brian Gates' study (*Religion in the Developing World of Children and Young People*, unpublished PhD thesis, University of Lancaster, 1976) distinguishes between children's intellectual capacity for handling religious concepts and their ability to understand before they can think in an adult fashion, questioning whether development researchers have measured what children really understand. Merlin Price's research, influenced by Jerome Bruner and Margaret Donaldson, goes further than Gates in showing that young children's degree of understanding of religious story partly depends on constructing the correct language approach and providing a framework of meaningful activities which enable a thorough exploration of their responses (*The Role of Story in the Religious Education of the First School Child*, unpublished MA thesis, University of Warwick, 1988).

Theoretical Research

Changing views of the nature of religious education reflect different assumptions about the nature of religion and of education as well as differing stances on the aims or purposes of the subject. Broadly speaking one distinction concerns whether its function is to transmit or to foster religious belief and culture or to develop a critical understanding of religion; another is the degree to which RE is concerned with the study of religions and the extent of its contribution to pupils' personal development.

The assumption that religious education in County schools should be a vehicle for fostering Christian faith and morality among pupils was all but universal until the late 1960s, with new developments inducing changes in content and pedagogy rather than in underlying aims. Thus the work of Ronald Goldman and of Harold Loukes (*Teenage Religion*, London, 1961; *New Ground in Christian Education*, London, 1965) precipitated child-centred or child-related approaches, with non-traditional content but retaining the assumption of a Christian world view.

Both writers were influential in shaping Agreed Syllabuses of the late 1960s (notably West Riding, 1966 and ILEA, 1968). Goldman's approach emphasised children's experience of Christian values such as caring, together with feelings of awe and wonder, as the foundation for a later, more cognitively based RE, while Loukes (influenced by liberal Christian theologians such as Paul Tillich, but also expressing his own Quaker outlook) advocated a method which starts with living issues relevant to young people, moving to an exploration of them in depth.

The work of Goldman and Loukes has been variously described as 'neo-confessional' to distinguish it from earlier straightforwardly traditional 'confessional' material, as 'experiential' to indicate an emphasis on the child's own experience of values, feelings and issues, and as 'implicit religion', since, Loukes (following Tillich), equated religion with elements of experience felt to be deeply important to people, while the curriculum material for younger children developed from Goldman's work left out explicitly religious topics in favour of 'life themes' exploring emotions associated with a Christian world-view.

Religious education writing from the mid 1960s to the early 1970s began to take account of the increasing secularisation and pluralism of British Society, notably Edwin Cox, *Changing Aims in Religious Education* (London, 1966) Ninian Smart, *Secular Education and the Logic of Religion* (London, 1968) and J. W. D. Smith, *Religious Education in a Secular Setting* (London, 1969). Although there are important differences in the argument of these writers, there was a general move (consistent with contemporary work in the philosophy of education and of religion) towards an epistemological justification of the place of RE in the curriculum based, not on religion's self-evident or publicly agreed truth, but on its role as a 'form of knowledge' (Hirst) or, more precisely, as a distinctive area of human experience.

Smart's ideas were particularly influential partly because they were the philosophical underpinning of the Schools Council Secondary Project on Religious Education (established in 1969 and based at the University of Lancaster under Smart's direction), but also because they responded to the increasing dissatisfaction of many RE professionals with dogmatic approaches to their subject still being adopted by Agreed Syllabuses. *Religious Education in Secondary Schools*, the project's widely-read working paper (Schools Council 1971), advocated the 'phenomenological' or undogmatic approach to RE which saw the subject as developing understanding without promoting any particular religious stance, a process drawing on scholarly methods to generate empathy with the religious faith of individuals and groups.

The working paper provided for many teachers their first encounter with the phenomenology of religion. The term was probably coined by the nineteenth century Dutch historian of religion, P. D. Chantepie de la Saussaye, to describe the comparison of certain common features of different religions. As an academic approach which gained in popularity in continental Europe, the phenomenology of religion was influenced to an extent by Edmund Husserl's work in philosophical phenomenology, especially in its adoption of the concepts of epoché (suspension of judgement) and eidetic vision, the capacity to see the 'essence' of a phenomenon, in this case the phenomenon of religion. Although phenomenologists of religion themselves have characterised their discipline in different ways, the main proponents have aimed to 'bracket out' their own presuppositions when attempting to understand another's faith and to study parallel phenomena in different religions in order to expose basic structures and forms which give insight into the essence of religious reality.

The first of these aspects of phenomenology has had much more influence on religious educators than the second. The notion of an impartial study, with both teacher and pupil attempting to suspend their own presuppositions in empathising with religious believers, was appealing to the many teachers who found theologically loaded approaches to RE distasteful. With few exceptions, religious educators have been less influenced by the phenomenologists's concern to grasp the essence of religion. This is due in part to the complexity of the exercise, partly to the subjective element in 'eidetic vision', but has perhaps rather more to do with phenomenology's assumption that religion is an autonomous and non-reducible value-category. Many teachers would prefer to leave questions about the nature of religion open to exploration by their pupils. Nevertheless the practical activity of studying common features of different religions thematically – worship, rites of passage, sacred writings and so on – has become widely practised in RE, and this is one area where Geoffrey Parrinder has made a contribution through writings used extensively by teachers (e.g. *Worship in the World's Religions*, London, 1974) and material written for pupils (e.g. *Something After Death?* London, 1974).

Most significant contributions to thinking about RE since this time have been developments of or reactions to phenomenological approaches, some of the latter resurrecting the axiom of Goldman and Loukes that RE should be concerned with the development of pupils' values and beliefs while rejecting their assumed theological framework. Some contributers have also challenged the concept of education, with its attendant epistemology, implicit in the Schools Council Project's version of phenomenology.

At this point it should be said that many criticisms of phenomenology have been misinformed or directed at poor quality curriculum materials which themselves misunderstand, mis-apply or ignore writing on the phenomenology of religion. Phenomenology has been widely regarded by critics as a single and inflexible approach. A glance through a work such as Waardenburg's *Classical Approaches to the Study of Religion* (The Hague, 1973) shows this not to be the case. Common criticisms of phenomenology assert that it denies the student a critical approach and in so doing propagates a form of relativism in which all religious claims are regarded as equally true. This is both to interpret phenomenology as being concerned solely with imparting information and to make the unwarranted assumption that the application of phenomenological methods necessarily precludes the employment of other complementary approaches. The key purpose of phenomenological methods in the classroom is to arrive at accounts of religious life that are expressed in the believer's or practitioner's terms. This process need not preclude other activities such as critical work or discussion of the implications of material studied for the pupil's own beliefs and values.

A look back at Smart's *Secular Education and the Logic of Religion*, for example, confirms that he envisaged young people developing critical skills for forming judgements about the truth or falsity of religious claims. A further criticism accuses the thematic approach associated with phenomenology of confusing children by presenting them with a surfeit of material from disparate world views, linked only by tenuous headings such as 'founders', 'buildings' or 'pilgrimage'. This is a valid criticism of bad thematic materials of the type that present children with a few hundred words on half a dozen traditions, with no attempt to encourage critical thinking or reflection, thus failing to help children to enter imaginatively the spiritual worlds of others. It is not a valid criticism of the thematic approach *per se*.

It is impossible to do justice in a few lines to the range and depth of some recent work in religious education, and I hope writers will forgive any distortions consequent on brevity. It is also impossible to mention all the work being done; the examples are selective, but illustrate some of the main lines of thinking.

Some writers have seen religious education as part of a wider values education. Edwin Cox, for example, (*Problems and Possibilities for Religious Education*, London, 1983) suggests that religious and secular beliefs about the nature of reality and of humanity should be explored by young people, probably as part of one subject, in order to help them come to terms with their own dilemmas and questions. Others have drawn attention to the interface between RE and other disciplines, with John Hull doing significant work on the relationship between theology and religious education (*Studies in Religion and Education*, Lewes, 1983).

One line of thinking has emphasised the need for pupils to have some personal experience of religion or spirituality in order to understand it, a stance sometimes coupled with a critique of phenomenology. Edward Robinson, for example, has argued that the phenomenological approach has 'encouraged curiosity at the expense of involvement'. Children, says Robinson, may learn a lot about religion without knowing what religion is about (*The Original Vision*, Oxford, 1977). Drawing on data from the Religious Experience Research Unit (RERU), Robinson postulates a unique and universal spiritual dimension of experience that can be awakened through religious education. Rather than studying religions, Robinson advocates the practical use of the creative arts as well as reflection on examples of modern secular art (regarded as evidence of contemporary man's inborn spiritual hunger). Good religious education consists in enabling pupils to exercise their spiritual curiosity, fostering in them an imaginative openness to the infinite possibilities of life. At times his writing borders on an argument for theism from religious or spiritual experience: 'it is in this openness that we become aware that reality is not neutral, it is not indifferent to our search; that there are powers and forces so sensitively responsive to our initiatives that we can only describe them in personal terms' ('The Experience of Transfiguration', unpublished paper, International Seminar on Religious Education and Values, Kemptville, 1984).

One problem with Robinson's position is that in emphasising a particular form of spiritual experience he confines RE to its exploration and effectively divorces the subject from engagement with the major religious traditions. There also tends to be a blurring of the distinction between religious and aesthetic experience and a lack of critical analysis of personal accounts of spiritual experience, which loads the approach towards confessionalism (e.g. the passage quoted above which is open to the standard philosophical criticisms of arguments for theism from religious experience).

David Hay, Robinson's successor at the RERU, has conducted more research on religious experience (*Exploring Inner Space*, Harmondsworth, Penguin 1982). He has produced writing and research on religious education and, in association with others on the Religious Experience Research Project, has developed materials for use by teachers and pupils. He agrees with Robinson's critique of earlier approaches and shares his view that religions derive their 'energy and cultural forms' from a unique and universal spiritual dimension. Unlike Robinson, however, Hay draws on techniques used in religions and the fields of counselling and humanistic psychology in order to develop practical activities aimed at helping young people to focus on personal inner experience as a preparation for deeper religious understanding. His intention is to help children to gain insight into areas of human experience which are of major concern to religious believers without being evangelical or indoctrinatory. The Religious Experience Research Project has devised classroom activities (Alison Jones, ed., *Making RE More Affective*, University of Nottingham, 1986) and at the time of writing is completing a handbook for teachers on experiential learning in RE. Many of the exercises in Jones (1986), if used in conjunction with material from religious traditions, would undoubtedly produce some exciting and valuable RE. Despite Hay's criticisms of phenomenology, his own approach is not fundamentally anti-phenomenological. His and his colleagues' preoccupation with sensitizing young people to elements of spirituality has features in common with 'eidetic vision'. However, as with phenomenology, his approach is also open to the objection of regarding a universal, autonomous area of religious experience as a given.

One criticism of approaches that have a high degree of pupil involvement, but limited or even no engagement with the religious traditions, is that they tend to universalise a view of religious experience that may be inconsistent with examples in the practice of religions. Some religious educators have tried to avoid this by devising approaches based on an interplay between the study of religions and the personal development of pupils (*The Fourth R*, an Anglican report on RE published by SPCK in 1972 advocated an approach along these lines). Jack Priestley's work is one example, though he gives more emphasis to the process rather than to the content of RE. Priestley argues that RE is essentially about 'educating *through* religion' rather than 'teaching about' or 'teaching that'. The focal point is the child or student and the 'truth' of the content is simply the Coleridgean maxim of 'whatever speaks to me is true'; the efficacy of religious material – like poetry – is whether or not it articulates inner experience and aids personal growth. (*Moral Education and Religious Story*, unpublished PhD thesis, University of Exeter, 1988).

An example giving closer attention to the religious traditions is the work of Michael Grimmitt ('World Religions and Personal Development' in Jackson, ed., 1982; *Religious Education and Human Development*, McCrimmons, Great Wakering, 1987). Unlike the *The Fourth R* which suggested reflection on 'ultimate questions', Grimmitt recommends the exploration of the various 'models of the human' provided by different religions and philosophies. It is the existence of a variety of 'models of the human', says Grimmitt, that constitutes the educational value of studying world religions. Education is defined by Grimmitt as 'a process by, in and through which pupils may begin to explore what it is and what it means to be human'. An exploration of various 'models of the human' by pupils involves them both in evaluating their understanding of religion in personal terms and in evaluating their own understanding of self in terms of the religions being studied. The kind of material from religions that Grimmitt hopes teachers might use with children includes themes of particular significance for personal growth and what he calls 'human shaping' (see the many examples in Part Two of his book). The skilful teacher, says Grimmitt, could marry such themes with the pupils' own concern with self-understanding in such a way that they both increased their comprehension of the nature and purpose of the spiritual or religious quest within different religions and were encouraged to reflect on the implications that the adoption of a religious view of life would have for their own understanding of self, and their consequent development as persons. The concern to engage the pupil found here is welcome, but the danger remains that a selection of material from a religion based on a theoretical framework imposed from outside it can result in a portrayal that adherents and specialist scholars alike regard as a distortion.

My own current work develops curriculum material from ethnographic field studies of religion, attempting to combine personal views of religious faith and practice – from children as well as adults – with active learning methods which engage pupils and raise issues for reflection and discussion ('Religious Education: From Ethnographic Research to Curriculum Development', in R. Campbell and V. Little, eds, *Humanities in the Primary School*, Lewes, 1989).

There is no space to tease out and discuss the different definitions of religion and education that are implicit in some of the work summarised above. Suffice it to say that there is a healthy range of ideas in circulation and a welcome return to the practice of linking empirical and theoretical research with practical experiments in curriculum development. New areas are also emerging discussing the implications for RE of topics such as critical theory, feminism and inter-faith dialogue, and promoting action-research in the field of 'early years' RE.

The Professionalisation of RE

A number of developments in the decades since 1944 have offered teachers of RE professional support of varying kinds, though against a general climate of underfunding. The Christian Education Movement is one body whose range of assistance through conferences and publications has been considerably wider than its name might suggest. In 1984 CEM's Professional Committee for Religious Education merged with the Association for Religious Education to form the Professional Council for Religious Education, a body offering associate membership to all professionally involved in religious education. The Shap Working Party on World Religions in Education brings together a group of around 35 teachers and scholars from all levels of education to encourage accurate and sensitive treatment of religions in schools and higher education. Shap has supported RE teachers through regular conferences, an information service, the publication of books (e.g. A. Brown, ed., *The Shap Handbook on World Religions in Education*, London, 1987 and A. Wood, ed., *Religions and Education: The Shap Working Party 1969–1989*, London, 1989), and an annual mailing consisting of a *Calendar of Festivals* and a journal, currently called *World Religions in Education*. As a founder member and a Co-President until 1987, Geoffrey

Parrinder contributed significantly to Shap's work. 1989 marked the twentieth anniversary of Shap and the emergence of the European Association for World Religions in Education, a forum for an exchange of ideas between religious educators in different parts of Europe. International dialogue in RE was pioneered through the formation of the International Seminar on Religious Education and Values which has met biennially since 1978 alternately in European and North American countries. The formation in 1973 of the Religious Education Council of England and Wales and the Standing Conference on Inter-Faith Dialogue in Education has been most significant. Both bodies provide an important inter-faith focus on RE and wider educational issues.

Publications servicing RE teachers include the *British Journal of Religious Education*, the main outlet for reporting research and new thinking on RE, while *RE Today* offers very practical advice to teachers with an emphasis on helping non-specialists. *Resource*, published by the University of Warwick Institute of Education since 1978 and now distributed by the Professional Council for Religious Education, offers a mixture of reviews and articles concentrating on current issues and curriculum development. The bilingual *RE News* published by the Welsh National Centre for Religious Education based at Bangor University includes news, articles and reviews.

An important source of professional assistance to RE teachers has been the setting up of a small number of RE Centres involved in the in-service training of teachers. Two of these were initiated in 1973 by the DES (one based at Westhill College, Birmingham, and the other at West London Institute of Higher Education) and another two by the National Society for RE (an Anglican body) at Kensington and York. The Welsh National Centre for Religious Education has already been mentioned. These Centres have been an important stimulus in the regions which they serve and have supported teachers nationally through publications (such as York RE Centre's magazine *Reflect*) and curriculum development (e.g. the Westhill RE Project published by Stanley Thornes). Sadly, only a minority of Local Education Authorities have employed full-time specialist RE advisers and, with changes in funding and management consequent on the Education Reform Act, the number could decrease.

The development of the GCSE examination (launched in 1987) generated much thinking about aims and content of RE syllabuses as well as attendant teaching methods and modes of assessment. All syllabuses and examinations have to conform to national criteria and 'should be open to candidates of any religious persuasion or none and should provide a broad structure for the study of religion, emphasising its educational basis' (*National Criteria: Religious Studies*, HMSO, 1985). The syllabuses show a marked increase in the study of world religions and in the use of methods of continuous assessment.

Practice and Politics

A disturbing feature of the debate about RE during the passage of the Education Reform Bill through Parliament was the lack of attention by politicians to the research and thinking done about religious education during the last thirty years. The debate was often reduced to a crude wrangling over whether the content of RE should be 'Christian' or a multi-faith 'mish mash'. One effect was to produce a spate of statements from certain politicians supporting a form of religio-cultural exclusiveness, demanding the teaching of confessional Christianity as a means to preserving 'British culture' and ordering society morally (see, for example, A. Coombes, 'Diluting the Faith', *Education*, 26 August 1988 and my reply 'Fortifying Religious Education', *Resource* 11, 3, 1989).

Quite apart from the dismay felt by RE professionals that a vital area of the curriculum should be used as a theological and political football, the debate obscured the real crisis for religious education in England and Wales, namely the chronic shortage of resources in terms of staffing, training and materials. The Religious Education Council of England and Wales' paper *Religious Education: Supply of Teachers for the 1990s*, through detailed analysis of DES statistics, exposes the chronic shortage of teachers with RE qualifications in primary and secondary schools together with insufficient training opportunities at initial and in-service levels. It also points to inadequate time on the timetable and low levels of funding for books and other resources. This abysmal picture is confirmed by a survey of secondary schools conducted by the Culham College Institute (*Christianity in RE Programme News*, 1989).

There seems little point in engaging in research and curriculum development in RE when the subject continues to be resourced inadequately in schools. The most important issue seems to be not whether one approach to RE is superior to another, but whether *any* educative approach can be effective with severely limited time, with a teaching force largely deprived of the opportunity for thorough training and with poor funding for books and materials.

The Secretary of State's reasons for omitting RE from the National Curriculum seem plausible, but already the consequence has been to relegate RE to the second division as Foundation subjects benefit from well-funded and intensive programmes of in-service training. It is hard to see how the situation will improve significantly without DES funding targeted specifically at religious education. The Act does help through giving Standing Advisory Councils for Religious Education and governors responsibilities for ensuring that its intentions are carried out, and it gives parents the right to complain if a subject is being taught ineffectively. Do its clauses, however, mark a turning point for the better for RE? This depends largely on whether the subject is considered by society to be worth the investment of financial and human resources.

SUGGESTED READING

E. Cox, *Problems and Possibilities for Religious Education*, London: Hodder and Stoughton, 1983.

J. Hull, ed., *New Direction in Religious Education*, Lewes: Falmer, 1982.

M. Grimmitt, *Religious Education and Human Development*, Great Wakering: McCrimmons, 1987.

R. Jackson, ed., *Approaching World Religions*, London: John Murray, 1982.

J. Priestley, ed., *Religion and Spirituality in Schools, Perspectives* (9), University of Exeter, 1982.

N. Smart, *Secular Education and the Logic of Religion*, London: Faber, 1968.

M. Tickner and D. Webster, eds, *Religious Education and the Imagination, Aspects of Education* (28), University of Hull, 1982.

5. THE NEW EDUCATION REFORM ACT AND WORSHIP IN COUNTY SCHOOLS IN ENGLAND AND WALES

W. Owen Cole

School worship may be one of the few areas of religion which Geoffrey Parrinder has not dealt with in his own writings. However, the issues which it raises have never been far from his mind. The memory is still fresh of a broadcast service in the seventies when he used a passage from the *Bhagavad Gita* as one of the lessons. In schools, material from his pioneering *Book of World Religions* (1965, still in print) and extracts from his four anthologies *Themes for Living* (1973) have been widely used. His *Worship in the World's Religions* (1st edition 1961; 2nd edition 1974), is a book which might be ripe for reconsideration in the school worship context.

The Historical and Educational Context

Worship is part of religious education in the maintained schools of England and Wales. The reason is historical in the first place. Almost every school before the 1870 Education Act was a religious foundation to a greater or lesser extent. A major aim was to bring up children in the beliefs and values of Christianity. For many years after 1870, the qualified, but non-graduate teachers who staffed them came mainly from denominational training colleges, and access to them depended on a reference from a clergyman of one denomination or another. With the growth of secular education after 1870 this aim was endorsed, though the right of parents to withdraw their children from Religious Instruction (as it was called) and worship was granted and in board schools both worship and RI were to be undenominational and nonsectarian. To facilitate withdrawal the act of worship usually began the school day and was followed by a Bible story. The 'withdrawn' children came to school in time to receive their mark of attendance and then the secular curriculum (to use the terminology of the 1988 Act) began.

The 1944 Education Act made worship compulsory, retaining the clauses relating to withdrawal and denominational distinctiveness, and decreed that it should take place at the beginning of the school day, thus endorsing common practice.[1] The 1988 Act will be considered later, but broadly speaking it confirmed the clauses of its 1944 predecessor.

School worship is to be seen partly as the legacy of the history of church involvement in education, but also as symbolic of the fact that in England, though not in Wales, there is a Church which is established by law, and Britain as a whole is Christian.

Developments

Until the late 1960s the propriety of school worship was rarely challenged. Concern was more with matters of organisation and relevance. Separate gatherings related to age range were encouraged. So was experimentation with timing, especially of such festive occasions as the harvest celebrations or the carol service which parents were encouraged to attend. Worship in the round, instead of in the traditional serried rows, and pupil participation became the rule rather than the exception. Especially in the secondary school, modern hymns and protest songs ousted Wesley and Watts, with 'thou' being replaced by 'you' in prayers.

Round about 1967 some voices were raised against the whole notion of religion having a place in education, but these tend to be few and to fall silent as the confessional approach to religious education gave way to that encouraged, promoted, and developed by the Schools Council projects[2] and the Shap Working Party on World Religions in Education. However, this shift to the open study of religion in school classrooms resulted, one might say naturally, in questioning the expression and affirmation of religious beliefs in the hall through acts of worship. In addition to educational objections concern was expressed that collective worship led to assumptions of cheap faith and commitment. The most famous publication was John Hull's *School Worship an Obituary*; (London, 1975).

Silence was probably the commonest response, one which is clearly manifest in most *Agreed Syllabuses* which date from this period.[3] Before 1968 they usually included a section on school worship. Since then any references to it in such documents has been difficult to find. Discussion of the subject was evaded by the device of using the word 'assembly' instead of 'worship'. In practice many gatherings became activities devoid of any religious or spiritual element, 'secular assemblies' Hull called them, though that is not to say that they lacked worth.

The reason for this change was not merely the different approach to religious education. The subject's influence has never been that potent! Rather it lay in the approach to education generally and a new attitude among teachers.

British education until the third quarter of the twentieth century was concerned with nurturing children into a society which was considered to be white, protestant and superior. Scots and the Welsh, not to mention Irish from the republic, would argue that it was also anglosaxon. There was no questioning of the right of the English to conquer the Welsh and the Scots, still less the uncivilised inhabitants of India and Africa. Language teachers might attempt to convey the worth of Goethe or Balzac, but as these did not appear in literature courses as such, it was clear that they lacked intrinsic value. Music was detached from biography, so Beethoven was not explicitly German and anyway the best work was the *Messiah* by the Englishman, Handel! Not surprisingly religious education was Christian in the British, protestant, sense, that is biblical, and was taught by believers with the intention of inculcating faith. Objections to Christian belief might be discussed, usually with able sixth formers, but the purpose was apologetic.

School worship fitted into this context naturally and well. When, however, religions came to be studied in an open manner and even Humanism might occasionally be examined on its own terms rather than to demonstrate the distinctiveness of religious belief, worship began to appear inappropriate.

Perhaps more important was the way in which the teaching profession came to mirror society as a whole. By the late sixties it was no longer possible to expect that most teachers would be church goers when the average for the nation as a whole was moving towards the twenty per cent mark. Nor did one find, as hitherto, that it was considered prudent to feign belief even if one did not possess it or be silent. Teachers have never been vociferous in their demands that religious education should be open or be removed from the curriculum, but during the last twenty years they have come to question the conventional view that it is right to pass on one's own religious or moral views to children.

Until 1988 school worship seemed to upset teachers less than classroom RE. Its opponents were usually RE specialists who saw it as embarrassingly contradictory to their open approach to Religious Studies. There may have been three reasons for the silence of the majority of other teachers. First for a few, they were Christians and approved of what happened in the hall and wished to reestablish Christian RE. Secondly, the objector could easily absent himself/herself without anyone commenting.[4] Thirdly, and perhaps chiefly, the activity was so innocuous that it upset nobody! Where the Christian element was strong, that is evangelical, it did not fill church pews, and led to resentment rather than persuasion. Where it was weak, it was innocuous.

Some support for school worship remained among educationalists before 1988. Only a few months before the Act was passed. Brenda Watson argued that 'Pupils may be regarded as educationally deprived who are not given the chance of a significant encounter with the worship. This cannot be done in any meaningful way without the opportunity to participate in it'.[5] She did, however, distinguish between worship in church and worship in a believing community, and described the school as a 'worship-enabling community', recognising that worship cannot be compelled and the integrity of the child must be respected, but the overall purpose of the article was the justification of school worship against the opposition of its critics.

Most supporters before 1988 and during the debates on the Education Reform Bill, especially in the House of Lords, seemed to have no current experience of maintained schools. They supported school worship for motives related to nationhood. Their voices were raised almost in unison during the debates. Whether they really won the day, and if so at what cost remains to be seen.

Worship and the Education Reform Act, 1988

The provisions of 1944 have been reiterated and even strengthened in the main in the Education Act of 1988. School worship must be daily and compulsory, (subject to the conscience clause), 'for all pupils in attendance at a maintained school' (6.1).[6] This was the implication of the 1944 Act, but often it went by default in sixth forms and certainly in Sixth Form colleges. Flexibility in timing and in allowing separate assemblies to be held on the basis of age or school groups (not religious groupings), are permitted, but this merely recognised good practices developed during the last twenty years. Advice to reduce the 'daily' requirement was ignored by parliamentarians who spoke of 'dilution'.

Clause seven of the Act prescribes the nature of worship in a completely new way. The 1944 Act merely legislated for a 'daily act of collective worship on the part of the whole school'. It is now more precisely defined: 'The collective act of worship required in school by section 6 of this Act shall be wholly or mainly of a broadly Christian character' (7:1). Although the subsequent subclauses have the effect of toning down these words, and DES circular 3/89 goes further in this direction,[7] as will be discussed later, it is the two words 'Christian worship' which have engaged the attention of teachers and provoked hostility. They could go along with the kind of definition found in the influential Hampshire LEA handbook, *Paths to Understanding* (1980), 'Worship has to do with worth and worthiness. It is the recognition, affirmation and celebration of the "worthship" of certain realities and values, held to be of central importance to the community which worships' (ibid. 118).

There is no confidence that this definition any longer provides them with adequate protection from inspectors, HMIs, or parents who are seeking something more Christian, though in a National Curriculum Advisory Note to Hampshire schools (November, 1988), the RE Adviser for Hampshire shared none of these doubts, and many other specialists in RE would endorse his view, though the word 'Christian' must probably be treated with caution. If the lobby which demanded the insertion of 'Christian' has won, their victory may be phyrric. The price of resentment could be paid by religious education as a classroom subject, not merely school worship. Hostility is considerable and vocal. Scarcely a gathering of teachers takes place without the requirement for 'Christian worship' to be denounced. Feeling is so strong that it is doubtful whether more optimistic interpretations such as those expressed below are capable of being heard just yet.

The danger of over-defining which RE specialists have often warned against, valuing the 1944 Act in this respect, has been ignored. It now remains to be seen whether the tendency to over-interpret can be avoided. The signs are not good. If interpretation is too narrow, school worship will become contentious to the point of being unacceptably divisive. Terence Copley, a former deputy headteacher, notes that it has become 'one of a number of potential flashpoints in the life of a manager' (1989: 26). One parent group may complain that worship is not Christian enough, another may object to it being too Christian. Muslim parents may ask for separate assemblies to be conducted by the imam. The machinery exists to deal with these situations, as though, from the outset it was realised that provisions for school worship would not work. Standing Advisory Councils on

Religious Education (SACREs), optional under the 1944 Act, but now mandatory, may decide whether the requirements of the Act can be waived in particular cases. They may make a 'determination' which permits 'broadly Christian worship' to be replaced by something else. (Ealing has made a number of determinations in favour of multifaith acts of worship already, many others have granted determinations for Muslim acts of worship in school which are overwhelmingly Muslim in composition). The Act has also, for the first time, made provision for a complaints procedure which parents may use if they are dissatisfied with the RE or school worship in the school which their children are attending. A litigious attitude is being encouraged in areas where good will has hitherto prevailed and which rely on an atmosphere of sensitive reasonableness to be effective.[8]

Headteachers and school governors faced with so many management issues as a result of the 1988 Act are unlikely to respond positively and sympathetically to those arising from worship when, for decades, they have placed it low on their hierarchy of concerns. Now, however, there is a recognition that whatever they do, they cannot ignore it. The present government at least expects the requirement of the Act to be implemented. Heads may, of course, plead the conscience clause and pass the responsibility to others, either members of staff or outsiders designated by the governors or SACRE to fulfil the obligations of the law.

At first glance the solution of handing over the conduct of school worship to outsiders may be attractive. The law permits it and it is one less burden for the headteacher and colleagues to bear. Things are seldom as simple as they appear, however. The responsibility is still that of the headteacher for whatever happens in the school. The irate parent will still beat a path to the head's door and not be put off by statements that s/he was not present or had, through the governors, given the job to someone else. There is no lack of people who would like to lead school worship among those who are outside the teaching profession, but *caveat emptor* applies here as elsewhere. Visitors coming to participate in school activities of any kind and for whatever reason should have their credentials checked and be briefed concerning what they may properly do and say.

Faced with the demand to provide for worship and aware that changes in the law, though desirable, are unlikely, we must ask whether it is possible to use the present legislation to advantage. I am sure that the intention is that we can. Much skill, as yet not wholly appreciated, went into helping the Bishop of London respond to the rather unexpected moves of those who used the Baroness Cox as their focus to ensure that school religion should be predominantly Christian. The glosses, 'broadly', 'collective', considerations of 'ages and aptitudes', and 'any circumstances relating to the family backgrounds of the pupils', are to be explored, and especially the requirement that the collective worship 'shall not be distinctive of any particular Christian or other religion denomination', while 'reflecting the broad traditions of Christian *belief*' (my italics).

Interpreting the New Act

Reflecting upon these words with reference to worship we must note the breadth of belief, from unitarian (regarded by some as Christian) to the strict biblicism of the Free Presbyterians, ranging through the Society of Friends and the Orthodox Church on the way. Broad is very broad indeed. Picking up verse anthologies one may find the Wesleys and Isaac Watts represented, but also Hardy, Hopkins, Blake, Dylan Thomas and Wilfred Owen.

'Collective' does not mean the same as communal or corporate. The Concise OD defines it as 'Formed by of constituting a collection, taken as a whole, aggregate' or 'of or from many individuals'. The strong democratic spirit of Britain, reinforced by an approach to education which encourages an element of individuality and invites pupils to think for themselves, denies any interpretation of worship which would inhibit this freedom.

'Age', and 'aptitude' are factors which teachers must keep in mind when delivering any part of the curriculum. In history, geography, music, and especially mathematics, languages and the sciences, we pay attention to the individual child's experience and intellectual development. They are not yet ready for abstract reasoning in certain things such as mathematics, the use of the subjective, factors influencing soil erosion, or the use of diminished sevenths in composition. We know that it is pointless and unhelpful to teach them too early; we should realise that to introduce children too soon to the doctrines of the Atonement or Trinity is equally ill advised. The full blown worship of Christian faith communities is not for young children, even if the 1988 Act permitted it, which it does not!

As for 'family background', this can relate to faith, Christian or Bahai, or lack of it. Even in rural areas like West Sussex, it is not always safe for teachers in denominational schools to assume church attendance or even a positive attitude towards religion on the part of parents. 'Family background' may warn teachers who are concerned for the development of religious understanding of their children, or the Christian faith, no to use explicitly Christian material of a traditional kind, especially in hymns and prayers. Here they might also take account of good practice in denominational youth clubs which attempt to include a spiritual element in the programme. They realise how far their young people are from the Church and try to meet them where they are, rather than from their own position of faith.

Finally, we remind ourselves again that we are concerned with 'school worship' which is not distinctive of any Christian denomination. Things relating to schools must be determined by educational principles. The sum of the terms discussed above must be acts of worship which are educationally justifiable and can be defended by educational arguments. If the over-precision of the Act has done anything, it has brought us to the realisation that school worship should not be a diluted form of church worship. For this we shall increasingly have cause to be thankful.

Working with the Act

It is the strongly held view of this writer that school worship can be worthwhile and unthreatening and, at the same time, legal. Furthermore, an element which has often been missing in school worship may now be introduced, namely that of meaningful sprituality. Liturgies based on church worship, using the great hymns and prayers of the faith, fail to affect young people either because of the difficulty of the unfamiliar language, or because the concepts are beyond their comprehension. 'Safe' assemblies, the 'secular assemblies' to which John Hull referred, might have no spiritual element at all. Perhaps the requirement to engage in broadly Christian worship might encourage teachers to explore those things which have to do with the human spirit, but not in a narrowly religious way.

Terence Copley has pointed out (1989: 17–18) that 'the legislators in 1988 were keen to eliminate what many politicians felt to be a multifaith mishmash', or the 'cocktail of faiths' to use the more original phrase of the Chief Rabbi. It remains to be seen whether, if this was their wish, they have been successful. Determinations for such acts of worship in multifaith schools have been given. As yet none of them has been contested in a court of law. There are those who would endorse the view expressed in the British Council of Churches booklet, *Can we Pray Together?* (1983) that these are possible even within the constraints of 'wholly or mainly of a broadly Christian character', for here, again, the Act goes on to say that this does not necessarily apply to every act of worship but, 'taking any school term as a whole' most acts should. Paragraph 34 of DES circular 3/89 *The Education Reform Act 1988: Religious Education and Worship* adds the following gloss to this phrase. It reads: 'In the Secretary of State's view, an act of worship which is "broadly Christian" need not contain only Christian material provided that taken as a whole, it reflects the traditions of Christian belief. Any such act of worship should not be distinctive of any particular Christian denomination. It is not necessary for every act of worship to be of this character, but within each school term the majority of acts must be so.' (para 34).

This paragraph may be regarded as permissive in the extreme, and evidence of the intention of the Act as finally passed to allow the developments which took place in the seventies and early eighties, until 1988, to continue. It even endorses, one might argue, Geoffrey Parrinder's use of the *Gita* in a Christian service. Perhaps it also calls for someone to take over where he left off and attempt not only to explain and analyse forms of worship in the different religious traditions, but to try to explore, if not answer, the question 'What is worship?'

The headteacher of a multifaith secondary school should find it possible to continue pre-1988 practices and obey the law in accordance with the paragraph quoted above. That is not a satisfactory situation, however. The school's faith traditions must be included for their own intrinsic worth and out of respect for them, not by interpreting the phrase 'broadly Christian' in an all-embracing manner. That smacks of paternalism. Multifaith acts of worship provide the only wholesome way forward in many schools in our major cities. The alternative of separate gatherings of Jew, Sikhs, Muslims, a few Christians, (not to mention those who belong nowhere, the disaffected of all these and those never reached by any of them), scarcely bears contemplating. It could lead to the kind of divisiveness which is just diminishing in Liverpool and Glasgow, not forgetting Northern Ireland where it still thrives, and which has not hitherto been an aspect of life in Bradford or Leicester. If it was the intention of the

1988 Act to reinforce a certain concept of nationhood and to marginalise groups which did not come within it, the religious clauses countered it with some success. They must now be exploited skilfully, not used to endorse it. *Can we Pray Together?* and the more recent BBC discussion document on school worship show ways in which it can be done. It is to be hoped that other faith groups understandably angry at having been consulted usually only by the Bishop of London and his advisers, who recognised the importance of including them, will realise that they will suffer as much as anyone else in a racially divided society. It would be a mistake for them to think that they may improve their chances of obtaining their own schools by using rights of withdrawal and winning determinations of separate acts of worship (Copley 1989: 17–18).

In Practice

In practice this would mean, in secondary schools, something in the nature of a 'thought for the day', an opportunity for reflection rather than affirmation. Let us take Holy Week and Easter as an example. A five day preparation could be as follows.

Day 1: (a) Brief explanation of the coming series of acts of worship.

(b) Slide of the Crucifixion projected and, on another screen, a slide of contemporary human suffering; brief explanation of why Christians observe Holy Week and Easter; reading of Isaiah 53: 2–12; invitation to think of the suffering of Jesus or some other suffering in a moment of silence. Departure to classes as suitable music is played, it could be popular (e.g. Dylan, the Beatles) or classical.

Day 2: Practices and customs associated with the season, bring out the symbolism of, for example, hot cross buns and Easter eggs. How Lent may be kept, Easter vigils, celebrations in other countries if staff or students have experiences they can share. Reflection on a poem or song.

Day 3: An art teacher, not necessarily Christian, shares her/his response to the crucifixion slide which was shown on day one and s/he had chosen. Explains selection.

Day 4: Reflection on a poem by one of the English department. Again not necessarily Christian, and the poem need not be religious or explicitly about Easter.

Day 5: A group of Christians tell the assembly what Easter Day means to them, read a Bible passage, sing an Easter hymn to guitars and/or piano. Words projected for all to read. Those who wish may join in.

Now, of course, this outline is merely the end product. For the series to be successful there must be an already existing ethos which encourages members of staff and pupils to expose themselves to different viewpoints and to share them without inhibition. The Christians must not, afterwards, be ridiculed as the 'God squad', and they must realise the bounds of propriety within which they are witnessing. Those who want to join in must feel free to do so without embarrassment. This healthy climate should, anyway, be one which the community is striving for. If respect for diversity of opinions cannot be developed, can schools serve any useful purpose beyond that of preparing children for the world of work (which anyway, they are often alleged to do badly!.)?

Isaiah 53 is only Christian by adoption, which may not seem to matter in a so-called monocultural school, though antisemitism is by no means confined to people who have actually met Jews (frequently the opposite is true). Sometime, not in this period of assemblies, the Jewish interpretations of Isaiah 53 need to be discussed in RE, probably under the heading 'Messiah'. If there are Jews in the school or perhaps the wider community, in Leeds or Manchester, for example, one of the week's assemblies might be a Jewish reflection on either the death of Jesus, or suffering. The visitor could decide how to respond to Isaiah 53, it could be by ignoring it or by providing a Jewish view. S/he would be a frequent visitor to the school. This Holy Week series is not a time to trundle in strangers.

Islam teaches that Jesus was not crucified. If the school had Muslim pupils, this might be explored now or a Muslim could reflect on suffering or on the prophet Isa's place in Islam.

The Need for Planning

We are beginning to see the need for planning. 'The place of Jesus in Islam' could feature at Christmas, or at Easter, but not at both. Which? Assemblies could become too cerebral, alternative RE lessons almost. How should they relate to RE? Clearly there is a need for a management group to look after school worship, to produce a policy and a programme, and to keep the school, students and staff informed and, above all, consulted and involved. The RE department should be represented, despite their understandable wish to distance themselves from worship, especially if it is understood in the traditional sense. The kinds of activities which I have in mind are too important for any group of teachers to ignore them. Incidentally, pupils too should be involved as much as possible. They, after all, are the principal consumers!

The secondary school problem is actually easier than that of the primary school, once it is admitted that the purpose of school worship is to reflect rather than affirm. Where teachers are sensitive, they will not require pupils to practise hypocrisy; where they are not, resentment will lead to rejection. Younger children can be persuaded to do almost anything. They will sing with enthusiasm and say 'Amen' loudly, though they do not know what it means. Here the burden is upon the teacher not to take advantage of their openness and trust by inviting them to affirm what they do not yet believe.

Proposals

School worship is too important to be the subject merely of a survey article. It is a symbol intended to be as potent as the flag in schools in the USA. It deserves to be taken seriously. At school level this means that time and resources need to be given to planning it and producing a policy. It should have its place when the purpose of in-service days is being considered. It should be seen as the responsibility of the whole community, parents, pupils and governors, as well as staff, and the Religious Studies department should regard it as one of their priorities for reasons which should already have become apparent. However, it should be regarded as a distinct area of the curriculum, though related to all others.

The Council of Churches for Britain and Ireland might set up a working party to monitor school worship and bring proposals before the government for reforming it. This should be the work of the DES, but there is no indication that it intends to concern itself with this curriculum area. It is well known that the government listens to the Church of England and only through them to professional teachers on the subject of religion in schools, so there is little point in a non-church body such as the Religious Education Council of England and Wales taking such an initiative.

This working party should include people of all faiths found in Britain today, and none. They should be drawn from the teaching profession and from many other walks of life, but all should have been educated in the maintained system. Too often those who do not use it decide what is good for those who do!

Meanwhile there are changes to be considered now. For example, the churches, when asked before the Act was contemplated, whether they would object if the requirement to worship daily were amended, indicated sympathy for a proposal which would alter the existing obligation. Opposition came from elsewhere and nothing was done. A move to reduce the 'daily' requirement to weekly would alleviate the very real difficulties of headteachers.

At the end of the day we are still on the horns of a dilemma. If history did not exist, it is doubtful whether anyone would seriously suggest that an act of worship should be part of the daily life of all pupils in maintained schools in England and Wales. However, it is part of the heritage of those countries and in England, where there is an established church, it is inconceivable to many people that education should be wholly secular. The abolition of school worship would be understood as an admission that England is no longer a Christian country. Could a weekly voluntary act of worship at a time when no other activities were allowed to compete with it, provide an acceptable alternative?

On the other hand retention, especially with a requirement that it should be 'wholly or mainly broadly Christian', wilfully ignores reality not only in multifaith cities, but in the rest of pluralist Britain, including parliament. Perhaps this is something adults can cope with, but pupils, those of secondary age especially, find themselves asked to take part in a daily act of hypocrisy which diminishes the respect for religion which it is supposed to enhance and uphold. It also carries with it the perennial threat that 'broadly Christian' may be challenged by Christians who think the interpretation is too broad.

Fluctuations in religious attitudes are notoriously difficult to predict. A Christian revival might be on the way which would result in packed churches and a teaching force which mirrored society. Leaving aside (where they are already) Jews, Hindus, Buddhists, Muslims, Sikhs, and Humanists, we might have schools where the affirmation of Christianity through worship was possible. Would it be appropriate and desirable? At the end of the day the school worship issue merges into something even greater, namely the question of whether the purpose of education is to endorse prescribed values, and prepare children and young people for entry into a certain kind of society, or to help them to challenge, question, and arrive at their own conclusions? Instead of prefixing the inhibiting word 'worship' with the prescriptive adjective 'Christian', perhaps it is time to remove it altogether and instead use 'assembly'. Some kind of collective gathering is considered desirable by most teachers for a number of purposes, including the collective exploration of and reflection upon values and beliefs, though they would not necessarily wish it to be on a daily basis.

NOTES

[1] The clauses of the 1944 Act relating to school worship are: 'the school day in every county school shall begin with collective worship on the part of all pupils in attendance at the school, and the arrangements made therefore shall provide for a single act of worship' (section 25); 'the collective worship shall not be distinctive of any particular denomination' (section 26); 'if the parent of any pupil requests that he (sic) shall be wholly or partly excused from attendance at religious worship he shall be excused' (section 25).

[2] *Schools Council Working Paper 36, Religious Education in Secondary Schools*, Evans/Methuen, 1971, is the most important document to have been produced by the projects which were based at Lancaster University. It is essential reading for anyone seeking to understand developments in RE in England and Wales in the last twenty years.

[3] An *Agreed Syllabus* is a document which prescribes what RE should legally be taught in any local authority in England and Wales.

[4] Section 30 of the 1944 Act states that 'no person shall be disqualified by reason of his religious opinions or omitting to attend religious worship from being a teacher in a school' (section 30), a position endorsed by the 1988 Act, chapter 40, section 86; 4, page 87. It has always been expected that, other than for reasons of conscience, all teaching staff would attend acts of worship, though this seems to be a matter of tradition rather than law. DES Circular 3/89 para 46 refers to 'teachers' freedom under the 1944 Act not to attend collective worship'.

[5] Quoted in B. O'Keefe, ed., *Schools for Tomorrow*, 1988, p. 102.

[6] Clauses in the 1988 Act relating to worship which differ from those of 1944 are; 'arrangements for the collective act of worship may, in respect of each school day, provide for a single act of worship for all pupils or for separate acts of worship for pupils in different age groups or in different school groups' (section 6); 'the collective worship required in the school shall be wholly or mainly of a broadly Christian character' (section 7:1); such worship 'shall be such as is appropriate having regard to any relevant considerations relating to the pupils concerned . . . those considerations are: (a) any circumstances relating to their family background (b) their ages and aptitudes' (section 7:4c and 5:a and b)

[7] DES Circular 3/89 says, 'One factor which may inform a headteacher's decision to make an application to the SACRE [for permission to allow alternative acts of worship] is the extent of withdrawals from Christian collective worship' (para. 36). It also outlines complaints machinery which parents may use (paras. 52, 53) under section 23 of the Act. See also DES circular 1/89.

[8] See *What Can Muslims Do?*, Muslim Educational Trust, 1988; also *The Assemblies' Loss of Faith*, Guardian, 1 August 1989; and Sardar Indarjit Singh, Thought for the Day, BBC Radio 4, 10 August 1989.

SUGGESTED READING

W. O. Cole and J. Evans-Lowndes, *Religious Education in the Primary School*, Exeter: Religious and Moral Education Press (forthcoming)

T. Copley, *Worship, Worries, and Winners*, London: National Society, 1989.

E. Cox and J. M. Cairns, *Reforming Religious Education*, London: Kogan Page, 1989.

J. Hull, *The Act Unpacked*, London: CEM, 1989

——, 'Editorial', *British Journal of Religious Education*, vol. 11/3, summer 1989.

B. O'Keefe, ed., *Schools for Tomorrow*, Brighton: Falmer Press, 1988.

Ian Ramsey, *The Fourth R* (The Durham Report), London: SPCK, 1970.

6. RELIGIOUS STUDIES AND INTERFAITH DEVELOPMENTS

Marcus Braybrooke

It was on my first visit to Younghusband House, then the headquarters of the World Congress of Faiths (WCF), that I first met Geoffrey Parrinder in 1965. I had gone to hear him speak and to see if he would accept me as a post-graduate student. I never suspected that that evening would be the start of my active involvement in WCF.

In those days interfaith dialogue was neither religiously nor academically respectable. 'All Faiths Services' might well be picketted and were the subject of a hostile motion in the Church of England Church Assembly. There was strong objection to allowing 'non-Christians' to use church buildings or to buy redundant churches. There was amongst church leaders suspicion of what Michael Ramsey, then Archbishop of Canterbury, called 'The World Congress of Faiths ideology', although he later admitted that he was 'using words vaguely and inaccurately'.Invited to a meeting about 'Religion and the Future', the Archbishop rejected the view that religion was necessarily good or unifying. 'Far from regarding "religion" as the uniting banner, I believe that some rationalistic and non-religious modes of thought and behaviour are as relevant as some religions are. I cannot subscribe to the idea that "religion" itself contains a high view of man and the hope for the future.' The influence of Karl Barth's distinction between the Gospel and religions can be recognised here, as well as the sixties' talk of 'man come of age'. The Archbishop was willing, he said, to join with anyone in the assertion of human rights, but not on the basis of religion. This is a view subsequently often adopted within the World Council of Churches, where the basis for cooperation with people of other faiths has been shared humanity rather than any religious link. The Archbishop also felt that the World Congress of Faiths was being used 'by non-Christian religions in order to propagate their own belief in a 'diffused' view of deity and revelation at the expense of the distinctive Christian belief in particularity.'[1]

The academic climate was scarcely more favourable. Hardly any theologians were yet interested in the relation of religions. In Britain, at least, books on 'Religion and Society' or 'Religion and Ethics' were, in fact, only about Christianity's views. Those engaged in the study of religions were suspicious of the wooly unscientific approach of interfaith gatherings, assuming they all espoused a theosophical approach. Professor Bleeker, following the 1958 Tokyo Congress, summarised the general view of members of the International Association for the History of Religions (IAHR) like this: 'We should make a clear distinction between our scientific work and the Ecumencial movement or the World Congress of Faiths – we are only a congress for the scientific study of the history of religions.'[2] As Professor Zwi Werblowsky had argued, 'the discussion of the absolute value of religion is excluded by definition . . . There may or may not be room for organisations in which students of religion join with others to contribute their share towards the promotion of certain ideals – national, international, political, social, spiritual and otherwise. But this is a matter of individual ideology and commitment, and must under no circumstance be allowed to influence or colour the character of IAHR.'[3]

It was typical of Geoffrey Parrinder that he was prepared to put at risk both respectabilities for what he already recognised as urgent for the future. He saw that the study of world religions required meeting and talking with members of those faiths. He also saw that the church must reinterpret traditional claims in the light of a new awareness of the riches of other spiritual traditions. The subject of his talk to the WCF was 'Light from the East: A Contribution to the Honest to God Debate'.[4]

The Growth of Interfaith Organisations

Much has happened in the subsequent 25 years. 'Interfaith dialogue has become a concern for the many rather than a dream of a few.' Interfaith organisations and groups have mushroomed, so that it has become common to speak of the 'interfaith movement', just as people speak of the 'peace movement' or 'green movement' as shorthand for a wide range of concerns and activities. As with these movements, most of the work has been the voluntary, sacrificial work of dedicated pioneers. The religious communities have been very reluctant to commit any of their considerable resources to this task.

International interfaith contacts have increased rapidly. The World Congress of Faiths (WCF), founded in 1936, has arranged major conferences in Britain, with speakers of the standing of W. Cantwell Smith, Hans Küng and R. Panikkar. Its international influence has

spread, especially through the journal *World Faiths Insight*, which it
publishes jointly with the Temple of Understanding. The
International Association for Religious Freedom (IARF), which was
founded early in this century, has become increasingly interfaith in
character and composition, and now has a wide range of member
groups. New organisations have been formed. The Temple of
Understanding, inspired by Juliette Hollister, held its first 'Spiritual
Summit Conference' in Calcutta in 1968. Two years later, the first
Assembly of the World Conference on Religion and Peace (WCRP),
energised by Dr Homer Jack, was convened in Kyoto. In India, the
World Fellowship of Inter-Religious Councils was formed by Fr
Albert Nambiaparambil, following a gathering in Cochin in 1981. A
Centre for World Thanksgiving, conceived by Peter Stewart in 1961,
has been built in Dallas. In addition, the Council of World Religions,
which is funded by the Unification Church, has an international
network and programme of conferences. Increasingly other
international gatherings, such as the Global Forum on Human
Survival (Oxford 1988) and the conference on 'Seeking the True
Meaning of Peace' (at the University of Peace, Costa Rica, 1989)
have had an interfaith dimension. Other bodies, such as the
International Council of Christians and Jews, the fruit of the persistent
work of W. W. Simpson, concentrate on bilateral dialogue.

Religious communities themselves have set up departments for
interreligious relations. The Vatican Secretariat for Non-Christians
was established in 1964[5] and the World Council of Churches' Sub-
Unit on Dialogue in 1971. By the early seventies, major Jewish
organisations agreed to work together for dialogue with Christian
denominations through the International Jewish Committee on Inter-
Religious Consultations. The World Muslim League and the World
Buddhist Fellowship have become more active in multireligious
gatherings.

Developments in Britain have been of particular importance. As
early as 1974, Dr Stanley Samartha, Director of the WCC Sub-Unit,
wrote to me that 'it seems to me that those of us who come from
traditionally multi-religious societies have something to learn from
you in ways in which you are facing what to you are new situations.'[6]
The Interfaith Network, to be mentioned below, is already serving as
an example for other parts of the world, such as North America.

In 1965, besides the WCF, the Council of Christians and Jews and
the London Society for Jews and Christians were already active. Both
organisations have expanded their work and influence, and whilst

Christian-Jewish dialogue retains its specific character, it has become more related to wider interfaith dialogue. In 1977, the British Council of Churches Committee for Relations with People of Other Faiths was formed, with Kenneth Cracknell as first fulltime secretary whose successor is Clinton Bennett. Several denominations now have special committees for interfaith reflection and dialogue, some with, at least, part time officers.

There has been considerable growth in the number of local interfaith groups and of voluntary groupings, such as the Interfaith Association – now merged with WCF. There are some thirty local groups, each with their own fascinating story, of which Wolverhampton, led by Ivy Gutteridge, Leeds Concord group, inspired by Peter Bell, and Glasgow, stimulated by the unforgettable Stella Reekie, are best known. Interfaith gatherings are held quite widely, especially in connection with the Week of Prayer for World Peace. There are study centres, particularly in Birmingham with its MultiFaith Centre, the Centre for the Study of Islam and Christian-Muslim Relations and the Centre for the Study of Judaism and Christian-Jewish Relations. Several conference centres, such as Ammerdown or, until its recent closure, Spode House, include interfaith conferences and retreats in their programmes.

Religious education has changed considerably. In his 1965 lecture, Geoffrey Parrinder called for 'much greater study of what the major religions teach'. Thanks to the SHAP Working Party, the Standing Conference on Interfaith Dialogue in Education, the RE Council and other bodies plenty of books about world religions are now available and agreed syllabi usually include the study of world religions. Television, and particularly the Open University's series on the 'Religious Quest' have brought this new awareness to a wide audience.[7]

These many developments have led some people to ask how the various activities could be related more effectively to avoid duplication and to increase their impact. In 1985 I invited representatives of many of the international interfaith organisations to meet at Ammerdown, near Bath. Initially there was talk of a 'World Council of Religions', but such a model was soon felt to be too structured, especially as some religious traditions do not have designated leaders. Yet from subsequent meetings there has been agreement that four organisations – IARF, the Temple of Understanding, WCF, and WCRP – should together mark 1993, the centenary of the 1893 World Parliament of Religions held in Chicago, as 'A Year of Interreligious Understanding and Cooperation'. A major gathering will be held in India. Already other plans are being made for conferences in Chicago, Vancouver and elsewhere. The hope is that many places of worship, schools and institutions will observe the year. Even so, the idea of some World Council of Religions keeps re-emerging, which suggests that the right structures for inter-religious cooperation have not yet been devised. The present structures seem clearly inadequate for the likely needs of the next century.[8]

In Britain, in 1977–8, Canon Peter Schneider, Rev Jack Austin and I, with some others, made tentative moves to explore forming a 'Consultative Interfaith Council'. In a memorandum, Canon Peter Schneider outlined the possiblities. On the projected Council, compared to the BCC Committee on Relations with People of Other Faiths, 'members of various Faith Communities would meet and discuss as equal partners. All are hosts and none are guests'. Compared to WCF, which was based on individual enthusiasts, the Council 'would consciously relate to the various Faith Communities as a whole and seek to provide a structured forum of meeting and discussion'. 'The aims of this Council can be seen as facilitating a more comprehensive meeting and acquaintance and knowledge of different Faiths than is at present the case. Further its purpose would be that issues of common interest and concern could be discussed and if it seemed proper decisions reached. In times of crisis the Council would be the obvious framework for urgent consultation and possible united decision, provided this had the support of the Faith Communities represented in the Council.'[9] Nothing came of these moves, partly because of the death of Peter Schneider, and because of lack of support from the religious communities. A little while later, however, the publication of *Interfaith News*, as a cooperative venture, helped to bring cohesion to interfaith work in Britain.

Recently, after much patient work by Brian Pearce, many of the British groupings have come together in the Interfaith Network. Formally established in 1987, the Interfaith Network links over sixty existing organisations and groups, including representative bodies from within different faith communities, existing countrywide organisations, local interfaith groups and bodies concerned with religious education on a multifaith basis and related academic institutions and study centres. The Network is already encouraging exchange of ideas on the implications of life together within a multifaith society.[10]

The Reluctance of Faith Communities to Change

Yet, writing in the wake of the Salman Rushdie affair, it is hard to be confident that Britain has become a more tolerant society. In part this reflects the political climate, where confrontation has replaced consensus, and the harsher economic situation. Elsewhere, as in the Middle East and Sri Lanka, religious passions enflame many conflicts. It still does not seem that religious leaders are heard clearly speaking together for moral and humanitarian values.

There has certainly been progress. More people are involved and increasingly they are in the main stream of their community's life. Dr Runcie, the present Archbishop of Canterbury, is often seen with other religious leaders. The Chief Rabbi has been made a member of the House of Lords. The Queen has been regular in her attendance at the Multifaith Act of Witness held in Westminster Abbey on Commonwealth Day. The Sir Sigmund Sternberg Awards for Interfaith Understanding have raised the profile of this work. Religious assemblies, such as the General Assembly of the Church of Scotland or the Lambeth Conference, have addressed the issue of dialogue.

Those involved in dialogue are moving beyond the stage of discarding prejudices and self-congratulation on the fact of meeting to discussing sensitive issues or what religious people can do together. The Manor House group of clergy and rabbis, for example, has grappled with the issue of forgiveness in Judaism and Christianity. The Joint Presidents of the Council of Christians and Jews meet annually to discuss major social concerns. At Assisi, religious leaders joined the Pope to pray for peace, and peace has been the focus of WCRP activities. Multi-religious groups are active as non-governmental organisations at the United Nations. Medical and social workers meet to discuss the needs of people of different faiths when they are ill, and especially when they are dying. Together, people of all faiths are showing concern about the enviroment.

Further, many people would testify to the personal enrichment that interfaith meetings have brought, both in terms of new friendships and spiritual renewal.

Yet to what extent do members of religious communities yet really understand each other? In November 1988, the World Congress of Faiths organised a conference at which scholarly members of the world religions responded to Professor Küng's book *Christianity and World Religions*. In the book he depends for his information about world religions on the writings of Christian specialists in this field. The two Muslim scholars made clear that, in their view, the Christian writers had failed to understand Islam, and the Buddhist scholars said the same of the descriptions of Buddhism. The Hindu scholar was too polite to suggest the same so clearly.[11]

The prerequirement for dialogue is that we begin to see and feel and understand as the other does – even if we do not share or agree with their vision or view. If distinguished scholars from outside a religion fail accurately to describe the religion of their studies, it should make us ponder whether, even yet, our communication is only superficial. Can members of one faith really enter into and have a feel for another religious world? It is so easy to read other texts with our presuppositions unchallenged. It is, for example, hard for Christians trained in biblical criticism to share a Muslim's feel for the Qur'an. Yet if it is not possible for a person of one faith to describe another faith, so that a member of that faith feels it is a fair and accurate description, there is little hope of progress. We need to refine our methods of study and give students more opportunity to immerse themselves in living experience of another religious world, as Klostermaier suggested in his book *Hindu and Christian in Vrindaban* (London, 1969).

One of the Muslim contributors, however, suggested that dialogue itself was a pointless activity, because religions are necessarily competitive. 'Any religion taking a linear view of history assumes its own finality, hence also exclusivity.'[12] The underlying hope of the interfaith movement, although not of the academic study of religions, is that in some way religions are complementary or convergent. Early suggestions that all religions really teach the same thing are seen to be facile. Significance must be given to the differences as well as the similarities. Yet there is the persistent (eschatological?) hope that different visions of truth may enrich each other – each being partial and pointing to an Ultimate Divine Reality greater than any single description. Dr Zaki Badawi ended his Younghusband Lecture on *Islam and World Religions* with this Sufi quotation, 'On my way to the Mosque, Oh Lord, I passed the Magian in front of his flame, deep in thought, and a little further I heard a Rabbi reciting his Holy Book in the Synagogue, and then I came upon the Church where the hymns sung gently in my ears and finally I came into the Mosque and watched the worshippers immersed in their experience and I pondered how many are the different ways to You – the one God.' Rabbi Dr Norman Solomon, in his lecture, spoke of the dialogue of faiths as a natural outgrowth of the mission of Judaism. Dr Runcie in his lecture quoted Paul Tillich, In the depth of every living religion there is a point at which religion itself loses its importance, and that to which it points breaks through its particularity, elevating it to spiritual freedom and to a vision of the spiritual presence in other expressions of the ultimate meaning of man's existence. That is what Christianity must grasp in its encounter with the world's religions.'[13]

There is the further hope that, despite sharp disagreements on particular moral issues even within religions, there are ethical values held in common by the great faiths and that together they can uphold human dignity and the sacredness of all life.[14]

Such an understanding of religions' inter-relationship and common calling requires a change in each religious community's self-understanding. It cannot claim to be already in possession of the whole truth. Convergence implies the possibility of revision and new insights – what has been called 'mutal transformation'. Nor can a religion claim that it has a monopoly of salvation, so that the only hope for others is to join the one true religion. This requires, in most religious traditions, a rethinking of traditional teaching and the rejection of proselytism. Missionary activity directed at the adherents of one religion by members of another destroys the possibility of a new cooperative relationship.

There are those in different faiths who are willing to make the necessary adjustments, but there is little evidence that representative leaders or their followers are willing to moderate traditional claims. Indeed such moderation may mean that 'liberals' are replaced by more 'fundamentalist' leaders. This may reassure the faithful, who seem in every tradition to be becoming more 'fundamentalist', but does nothing to stop the steady erosion of faith communities as more people find themselves unable to accept the dogmatism of the past.

Yet to drift away may be to forfeit the spiritual vision at the heart of the faith tradition and to be submerged in the prevalent cynicism, secularism and superstition. The growth of new religions and new age groups suggest that many seek after a spiritual vision, but cannot discern it within the great religions because their shell is almost impenetrable. As Jacob Needleman said in his book *The New Religions*, 'the contemporary disillusionment with religion has revealed itself to be a religious disillusionment'.[15]

Those who remain members of a living religious tradition, but who are also committed to interfaith dialogue, have both to witness to the world that at the heart of their religion there are spiritual resources of inestimable worth for the new age and to persuade their co-religionists that these spiritual riches are to be generously shared, not defensively protected. It has been said that the next century will be a spiritual century or there will be none at all. Only religions together offer the spiritual basis without which world community and global survival are unlikely.

The hardest task of the interfaith movement is not to establish co-operation between some members of each religion, but to effect inner change within each religion. There may be growing appreciation of the nees for understanding between religions, but there is still reluctance to start the rethinking that seeing other religions as partners rather than rivals requires. There is even greater reluctance to make resources available for the work of interfaith dialogue and cooperation. As with the nations, so with religious institutions, self-preservation and self-interest are stronger than a world vision.

Being awakened to a unity that transcends religious divisions has been called a 'second conversion'. It has to be an individual discovery. It takes time for the circle of those who have made this discovery to grow. The dream of the few may have become the concern of the many, but the many are still too few to effect the radical change urgently necessary not just for religions' sake but for the sake of the world.

Geoffrey Parrinder made the discovery early in his ministry and has helped many others to make this discovery for themselves. As he said in 1965, 'There are many problems', but we seek 'a realisation of the need to co-operate, to learn from each other, in charity and humility, and to be fellow-seekers after truth'.[16]

NOTES

[1] Correspondence with Dr Edward Carpenter, 25.10.69 and 17.11.69.
[2] See my *Inter-Faith Organizations*, Toronto and New York: Edwin Mellen Press, 1980, pp. 12–13.
[3] Ibid.
[4] *World Faiths*, No 62, March 1965, p. 9
[5] Now renamed as The Pontifical Council for Interreligious Dialogue.
[6] In a letter dated 6.5.74.
[7] See the earlier chapters by Terence Thomas and Robert Jackson in this book.
[8] *World Faiths Insight*, New Series 12, Feb 1986. *Interfaith News*, Summer 1985, and David Edwards in *The Futures of Christianity*, London: Hodder and Stoughton, 1987, pp. 275–6.

[9] Memorandum 26.6.78.

[10] Paul Weller in *Discernment*, Autumn 1989, vol. 3, no 2, pp. 30–4.

[11] The papers are in the 1989 issues of *World Faiths Insight*. Küng's book is published by Collins/Doubleday, 1987.

[12] Dr Yakub Zaki in his paper to the WCF conference.

[13] The Sir Francis Younghusband Lectures for 1984, 1985 and 1986, printed in *World Faiths Insight* New Series, nos 12, 13 and 14. See also John Hick and Hasan Askari, eds, *The Experience of Religious Diversity*, Aldershot: Gower, 1985.

[14] See my chapter in Eric Moonman, ed., *The Violent Society*, London: Cass, 1987.

[15] J. Needleman, *The New Religions*, London: Allen Lane Penguin Press, 1970. Preface.

[16] *World Faiths*, no 62, 1965, p. 10.

SUGGESTED READING

M. Braybrooke, *Inter-Faith Organizations, 1893–1979: An Historical Directory*, Toronto and New York: Edwin Mellen Press, 1980.

——, *Time to Meet*, London: SCM Press and Philadelphia: Trinity Press International, 1990.

F. Clark, ed., *Interfaith Directory*, New York: International Religious Foundation, 1987

J. Hick and P. F. Knitter, eds, *The Myth of Christian Uniqueness*, New York: Maryknoll Orbis Books, 1987, and London: SCM Press, 1988.

P. F. Knitter, *No Other Name? A Critical Survey of Christian Attitudes towards the World Religions*, London and New York, 1985.

H. Küng, *Christianity and the World Religions*, London: Collins and New York: Doubleday, 1987.

PART II

TURNING POINTS IN THE DEVELOPMENT OF
SOME ACADEMIC SUBJECTS AND THEMES

7. HINDUISM

Friedhelm Hardy

What is 'Hinduism'?

Concepts create their own reality. When used for long enough, particularly by politicians and ideologues, they can objectify themselves and acquire something 'out there' to which they refer. 'The Hindus' and 'Hinduism' (just as 'Asian' in common British parlance) are good examples of such a process. It goes without saying that there are now people who refer to themselves as 'Hindus', using the label to define their own identity within a wider social context (both in India and in Britain). But when lining up the answers that different individuals and groups give us about their beliefs and practices, about what constitutes for themselves their 'Hinduness', the range and variety are staggering. Is this a sign of the incomprehensible mysteries of the East? Not at all. All that is required is, instead of trying to project a preconceived 'Hinduism' on to this variety, to acknowledge its irreducible internal differences. There is no 'ism', at least not in any sense that words formed in this way are normally used in English. Instead we are dealing with a large cluster of religions, some of which may have more in common with what is popularly called 'Buddhist' or 'Sikh' than with other members of the cluster itself. Although in popular writing the alleged content of 'Hinduism' is rapidly developing a monolithic and stereotyped character, this is no more than a fairly arbitrary abstraction from a random set of facts. Here is not the place to enter into complex history of this abstraction itself. But what is essential to state at the outset is that to comment on the history of the study of 'Hinduism' inevitably will involve comments on the nature of 'Hinduism' itself. To study 'Hinduism' is not the same as to study Buddhism, for unlike the latter, the former is not a defined (or probably, definable) entity. In fact, major problems in the understanding of 'Hinduism' arise from the imprecision in determining its nature, and not from the material itself. The case of the 'gods' and 'God' mentioned below is a good illustration. In other words, we are dealing with a jungle. The ideal would be to describe it as a total eco-system, but this will never be achieved. But it is still possible to do more than just pluck a few flowers. There are elements of an order here; it is just extremely important to know whose order or 'map' one is using.

Is there Life after the Vedas?

Early nineteenth century culture in Europe, busy with developing scientific and academic methods and interested in origins and evolutions, could not fail to be impressed by the Vedas. This corpus of religious scriptures had been handed down by meticulous oral means from the second millennium BCE onwards. Its discovery triggered off comparative philology alongside comparative religion, besides the study of Sanskrit (the language of the Vedas) in its own right. General categories (like 'polytheism' and 'nature worship') that still haunt comparative religious literature were derived from this material, just as – inevitably – the idea that the Vedas are the foundation of what eventually became known as 'Hinduism'. Unfortunately, the earliest Vedic material is poetry, and extremely elusive poetry at that. To gain any kind of idea of the wider religious context, materials from much later ages had to be used. More often than not, no historical questions were asked and more than one millennium of religious history telescoped into one total, and supposedly coherent, system. Matters of particular interest to us here concern the ideal of the true Vedic religious life, and the nature of the 'gods'.

Man finds his religious fulfilment by leading a life strictly regulated by the rules of *dharma*. This 'cosmic order' is spelled out in minute and positivist detail in the *Treatises on dharma (dharmashastras)*. The whole of society is divided into two primary categories: those who are entitled to the full Vedic religious programme, and those who are not. The first category is subdivided into three groups, led by the brahmins, the traditional and professional guardians of the Vedic heritage. Now each group of the four has its own specific *dharma*. Moreover, a life is divided into four stages (student, householder, etc.) each of which has its own dharmic rules (for example, celibacy for the student, enjoyment of marital love for the householder, etc.) All this is very neat and appears to contain the whole religious life of a 'Hindu'. Certainly this is the way it is even today presented in the majority of the popular books. From this point of view, the study of

'Hinduism' exhausts itself in analysing the Veda and these related matters.

But there are various flaws here, the discovery of which can be regarded as one major turning point. First of all, rather rashly only one of the many *dharmashastras*, viz. that attributed to Manu, tends to be consulted. But what does it mean that we have many such works, often diverging quite considerably on details and intention? While this fact breaks up the historical and social monolith called 'true Vedic life', a second point is even more important. Naively it has been assumed that what the *dharmashastras* lay down as rules corresponds to actual life. In fact, it is no more than an ideal, a blueprint for a perfect society. Precise figures are obviously not available, but it is hardly conceivable that many more than one per cent of Indians ever actualized this programme fully in their own lives. This would leave us with as much as 99 per cent of the population. Should their religion not be looked at?

From this follows that a considerable amount of religious life has been going on that is not as such described in the books on the Vedic *dharma*. No doubt these books, along with the belief in the Vedas etc., played a far wider role as prestigious norms and ideals than such a hypothetical calculation reveals. But they prescribe, not describe. Once it is realized that things need not actually be what they are supposed to be, according to some normative interpretation, it becomes possible to look at them in their own right and not write them off as 'unorthodox distortions' or 'sectarian developments' when acknowledging their existence at all. Thus a vast realm is opened up for the study of a 'Hinduism' after and outside the Veda *in senso stricto*.

God in the Plural

The rituals of the Vedas are addressed to non-human beings called *devas*; nearly a thousand have been counted. Given that different *devas* are often addressed for different specific purposes (like victory in battle, the birth of many strong sons, or abundant cattle), it might have been tempting to translate the word as 'saint'. Structurally this would have made better sense than 'god', which unfortunately has universally been chosen, no doubt on the basis of the (linguistically) related Latin *deus* and Greek *theos*. Since there are many, we must be dealing with 'polytheism'. As far as the interpretation of ancient

Vedic religion itself is concerned, this is not as important or as misleading as something else that has been derived from it. Superficially it looks as if the Vedas once for all have laid out the range of *devas*. Thus when we do meet 'gods' at a later period and in different kinds of scriptures, such an assumption allows for only two possibilities. Either such a *deva* carries a name found also in the Vedas, or not; what he represents in theological terms is then defined either directly by looking at his Vedic function, or indirectly by making him an 'aspect' or a 'form' of a Vedic god. For a long time nobody bothered to read what was actually said about such a god in the later treatises. It was another important turning point in our understanding of 'Hinduism' when scholars began to take the treatises themselves more seriously.

The way that certain religious movements and their books speak of a particular *deva* demonstrates beyond all reasonable doubt that we are dealing here with true monotheism. This was obviously difficult to acknowledge, because traditionally 'monotheism' was a category exclusively reserved for the Semitic traditions. Moreover, superficially even these 'monotheistic-sounding' groups and texts could be relativized (and thus accommodated under the customary 'polytheism'), because a number of different God-figures could be listed. But just as nobody would relativize Christian monotheistic belief, merely because there are Christians, Jews, Muslims, Sikhs, Hindus, etc. living in Britain, such a monotheistic religion cannot be relativized in India. This is a striking illustration of how a misconceived concept like 'Hinduism' (as the whole that relativizes the parts it contains) can distort our perception. As early as 1912, the German missionary H. W. Schomerus produced a sizeable book (*Der Shaiva-Siddhanta – eine Mystik Indiens*, Leipzig) on the theology of a particular movement which has Shiva as its God. Five years later, also Rudolf Otto (*Vishnu-Narayana*, Jena, 1917), though on a smaller scale, explored the theology of some Vishnu movements.

But such examples of a theological recognition of monotheism in India remained without much effect over the next few decades. It is difficult to say why this should have been; I can think of two major reasons. One is that the material dealt with by Schomerus (and Otto) was South Indian and predominantly in the vernacular Tamil. Without further research, it was difficult to correlate it to the nominal 'mainstream' of Hinduism. Another one is the fact that during the first five or so decades of the twentieth century, the concept of 'philosophy' came to dominate the access to Indian material. It was only when 'theology' once again emerged as an acceptable category of investigation, that a turning point could be achieved. On the basis of Kirfel's epoch-making research into the Puranas – the fundamental scriptural sources of monotheistic Hinduism – Paul Hacker (*Prahlada*, Mainz-Wiesbaden, 1959) evaluated the theological content of many of these texts in a global manner. Zaehner drew attention to the seminal role of the *Bhagavadgita* (Oxford, 1969) in Indian theism, and Geoffrey Parrinder (in his *Avatar and Incarnation*, London, 1970, a book derived from his Wilde Lectures at the University of Oxford 1966–1969) offered comparative reflections on a key concept (that of the *avatara*). Dhavamony, for the Shaiva-Siddhanta, and Carman (to be followed more recently by Lott and Lipner), for Srivaishnavism, resumed the line of investigation begun by Schomerus and Otto. The concept of 'God' (whether Vishnu or Shiva) has, at least in certain quarters, become accepted as a genuine category of traditional Indian religious life. Instead of saying that 'Hinduism' *is* a philosophy or a 'way of life', this material shows that it *contains* within its jungle-like growth true monotheism. Ambitious projects have meanwhile been initiated that aim at making the Epics and the Puranas available to the English-speaking world in critical translations. Since 1970, under the general editorship of J. L. Shastri, volumes have appeared from Benares of the Puranas; J. van Buitenen published in 1973 the first volume of his *Mahabharata* translation from Chicago, and in 1984 the *Ramayana* began to appear from Princeton, by R. Goldman and others.

Both Shiva and Vishnu have roots in the Vedas (however tenuous they may be), but Krishna has not. Yet once the conventional idea of Krishna being (merely) an *avatara* (incarnation) of Vishnu is questioned, it becomes possible to recognize also in him a genuine Hindu God-figure in his own right, as I have tried to show (*Viraha-bhakti*, Delhi, 1983). Moreover, by looking both at 'mainstream' Sanskrit and vernacular (particularly Tamil) material, I have attempted to bring into better focus the interaction between vernacular, regional religious cultures and the Sanskritic brahmin tradition. More recently, Brockington and Whaling have looked at another non-Vedic figure, viz. that of Rama, and Courtright that of Ganesha. It is highly regrettable that even a recent (and presumably influential) work like the *Encyclopedia of Religion* basically ignores all this as 'sectarian'. It is another question when these genuine theological matters will begin to affect the popular treatment of 'Hindu myths'. Conventionally this material typical of the Puranas has been treated as interchangeable and subjected to structuralist and psychoanalytical study without concern for the theological intentions (more often than not expressly stated) of the specific version of a particular myth. Thus there is a fundamental difference in such a story, whether it is told from the point of view of a Vishnu or a Shiva devotee about Shiva or Vishnu. It is of equally fundamental importance when such a myth is told about a particular place of pilgrimage. Shulman (*Tamil Temple Myths*, Princeton, 1980) has pointed into the direction of such a 'localized' approach.

Another area that can be regarded as being at the forefront of current concern is the fact that 'God' can be a woman. Feminist interest and concern has created a very lively scene of indological investigation; the exploration of monotheistic Hinduism centering around a 'Goddess' is still in its infancy. I hope to be able to publish relevant material in the not too distant future. The conventional obstacles to such a perception are many. Goddess religion in 'Hinduism' is on the whole low–caste, and even when expressed in highly sophisticated Sanskrit treatises, tends to get 'emasculated' by saying that the goddess is Shiva's 'consort' (read: respectable married and obedient wife) or his *shakti*, 'energy' (naturally controlled by him). The Vedas themselves know of extremely few *devis* (viz. female *devas*). While it is relatively easy to correlate for example Ramanuja's Vishnu with 'God' and then develop his theology, our culture is not familiar with 'God' as 'Goddess'. However, in spite of these obstacles I do envisage another turning point in our understanding of 'Hinduism' when the concept of 'Goddess' becomes accepted as another legitimate category.

The Swinging Sixties

Strange though it may seem, much of the theological discovery of Hinduism went on during the sixties. But this is certainly not what one would expect from a general survey of books on the Indian religions written during that period. In fact, there were a number of turning points which certainly must not be reduced to the one 'funk' of the swinging era. At least from hindsight it is possible to point at another three or four areas in which our understanding of 'Hinduism' changed considerably or was enriched substantially. But change does not automatically mean for the better; the 'funk' included also some *cul-de-sacs*.

In a cultural milieu in which the concept of 'philosophy' acted as the central tool of making sense of Hinduism, and that of 'theology' was only in the process of breaking loose from that stranglehold, to draw attention to certain 'mystical' elements was a major turning point. To provide this with some kind of academic precision was the achievement of Zaehner (*Mysticism – Sacred and Profane.* Oxford, 1957; *Hindu and Muslim Mysticism*, London, 1960.) Working on one's mind, not intellectually but by means of meditational exercises, and achieving 'altered states of consciousness' was recognized as a major rationale behind all kinds of seemingly 'non-sensical' statements. It remains to be seen what results a more recent and more experimental approach on meditation will come up with. But already now it is possible (and invaluable) to distinguish intentionally philosophical (and theological) statements from those that are meant to refer to meditationally gained experiences.

The period also produced a number of books on figures that till then had hardly been taken seriously or even known. The spirit of rebellion against any kind of establishment searched for soul-mates, and many could be found on the Indian side. A number of books introduced antinomian figures and movements that in one form or another had challenged a religious establishment which had lost (or at least was perceived to have lost) its inner life and had become ossified. Ramanujan's *Speaking of Shiva* on the Lingayites (Penguin Classics, 1973), Zvelebil's *Poets of the Power* on the Tamil *siddhas* (London, 1973), Vaudeville's *Kabir* (Oxford, 1974), Bhattacharya's *The Mirror of the Sky* on the Bengali Bauls (London, 1969) and other books drew attention to a strand in Hinduism that emphasized religious purity and freedom as opposed to institutionalization and social oppression in religion. The monolith is shown to be broken from within itself.

Closely related are developments in another area, where again the earlier efforts of a missionary were resumed. As early as 1900, G. Pope produced a translation of Shivaite poems in Tamil (*The Tiruvacagam*, Oxford). Then in the 20s Abbott brought out a whole series of translations from Marathi with the poetry of devotional, theistic saints. Similar material, but with a much more overtly erotic flavour, began to appear, on Candidas, Vidyapati, Mira-bai, etc. In a sense, this theistic poetry fitted in nicely with the previously mentioned material, because many of these vernacular poets, who often were low-caste, propagated antinomian attitudes and challenged the orthodox (and non-theistic) establishment. But its eroticism links it with the following.

Probably of far greater appeal to the popular imagination, although in various respects a serious regression in our understanding of

Hinduism, was the invention of a new -ism, 'Tantrism'. One of its roots are the highly esoteric writings of Avalon of the 20s, where the emphasis is nevertheless still on actual texts (the Tantras) and what they say. From it a generic 'tantric' was extrapolated by Ajit Mookerjee and projected on to a relatively random assortment of *objets d'art*. With Philip Rawson 'Tantrism' evolved then as the catch-all title of a new religious system, 'the cult of ecstasy'. Material taken from Jaina cosmology and astronomy. Hindu monotheism involving the Goddess, secular eroticism, folk-religions, regional cultures, mainstream Shiva, Vishnu, and Krishna religion is mixed up with genuine 'tantrika' material (viz. actually found in one of the innumerable texts called Tantras). The heterogeneous elements are imaginatively put together and the resulting whole is presented as the system of 'Tantrism'. Another conceptual veil was thus created that obscured the realities of religious life in India. (A London bookshop actually listed for a while all its books on Hinduism under the category of 'Tantrism'.) Speaking of turning points, this was a decisive turn backwards in many respects. Nevertheless, however inadvertently perhaps, Mookerjee, Rawson and others made highly interesting visual material accessible which otherwise and in a different social climate would have remained in the locked cupboards of libraries. But the arduous task of studying what ideas and practices the innumerable Tantras actually contain has barely begun (by Sanderson, Gupta, and others.)

Complex rituals are least interesting when studied in texts, while from the performer's (and to a lesser extent, the observer's) point of view they can be most appealing and satisfying. Hindu literature dealing with such rituals is enormous, but predominantly it wants to be practical advice, not theory or 'philosophy'. Apart from the Tantras, there are other categories of texts which deal with the rituals performed in the temples of various monotheistic groups. Academic interest in these is relatively recent. Goudriaan and Colas have worked on Vaikhanasa material, and Daniel Smith on the Pancaratra.

Regional Variations

The scope of the present essay does not allow for a survey of the anthropological work carried out in India. But it may be permitted to make some general comments here. From the point of view of the student of 'Hinduism', much of the relevant material has no more than incidental relevance. I believe this to be due to the traditional definition of British 'social anthropology' (with its emphasis on social relations, its pursuit of the nebulous 'caste system', its refusal to take textual and historical material into account, and its concentration on the isolated village context). This is not a comment on the value of the enterprise on its own right. But it means that other kinds of anthropological and ethnological studies from outside Britain yield more immediately and centrally relevant insights into the complexities of 'Hinduism'. On the whole ignored by classical indology and only accidentally picked up by social anthropology are a host of regional religious cultures. 'Region' may denote here areas as large as some European countries, yet much smaller than the whole Indian sub-continent. Out of the interaction between 'mainstream' (or normative) Hinduism and folk-religion, interesting and often highly complex forms of religion evolved which deserve study in their own right, as yet further expressions of what is contained in actual 'Hinduism'. For Maharashtra (and neighbouring Karnataka) work has been done by Tulpule, Sontheimer, Dhere and others on such cults as those of Khandoba, Yellamma, Gaja-Lakshmi, Biroba, Mhaskoba, etc. For regional cults in Gujarat and neighbouring areas we have the work by Westphal-Hellbusch, E. Fischer, J. Jain, H. Shah, etc. Dimock, Smith, and others have produced interesting material on Bengali cults such as those of Manasa, Candi, etc. For Tamil Nadu, various works deal with the religions associated with Mariyamman (by Nishimura), Ankalamman (by Meyer), Aiyanar (by Reiniche), Kattavarayan (by Shulman), Pattini (by Obeysekere), and the names of Brubaker and Hiltebeitel ought to be mentioned in this context. John Smith has worked on the cult of Papuji in Rajasthan. This is clearly an area of very lively current scholarship which is bound to throw much new light on the relationship between the prescriptive 'classical' Hinduism of brahmin, Sanskrit religion and the 'Hinduism' of the majority of the populace.

Among these regional religions, we notice some that developed a distinct social position, partly by consciously rejecting certain ideological features of the mainstream. The Lingayites of Karnataka have been mentioned previously. Tulpule and Feldhaus have done interesting work on the religious movement of the Manbhavs in the neighbouring Maharashtra.

The 'Modern' Period

It is perfectly possible to travel to India today and observe Hindu religious life of a kind that allows for a relatively uncomplicated extrapolation of what it was like hundreds of years ago. It is equally well possible to observe other forms of Hinduism which, due to the century-long presence of Islam, have developed much further away from the nominal 'classical' archetype. Similarly, there are expressions of Hinduism which take into account a variety of Western features. It has been customary to present a series of important names of thinkers under the heading of 'neo-Hinduism' or 'modern Hinduism' (Ram Mohan Roy, Dayanand Sarasvati, Rabindranath Tagore, Ramakrishna, Vivekananda, Aurobindo Ghose, Radhakrishnan and – most important of all – Mohandas Karamchand Gandhi, the Mahatma). An enormous amount of literature has been, and is still being, produced that explores their thought and their relevance. Thus it may seem pedantic to point out that comparable figures (like Narayana Guru of nineteenth century Kerala) who did not write in English have so far received hardly any attention, that 'modern' may cover up an ideological bias, and that sometimes a feature presented as typically 'Hindu' may have no parallels at all in other forms of Hinduism (or reveal themselves for instance as typically Jaina). Yet such pedantry is meant to highlight as much the historical dimensions as the potential for original creativity in 'Hinduism', while at the same time to point at the need to remain aware of the wider, and vastly more variegated, context in which such thought has occurred.

Moreover, what may appear as a merely academic concern (to understand 'Hinduism') actually has its practical relevance. Forms of 'Hinduism' are now part of British life and are labelled as such. An extremely lively branch of investigation has begun that concerns itself with this subject (particularly at Leeds and London). A vast amount of factual information is piling up about such varied groups as the Swami Narayanas, Hare Krishnas, Bhagawan Rajneesh, schools of Yoga, Transcendental Meditation, Vedanta, Sahaja Yoga, etc. Moreover, within the British context it is possible to say what it is to belong to the Swami Narayanas (possibly the largest group of Hindus in Britain) who constitute a well-defined religious movement and whose links with traditional Indian thought are relatively fixed. Thus again it would seem to be a 'merely' academic concern to try and define the position of this and of other movements within the overall umbrella term of 'Hinduism' or to ascertain to what extent the usage of Sanskrit terminology (particularly in some of the new religious movements) points at an integral link with traditional Hindu thought. Yet it is not just the university or college student who will ask what that 'Hinduness' is that the Hare Krishnas of TM are supposed to have in common with the Swami Narayanas. There are also the British-born children of Hindu immigrants who ask what it means to be a 'Hindu'. That will be a further, very major turning point in the study of Hinduism when a sensible answer to that question can be given. It is clear in light of what has been said previously that the answer cannot simply be a catalogue of all the things that happen to be called 'Hindu' in Britain, nor an arbitrary selection of them, or for that matter, of bits and pieces taken from India, nor of what one's grand-mother happens to remember of her youth in Gujarat or Kerala or Bengal or the Punjab, nor a neat, coherent system. Finally, the concept of 'Hindu' is bound to play an important role in all kinds of social, political and legal matters. The task is to work out what sense it could actually be given in such a context.

SUGGESTED READING

J. L. Brockington, *The Sacred Thread. Hinduism in its Continuity and Diversity*, Edinburgh: Edinburgh University, 1981.

R. Burghart, ed., *Hinduism in Great Britain. The Perpetuation of Religion in an Alien Cultural Milieu*, London & New York: Tavistock Publications Ltd., 1987.

F. Hardy, 'The Classical Religions of India' in S. Sutherland et al., eds, *The World's Religions*, London: Routledge, 1988, pp. 569–626; pp. 637–59.

K. Knott, *My Sweet Lord. The Hare Krishna Movement*, Wellingborough: Aquarian Press, 1986.

R. B. Williams, *A New Face of Hinduism. The Swaminarayan Religion*. Cambridge: Cambridge University Press, 1984.

R. C. Zaehner, *Hinduism*, London: Oxford University Press, 1966.

8. BUDDHISM

Paul Williams

I am not always sure whether the texts and events that I treat mark turning points or not. Time will tell, thirty years is too short a span – at least for one who lacks the omniscient and perfectly objective mind of a Buddha. And yet, from my own perspective the following are at least for me, given the limitations of space, some significant events in Buddhist Studies during the past three decades.

Lamotte's Histoire du Bouddhisme Indien

These decades have seen an unprecedented interest and growth in Buddhist Studies, and yet two events in particular mark our beginning – two events which are very different in nature but both contributing to the flavour of what was to follow. First, in 1958 Etienne Lamotte published his magisterial *Histoire du Bouddhisme Indien: des origines à l'ère Saka* (Louvain; English translation by Sara Boin-Webb, Louvain la Neuve, 1988). Lamotte, who died in 1983, was one of the greatest scholars of Buddhism whose translations of Buddhist texts, enriched with densely packed footnotes which amount to a series of mini-essays, have changed the face of Buddhist scholarship and also made available for those who do not read Sanskrit, Pali, Tibetan and Chinese accurate French versions (some of which are now being translated into English) of a number of the most important Buddhist sources. His *Histoire du Bouddhisme Indien*, over 850 pages long, is a complete survey of the historical, literary, archaeological, legendary and sociological developments of Buddhism during the crucial period from the time of the Buddha to about the first century CE. It is an encyclopaedia – almost everything is there; it is impossible to imagine what the study of early Buddhism in the last thirty years would have been like without this work, even where further discoveries, subsequent study, and later scholars have started to question some of Etienne Lamotte's perspectives and conclusions. Recent plans at Lamotte's old university of Louvain for adding further volumes in order to cover all-important later developments in Buddhism involve an international team of scholars as contributors. In terms of scholarship and influence Etienne Lamotte was larger than life; he can be replaced only by a committee!

The 1959 Tibetan uprising, and its significance for Buddhist Studies

The second event which marks the beginning of our period, but
very different from the cloistered scholarly work of Etienne Lamotte,
was the Tibetan uprising of 1959 against Chinese occupation, and the
flight of His Holiness the Dalai Lama to India together with many of
his fellow Tibetans. The destruction of Tibetan sacred places, the
razing of monasteries which were previously small cities, is now
well-known. What survives of the great Tibetan libraries is however
largely unknown. It seems that Tibetan books were used by the PLA
for toilet paper. There are also tantalising rumours of large numbers
of texts taken to Beijing and saved from the holocaust. Sanskrit texts
considered lost by scholars since the Islamic destruction of Indian
Buddhist centres of learning have in the past been discovered in
Tibetan monasteries. Who knows what now survives – or what may
have survived until the Cultural Revolution.

The destruction of Tibetan monasteries and texts, while a global
tragedy, would not in itself make the Tibetan exodus in 1959 a
turning point in Buddhist Studies. But for scholars there has been a
positive dimension to the Tibetan events. Many of the leading Tibetan
religious figures – scholars and holy men – did escape from Tibet and
followed His Holiness the Dalai Lama into exile. Often they brought
with them their precious texts. Since 1959 the four orders of Tibetan
Buddhism have been re-established in India, monasteries have been
built, the monastic education system has been restored, on the death
of lamas their reincarnations have been sought and found both among
the refugees and also among western followers of the Tibetan form
of Buddhism. Occidentals have indeed been rather attracted to
Tibetan Buddhism. Centres have blossomed in the West, and Tibetan
hierarchs, most notably the Dalai Lama, have visited the West to
teach and offer initiations. Westerners have become monks and nuns.
For the scholar it is now possible to consult with Tibetan teachers in
the USA, in the UK, France, Germany, Italy, not to mention India
and Nepal. It is no longer necessary to trek over the Himalayas, as
did scholars of a previous generation. It is much easier to visit
Dharamsala, the seat of His Holiness the Dalai Lama and his
government in exile, even if Indian trains can be uncomfortable and
buses lethal, than it was to reach Lhasa. Particularly important also
has been work among Tibetan refugees in publishing Tibetan texts.
These texts are now freely available from India in both traditional
Tibetan block-printed format and western-style books. Sometimes

texts have been printed in the West, and an American government-funded project for creating microfiches of Tibetan works published in India means that vast numbers of Tibetan texts are now available in fiche format as well. A number of editions of the canon can be found, reprinted in India, Japan, USA and on microfiche. The Tibetan canon includes translations of many, many texts from all phases of Buddhism which do not survive in Sanskrit. Centuries of Tibetan scholastic exegesis clarified, elaborated and refined Indian Buddhist perspectives and dogma. The increased availability of this material since the tragic events of 1959 has been of immeasurable importance, and the past thirty years in Buddhist Studies have been marked in particular, I think, by a growing knowledge (although still very, very incomplete) in the area of Tibetan Studies, and an increasing use of the vast Tibetan literature. The sad thing is that still so much seems to have been lost.

A Fresh Look at the Date of the Buddha

If we turn now to significant contributions to the study of early Buddhist history during the past three decades, there have been some notable advances. It may come as something of a surprise to non-specialists to realise just how uncertain scholars are about events in Buddhist history. Books often write as though the first date we can be reasonably sure about in Indian civilisation is the death of the Buddha in 486 or 483 BCE. Nothing could be further from the truth. The train of reasoning which leads to these dates is extremely suspect, and the German scholar Heinz Bechert has reopened the whole issue, re-examining the evidence and pointing out problems involved in this 'traditional' dating ('The date of the Buddha reconsidered', *Indologica Taurinensia* X:29–36, 1982). The upshot is that Bechert favours placing the death of the Buddha some hundred years or so later than is usually the case in western writings on Buddhism. This would have rather radical repercussions on our assessment of the nature of early Buddhism. For example it would considerably shorten the distance in time between the Buddha and the great Buddhist emperor Ashoka (d. *c.* 232 BCE) and increase the relevance of the relatively abundant Ashokan and post-Ashokan material for our understanding of early Buddhism. Bechert's re-examination and dating are taken very seriously by scholars. Richard Gombrich has commented that 'I think no one can seriously continue to claim that the Buddha was born as early as the sixth century BC' (1986: 15).

The First 'Schism'

It is still commonly stated in books on the history of Buddhism that the first 'schism' occurred when some lax monks who were infringing the monastic rule broke away from the orthodox body and formed their own sect. Called the Mahasamghikas, this sect eventually gave rise to the Mahayana. Such is to follow a traditional account from the Theravada, which sees itself as the orthodox body in the dispute. This is, however, no longer tenable. We know from examination of Mahasamghika texts preserved in Chinese translation that they also were aware of this dispute, but failed to identify themselves with the lax monks. Rather, the Mahasamghikas' view of their own history is that they were *opposed* to the schismatics, the lax monks, at the relevant council. Moreover, examination of the Mahasamghika monastic code shows that it was by no means lax, and in its totality the Mahasamghika code may have greater claims to antiquity than that of the Theravada. Heinz Bechert has again examined what exactly is meant in this context by the crucial term *samghabheda* – splitting of the Samgha, the Community, usually translated as 'schism'. He has shown that 'schism' in Buddhism is not a matter of doctrine, (and nothing to do with the laity), but is rather a matter of monastic rule. Thus it is clear now that in Buddhism there is no schism if monks happen to hold different doctrinal views. We are dealing here with an orthopraxy, not an orthodoxy. One repercussion of this is that Mahayana, which is a perspective on the spiritual path, and therefore in Buddhist terms in the broadest sense a doctrinal matter, was not in any way the result of *schism*, and cannot be identified with any particular Buddhist sect, that is, a group holding its own monastic code. There is no Mahayana monastic code in the way that, say, the Theravada or the Mahasamghikas have their own codes, and it is simply a category mistake to see Mahayana as emerging out of the Mahasamghikas. We know now that monks from a number of different sects adopted the Mahayana perspective. Outwardly, visibly, they do not appear to have differed very much from their non-Mahayana brethren who would often have inhabited the same monasteries.

Access to Very Early Buddhist History

In the course of three detailed volumes André Bareau has examined our sources for the life of the Buddha – best known in the Theravadin versions of the Pali Canon – preserved in Pali, Sanskrit, Tibetan and crucially Chinese translation. He has shown the growth of the legend of the Buddha, and stages in its development. In terms of gauging what can be known with reasonable certainty about the life of the 'historical' Buddha, however, Bareau's conclusions are very sceptical. This scepticism has characterised the attitude of many scholars during the last twenty-five years to the life of the Buddha, the Theravada tradition, and even sometimes the basic teachings of the Buddha. It is quite clear that there are no longer any grounds for speaking of the Theravada tradition as though it were simply and unproblematically the original Buddhism. Nevertheless now, I think, there is a tendency for some scholars to redress the balance, to argue that even if comparative textual examination leaves problems of detail and very little known *for certain*, still the monastic tradition including that of the Theravada can be shown in general to have been remarkably good at preservation of material (communal chanting is a more effective medium for accurate transmission than the written word), and anyway we have no grounds for thinking that later followers may have got the message of the Buddha radically wrong.

Having said that, however, an important methodological point concerning the study of early Buddhist history has recently been made by the American scholar Gregory Schopen. There is a frequently employed principle that where a number of versions of an event, teaching and so on found in different early Buddhist traditions agree, we can see this as evidence for a position which was held in common *before* the subsequent split between schools. Thus we can move beyond the existing canonical versions to a primitive 'pre-schismatic' position. Schopen has suggested that in reality the exact reverse is the case. There is evidence that as time passed texts were harmonised and brought into line. Schopen's argument must indicate even greater caution, greater scepticism, as regards our assumption with any precision of the details of very early Buddhism (1985).

Theravada Buddhism and Society

In the area of Theravada Buddhist Studies noteworthy work has been done in the past thirty years or so by those with an anthropological training who have examined the interaction between Theravada Buddhism and society in Theravada countries. Particularly striking in Richard Gombrich's readable and entertaining book *Precept and Practice* (Oxford, 1971) is the way in which he demonstrates quite clearly the untenability of a common dualism in the study of Theravada Buddhism. The dualism I mean is that between 'popular' and 'orthodox' Buddhism, often identified with another dualism, that of lay versus monk, and a further dualism, of seekers after merit for a favourable rebirth versus seekers after enlightenment. Thus the 'orthodox' Buddhist becomes the monk who alone seeks after enlightenment. 'Popular' Buddhism is found among the laity, whose concern is not with enlightenment but merit. Gombrich has shown that this will not do. It is impossible in practice to separate out these dualisms in traditional Theravada Buddhism. A monk will seek for merit and will take part in 'popular' practices. A layman may have greater knowledge of the scriptures and doctrines, perhaps meditation, than the local monk. All the evidence is that this has always been the case in Theravada Buddhism, as far back as we can go in history. There *is* a dualism in Theravada, Gombrich argues, but it is a dualism not of orthodox/monk/enlightenment versus popular/laity/merit, but rather precept versus practice, the mediation through human nature and ordinary day to day practicalities of the message of Buddhist tenets into social and political life. This dualism, moreover, cuts across the monk/lay divide as social groups. We are now beginning to realise, I think, that the dichotomy of popular from orthodox is always far too simplistic, an excuse for explanation which it would be better to abandon completely.

The Origins of the Mahayana

In an influential paper published in 1963 the Japanese scholar Akira Hirakawa argued that the origins of the Mahayana lay in an identifiable order of *bodhisattvas*, those who had taken a vow to the full enlightenment of the Buddha, composed of lay and monastic members of equal status, and centred on the *stupas*, relic mounds, and *stupa* worship. Institutionally these *stupas* were administered by the laity, and in certain rivalry with the monastic orders. Thus Mahayana originated in a reaction against monastic exclusivity, notably the decidedly inferior status given by monastic Buddhism to the laity. That the Mahayana arose under lay influence and initiative is a widely-held view particularly among modern Japanese scholars, and was also held by Etienne Lamotte. However, this hypothesis is beginning to look decidedly unlikely. Gregory Schopen has studied evidence for Mahayana found in Indian inscriptions, which serves to provide data for what was going on 'on the ground' outside that supplied by scriptural and doctrinal treatises. Schopen has suggested that if we look at Mahayana donor inscriptions, including those to *stupas*, by far the majority are connected with members of the monastic community, not excluding doctrinal specialists, and the proportion increased with the passage of time. He considers it clear that 'the cult of images was overwhelmingly a monastic concern . . . [and] . . . it was also – on the basis of the available information – a monastically initiated cult' (1985: 27). There was simply no radical separation of monastic from *stupa* Buddhism. The laity played relatively little significant role in the development of *stupa* cult or Mahayana. Schopen has also pointed out that the earliest use of the term 'Mahayana' in inscriptions is not until the sixth century CE, although terms with unique Mahayana reference can be found from the fourth century CE. This is some four or five hundred years later than a frequent estimation for the earliest Mahayana scriptures, and suggests that Mahayana had no separate social self-identity until well into the Common Era ('Mahayana in Indian inscriptions', *Indo-Iranian Journal* 21: 1–19, 1979). Moreover, Schopen has argued elsewhere that Mahayana *may* have originated in a series of separate 'text cults', centered on the following and worship of particular *sutras* felt to have special connection with the (or 'a') Buddha, perhaps even identified with his 'true body', his Dharma-body (*kaya*) and contrasted with the *stupa* cults (1975).

The Mahayana Sutras

One fascinating picture of the origins of these *sutras* is suggested by Paul Harrison's work on a *sutra* best known by the short title of *Pratyutpanna Sutra* ('Buddhanusmrti in the Pratyutpanna-buddha-sammukhavasthita-samadhi-sutra', *Journal of Indian Philosophy* 9: 35–57, 1978. Harrison has also translated the *sutra* in an unpublished doctoral thesis: Australian National University, 1979). This *sutra* was translated into Chinese in the late second century CE, which in terms of reliable dating makes it one of the earliest Mahayana *sutras*. In particular the *sutra* describes a meditation practice on Buddha Amitayus whereby the meditator can actually see Amitayus not with the spiritual but with the bodily eye. Amitayus gives him (or her) new teachings which the meditator then transmits to the world. In this astonishing *sutra* new teachings are said to spring from meditative vision, a continual revelation through meeting a living Buddha in ecstatic experience. These transmitted teachings perhaps formed the centre of Schopen's book-cults – cults monastically initiated, primarily a monastic concern, occurring well within existing 'non-Mahayana' monastic organisation, probably a minority interest quite possibly seen by others in the monastery as eccentric or rather crazy, the results of strange meditative experiences. Such at least is one picture that is beginning to emerge of the origins of the Mahayana.

Before leaving the Mahayana *sutras* we should note in passing the important work done in the last thirty years in translating these scriptures. Mention should be made in particular of Edward Conze's research on and translation of the *Prajnaparamita Sutras*, most of which was completed during this period. Perhaps the most valuable Mahayana *sutra* translation activity in recent years however has been Thomas Cleary's monumental translation in three large volumes of an entire Chinese text of the *Avatamsaka Sutra* (*The Flower Ornament Scripture*, Boulder, Colo. 1984–87). The *Avatamsaka Sutra* was the inspiration in East Asian Buddhism for the school of Hua-yen, particularly well-known for its systematic development of the *sutra's* key teaching of infinite interpenetration. In the past scholars have severely neglected this school of Buddhism, an important influence on Zen and the East Asian Buddhist perspective. This situation has now completely changed, and Hua-yen is becoming quite fashionable. Much of the credit for the present popularity of Hua-yen studies must go to Thomas Cleary himself, and also to the interesting if controversial work of Francis Cook. (See T. Cleary, *Entry into the Inconceivable*, Honolulu, 1983; and F. H. Cook, *Hua-yen Buddhism: The Jewel Net of Indra*, Pennsylvania, 1977).

Buddhism in China and Japan

Still within the field of East Asian Buddhism, the past three decades have seen the publication of works which are now standard texts for anyone researching in this area. Holmes Welch's series of books on twentieth century Chinese Buddhism, based on extensive textual study and also his own experiences and interviews in China, give a picture of a world now gone, the tragedy, triumph and disaster of Chinese Buddhism in our century. Erich Zürcher concentrates on the other end of Chinese Buddhist history, the difficult if fascinating field of the transmission of Buddhism to China, the reception, internalisation and domestication of an alien, indeed a barbarian, creed (*The Buddhist Conquest of China*, Leiden, 1972. Two volumes. First published in 1959). More recently Zürcher's work has been supplemented by a translation into English of the monumental two-volume study *A History of Early Chinese Buddhism* by the Japanese scholar Zenryu Tsukamoto (Tokyo, 1985. Two volumes. Transl. L. Hurvitz). Apart from these large-scale works so much research is now taking place in all areas of Buddhist Studies that our received views and ideas are constantly being questioned and revised. To take just one example we can refer to John McRae's work on the early history of Chinese Ch'an (Zen), showing how the traditional story of the sixth Ch'an patriarch Hui-neng defeating his rival for the patriarchate Shen-hsiu through a verse-writing competition on the monastery walls is pure sectarian propaganda rather than historical fact (*The Northern School and the Formation of Early Ch'an Buddhism*, Honolulu, 1986). Also worth mentioning is Alfred Bloom's short, but sympathetic account of Shinran's Jodo Shin Shu, so often portrayed in the past as almost a non-Buddhist form of theism. Bloom shows clearly the rationale for Shinran's system, its continuity with previous Buddhist history and key Buddhist principles, as well as the way in which it responded to the particular spiritual problems of Shinran's day (*Shinran's Gospel of Pure Grace*, Tucson, 1968). Among topics, we should perhaps note a growing interest in the subject of women in Buddhism, to which contributions by Diana Paul are particularly well-known. So much is happening in Buddhist Studies; as the Zen Master might say, 'Who can speak of it all?'

Buddhist Philosophy – Madhyamaka, and the Tathagatagarbha

In Indian Buddhist doctrinal history many of the significant contributions during the last thirty years or so concern a growing detailed exploration of Madhyamaka Buddhism on the one hand, and a realisation of the importance of the teachings and traditions centred on the *tathagatagarbha*, the Buddha Nature – that within each sentient being which enables him or her to become a fully enlightened Buddha – on the other. In both fields the name of David Seyfort Ruegg is particularly important. As we have seen, one of the hallmarks of Indian Buddhist scholarship during the past twenty-five to thirty years has been the significance of the Tibetan language and a study of the vast resources of Indian Buddhist material which survive in Tibetan translation. Previous writers on Madhyamaka thought all too often tried to understand Madhyamaka with reference to only the few works which remain in Sanskrit. Ruegg's survey of Indian Madhyamaka literature, using all the sources available, is therefore particularly important, both for his own philosophically sensitive treatment of the doctrines and also for his discussion of texts and dates, and summaries of a whole range of Indian Madhyamaka texts (*The Literature of the Madhyamaka School of Philosophy in India*, Wiesbaden, 1981). His book, although quite short, is indispensable to the study of Madhyamaka, as is Chr. Lindtner's *Nagarjuniana*, which attempts to establish which works can be attributed authentically to Nagarjuna, and offers editions, translations (from Sanskrit, Tibetan and Chinese), and textual comments on all the 'authentic' texts as well as an introduction to Nagarjuna's ideas which stresses their continuity with pre- and non-Mahayana thought as well as the wider Mahayana religious context (Copenhagen, 1982).

Ruegg's *magnum opus* (to date) is his *La Théorie du Tathagatagarbha et du Gotra* (Paris, 1969), a work which shows characteristically detailed textual scholarship of the highest order, and some subtlety in assessing those statements found in texts associated with the Buddha Nature which would portray it as a 'Self', a permanent immutable element within each sentient being (or even all things). Such statements are obviously problematic within Buddhism. What Ruegg's book does, among other things, is indicate the importance of this tradition to a study of Buddhist doctrinal history, and the complexity and problematic nature of its interpretation. It is highly inappropriate to assume here that we have a clear-cut case of Buddhism abandoning its central teaching of no-Self, perhaps in the face of some assumed 'Hindu' pressure or influence. Ruegg's book should be read alongside the study and translation by Takasaki of the principal Indian text for the *tathagatagarbha* doctrine, the *Ratnagotravibhaga* (Rome, 1966).

Another particularly significant event in Indian Buddhist doctrinal history during the past few years has been the opening-out to scholarship of a neglected area of Madhyamaka studies – Svatantrika Madhyamaka. Because so little Svatantrika material survives in Sanskrit, previous studies based on Sanskrit material alone have failed to appreciate the importance of the subschool of Svatantrika Madhyamaka, founded in the sixth century CE by Bhavaviveka apparently with a particular interest in applying to Madhyamaka the insights of Buddhist logic and epistemology. Svatantrika Madhyamaka may well have been the most important form of Madhyamaka in India until perhaps the tenth century. A number of young scholars, particularly in the USA and Japan, have been researching not only Svatantrika texts preserved in Tibetan and Chinese, but also indigenous Tibetan discussions of Svatantrika, and the controversies between Svatantrika Madhyamaka and its rivals.

The Study of Tibetan Philosophy – and the Vitality of Buddhist Studies

In the area of Tibetan thought, particularly Madhyamaka, the greatest contributions have been made by Jeffrey Hopkins and his students. A Buddhist, and sometime interpreter for His Holiness the Dalai Lama, Hopkins largely works to transmit accurate accounts of Tibetan positions and disputes using texts and also relying on consultations with modern Tibetan teachers. He is very careful to give exact sources, oral and literary, for all his material, and his own critical comments are slight. Jeffrey Hopkins has written and translated a very large number of books, concerned in particular to expound in detail the Madhyamaka teachings of the dGe lugs (pronounced: Geluk) school of Tibetan Buddhism – the so-called 'Yellow Hats' associated with the Dalai Lama. Hopkins' most significant work has been his very large *Meditation on Emptiness* (London, 1983), a comprehensive survey of the philosophical world-view of dGe lugs thought which shows how a number of assumptions and assertions on Madhyamaka made by Western scholars (that it has no views, is anti-rational or anti-language, for example) are contradicted by the centuries of scholastic refinement which occurred in Tibet. Nevertheless in Tibet there was no homogeneity of interpretation. It is to be hoped that in the future more work will be done on other, non-dGe lugs, Tibetan interpretations of Madhyamaka. Hopkins has established a centre for the study of dGe lugs thought at the University of Virginia, and his students have taken the Hopkins approach into other areas of mainly dGe lugs exegesis, for example a study of the tradition of Buddhist epistemology associated with the name of Dharmakirti, and Vajrayana or Buddhist Tantricism.

Among other institutional 'turning points' might be mentioned the programme in Buddhist Studies at the University of Wisconsin, initiated by a Canadian, Richard Robinson, a scholar of great promise who died tragically young. He, and the Wisconsin programme, have produced and inspired a number of young scholars who are now in the forefront of Buddhist research. We have also seen during these years the founding of the International Association of Buddhist Studies, which serves as a global forum through its conferences and journal, and the establishment of numerous publishing companies associated with Buddhism, often initiated and staffed by western Buddhists (Snow Lion, Wisdom, Shambhala etc.). All these indicate the vitality of Buddhist Studies both as a critical, questioning academic activity and a lived tradition thought to have relevance to the spiritual and intellectual problems of the contemporary world. Long may both perspectives continue – and may they never drift too far apart!

SUGGESTED READING

For further details on many of the works and doctrines referred to here, see Paul Williams, *Mahayana Buddhism: The doctrinal foundations*, London: Routledge, 1989.

A. Bareau, *Recherches sur la Biographie du Buddha dans les Sutrapitaka et les Vinayapitaka Anciens*, Paris: École Française d'Extrême-Orient. Three volumes, 1963, 1970, 1971.

H. Bechert, 'The importance of Asoka's so-called schism edict' in Hercus, L.A. *et al.* (1982) *Indological and Buddhist Studies*, Canberra: Australian National University, Faculty of Asian Studies, 1982, pp. 61–8.

R. Gombrich, 'The history of Early Buddhism: Major advances since 1950', *Indological Studies and South Asia Bibliography: A Conference*: pp. 12–30. Published in India, no further details available, 1986.

A. Hirakawa, 'The rise of Mahayana Buddhism and its relationship to the worship of stupas', *Memoirs of the Research Department of the Toyo Bunko*, Tokyo: Toyo Bunko, 1963, pp. 57–106.

G. Schopen, 'The phrase "sa prthivipradesas caityabhuto bhavet" in the Vajracchedika: notes on the cult of the book in Mahayana', *Indo-Iranian Journal* 17, 1975, pp. 147–81.

——, 'Two problems in the history of Indian Buddhism: the layman/monk distinction and the doctrines of the transference of merit', *Studien zur Indologie und Iranistik*, 10, 1985, pp. 9–47.

9. SIKHISM

Eleanor Nesbitt

Introduction

The word Sikh means a learner or disciple, more particularly a follower of Guru Nanak (1469–1539 CE) and of the nine Gurus or spiritual teachers who succeeded him. Except for a few western converts, Sikhs are Punjabi by language and culture, regarding the present Indian state of Punjab as their homeland. According to an English translation of the Sikhs' Code of Discipline, the *Rahit Maryada*, authorised by their supreme elected body: 'A Sikh is any person who believes in one God (*Akal Purakh*), the ten Gurus, the Guru Granth Sahib and other writings of the ten Gurus and their teachings and who believes in the tenth Guru's amrit and does not believe in any other religion.'

Amrit refers to the ceremony of initiation into the *Khalsa* (the body of 'pure', committed Sikhs). Sikhism is the name originally conferred by westerners on the Sikhs' religion for which in Punjabi the word *Gurmat* (the religious principles of the Guru) is used.

Sikh Studies have not yet achieved recognition as a distinct subject in Britain's universities. Opinions vary on what exactly the term should cover. Nonetheless there is a fair degree of consensus, and it is possible to indicate what is generally meant by the term.

Sikh Studies covers the study of the origins of the Sikh faith and community (*panth*), the lives and message of the ten Gurus including their religious and political background, and the study of the text of the Guru Granth Sahib (scriptures) and other respected writings. These include the compositions of Bhai Gurdas and Bhai Nand Lal 'Goya' (both contemporaries of the Gurus) and the Dasm Granth which was composed by Guru Gobind Singh, the tenth Guru, with contributions, some scholars would argue, by contemporary poets. Sikh historical literature also includes the *janamsakhi*s (hagiographic accounts of Guru Nanak's life) and *rahitnama*s (codes of discipline of which the earliest date from the eighteenth century). Also subsumed under the heading of Sikh Studies is the history of the evolution of the *panth* during the eighteenth and nineteenth centuries including the reign of Maharaja Ranjit Singh and the annexation of Punjab by the British. The developments of the twentieth century with the growth of a diaspora population of over a million Sikhs resident outside India constitute a significant area of contemporary Sikh Studies.

Sikh Studies draw upon and enrich a number of academic disciplines – notably history, language, literature, philosophy, theology and ethics, art, architecture and music, anthropology, sociology and political science. Most recently women's studies have been added to the list.

I shall examine Sikh Studies in Britain since 1960 with reference to materials published for use with school children as well as works of scholarship intended for advanced study. Sikh Studies in the United Kingdom are also viewed in the global context of Sikh Studies overseas, principally in North India and North America.

This survey is prefaced by a swift overview of the scholarly study of Sikhs and Sikhism prior to 1960. This is because the growth of Sikh Studies since 1960 exhibits several characteristics which have their origins in the previous century or for which instructive parallels can be found during this earlier period. In particular the responsiveness of Sikh Studies to the political vicissitudes of the Punjab and the use of English as a major language for Sikh Studies are evident from the middle of the nineteenth century.

The Beginnings

Europeans began writing about the Sikhs at the end of the eighteenth century. In 1777 A. L. H. Polier published *The Siques* and 1798 saw the publication of George Forster's *Journey from Bengal to England* in which he described the Sikhs' religion. In 1812 John Malcolm published his *Sketch of the Sikhs*, and in 1849 appeared J. D. Cunningham's *History of the Sikhs* which brought him into official disfavour with his British masters.[1]

Clearly in Britain scholarly and more general public interest in the Sikhs was inseparable from Britain's imperial expansion and the annexation of Punjab in 1849. During the latter half of the nineteenth century and the first half of the twentieth century extremely detailed accounts of the traditions and practices of the many constituent parts of Sikh society were produced by such able and dedicated British administrators as Ibbetson, Rose, McLagan and Darling. The writings of some British historians show how they wished Sikhs to interpret their history.[2]

Sikh writing, hitherto purely devotional, was also reactive to the circumstances of imperial rule. Largely as a result of British involvement in Punjab, and particularly in response to missionary-run education, actively reformist Hindu, Muslim and Sikh movements came into being, among them the Singh Sabha which aimed to regenerate Sikh teaching and practices. The Singh Sabha strove to eradicate brahmanical influence on Sikhism and promoted a new, powerful sense of a Sikh identity, distinct from Hinduism, which still prevails. During the first decades of the twentieth century scriptural commentaries were compiled in Punjabi, two of the most significant resulting from the labours of the distinguished Sikh writers, Principal Teja Singh and Bhai Vir Singh. Another notable work of reference was Kahn Singh Nabha's *Mahan Kosh* (1930, repr. 1974, Patiala, Punjab), an encyclopaedic compilation of Sikh history. His earlier essay 'Ham Hindu Nahin' ('We are not Hindu') was a significant contribution to the definition of Sikhs and Sikhism.

Working in consultation with Kahn Singh Nabha and other Singh Sabha intellectuals, the British civil servant M. A. Macauliffe produced in 1909 *The Sikh Religion* (repr. 1963, New Delhi), an English narrative rendering of the Sikh scriptures, arranged chronologically in the context of the Gurus' lives. This still commands the respect of Sikhs, and it helped to compensate Sikhs for the injury caused by a German missionary's unkind translation of part of the scriptures. Writing in his preface Macauliffe emphasised his commitment to writing only what was acceptable to learned Sikhs.

Now, almost a century later, the mutual trust and respect of insiders and outsiders, so strongly emphasised by Macauliffe, remains crucial to the advancement of Sikh Studies. Confessional and critical stances need to be delicately balanced. Of recent years some of the best contributions to Sikh Studies have been the fruit of partnership and friendship between Sikh and non-Sikh.

The study of Sikhism continues to be conducted almost exclusively in the English-speaking world even in this post-imperial age. Despite the establishment of Sikhism in many countries it is political change in the Indian state of Punjab, where most Sikhs live, which continues to be inseparable and uniquely linked with Sikh Studies, both as content for study of the contemporary scene and by keeping Sikhs and Sikhism firmly in the public domain.

Sikh Studies 1960–1990: North India

After India gained independence in 1947, scholarly writing on Sikh
subjects continued in Punjab, the major figures being Dr Bhai Jodh
Singh and Dr Ganda Singh at Khalsa College, Amritsar, the college
founded in 1892 by the Singh Sabha. When, in 1962, Punjabi
University was set up in Patiala, Dr Bhai Jodh Singh was appointed
as Vice-Chancellor and he chose Dr Ganda Singh as Head of the
Department of Punjab Historical Studies. In the next few years Sikh
Studies took off as never before. Speaking in Berkeley, California, in
1982 about Sikhism, Professor Harbans Singh of Punjabi University,
Patiala, described the years 1965–69 as 'the creative half-decade'.
During these years, after a sustained political struggle by Sikhs, the
present boundaries of the Indian state of Punjab were fixed. Punjab,
as demarcated in 1966, is a state in which for the first time the official
language is Punjabi. What is more, it is Punjabi written in the
Gurmukhi script, the alphabet hallowed by its use for the Sikh
scriptures. For the first time in their history Sikhs constituted the
majority in an Indian state. At the same time the Green Revolution
was transforming the agriculture of Punjab, bringing unprecedented
prosperity to its farmers, most of whom are Sikh. Moreover, in 1967
and 1969 significant anniversaries of Sikh history were celebrated on
an unprecedented scale. In 1967 Sikhs commemorated the
tercentenary of the birth of Guru Gobind Singh, their tenth Guru,
and in 1969 the quincentenary of the birth of Guru Nanak, the Sikhs'
first Guru, was celebrated.

Not surprisingly these years of political affirmation, economic
growth and proud historical retrospect were ones of new expansion
and self-confidence for Sikh Studies in Punjab. A spate of publications
on Sikhism appeared, especially on the Gurus whose anniversaries
were honoured, and institutions of higher education dedicated to
Sikh Studies were established. The Guru Gobind Singh Department
of Religious Studies in Punjabi University began functioning in 1967.
The inspired architectural design of the Guru Gobind Singh Bhavan
in which it is housed underscores the department's emphasis on interfaith studies. Gurmat College was established, also in Patiala, where
students for a Master's degree could study Sikh religious texts, history
and philosophy. In Amritsar, in 1969, the Guru Nanak Dev
University was inaugurated. Under the auspices of the University
Grants Commission chairs for research on Guru Nanak and on Sikh
tradition more generally were established in Chandigarh, Amritsar,

Banaras, Calcutta and Madras. In 1974 the Guru Nanak Professor of
Sikh Studies at Chandigarh, Dr Harnam Singh Shan, illuminated the
current state of Sikh Studies.[3]

Although Sikh Studies are underway in Indian universities far from
Punjab, it is this state, the homeland of the Sikhs, which has naturally
continued to be the hub of Sikh Studies. In addition to individual
research and publications useful reference books have been produced
and excellent journals flourish. The largest reference project is the
several thousand entry *Encyclopaedia of Sikhism* (Patiala: Punjabi
University, in preparation) under the editorial oversight of Professor
Harbans Singh. This will be an invaluable aid to all who are engaged
in Sikh Studies. The Department of Sri Guru Granth Sahib Studies at
Punjabi University, Patiala, has also prepared other research aids such
as a dictionary and concordance of the Guru Granth Sahib and a
glossary and index of the Dasm Granth.

Sikh Studies are also pursued vigorously in India's capital city,
New Delhi: in Delhi University and in its affiliated Sri Guru Tegh
Bahadur Khalsa College. Here a noteworthy thesis on the Akali
Movement (a twentieth century Sikh reform and protest movement)
was produced by Dr Mohinder Singh. He is now the Director of the
Guru Nanak Foundation in South Delhi which hosts conferences,
provides research facilities and publishes scholarly works on Sikhism.

Since 1981 the Guru Nanak Foundation has published a journal
entitled *Studies in Sikhism and Comparative Religion.* Punjabi
University, Patiala, publishes two journals of importance to Sikh
Studies, but not limited to them. These are *The Journal of Religious
Studies*, from the Department of Religious Studies, and *The Panjab
Past and Present*, from the Department of Panjab Historical Studies.
This department has also published, since 1965, the *Proceedings of the
Punjab History Conference.* From the Department of Guru Nanak
Studies in Guru Nanak Dev University, Amritsar, comes *The Journal
of Sikh Studies*, and since 1981 its Department of History has published
The Journal of Regional History. Together these journals provide a
forum for local and overseas scholars, Sikh and non-Sikh.

The names of the historians Dr Ganda Singh and Professor J. S.
Grewal must be mentioned, but space does not allow for discussion
of the notable work accomplished by them and by many other
scholars. The numerous subjects on which scholars in Punjab have
written during recent years include the history of the Golden Temple,
Sikh ethics and sectarian groups.

A valuable research tool in the rapidly growing field of Sikh Studies is Rajwant Singh's compilation of 'Information sources in Sikh studies', (*Studies in Sikhism and Comparative Religion VI*, 2, October 1987, pp. 143–55). This lists information sources such as indexing and abstract sources, bibliographies and dictionaries, both English and Punjabi periodicals and scholars and research institutions in India and overseas.

North America

North America is the second significant locale for Sikh Studies. Sikhs first entered Canada and the United States in the 1890s. There have been Sikhs living in both countries every since then, but Sikh Studies have developed only in the 1970s and 1980s, following the influx of Sikhs from the mid-1960s as a result of more liberal immigration legislation. In 1965 the immigration legislation of the United States was revised and national quotas for immigrants were eliminated. In Canada, in 1963, the immigration laws eliminated the distinction between whites and non-whites, and in 1966 selection of would-be immigrants was based on qualifications as opposed to country of origin. Among the resultant spate of recent immigrants are many highly educated Sikh professionals, whereas the first generation of Sikh settlers in North America were relatively uneducated manual labourers. The number of gurdwaras and Sikh organisations in Canada and the United States has increased dramatically during the 1970s and 1980s.

During the same period major international conferences of scholars concerned with Sikh Studies have signalled their growth and have considered future directions. The first of these conferences was held in 1976 in Berkeley. The papers which were presented were subsequently published as *Sikh Studies, Comparative Perspectives on a Changing Tradition* (eds M. Juergensmeyer and N. G. Barrier, Berkeley, 1979). These papers related to the contexts of Sikh Studies, to the origins of Sikhism, the texts of Sikhism and to the Sikh diaspora. Ten years later (1986–87) several conferences took place, including one in the University of Toronto. The volume of conference papers, entitled like the conference *Sikh History and Religion in the Twentieth Century*, marks another step in Sikh Studies.

In the University of Toronto courses on Sikhism have been set up and tentative plans have been made for Sikh and Punjabi programmes in other North American universities. Future realisation of these plans will depend on substantial private support. This demands trust between scholars and members of the faith. Already a Chair of Sikh and Punjabi Studies has been created in the University of British Columbia, Vancouver. To this Harjot Singh Oberoi has been appointed. Scholars who have made a significant contribution to Sikh Studies hold senior academic posts elsewhere, among them Mark Juergensmeyer, formerly Professor of Ethics and the Phenomenology of Religions at the Graduate Theological Union, Berkeley, now at the University of Hawaii.

Great Britain

Until 1960, in Britain as elsewhere, Sikhism was all but ignored in books on world religions. For example, *The Concise Encyclopaedia of Living Faiths* (London, 1959), edited by R. C. Zaehner, included just 27 lines of one column of print on Sikhism. This was under the heading 'Hinduism'.

That the situation has changed since then is chiefly due to the arrival of Sikhs from India and East Africa to live in Britain. Thus Sikhs became a visible presence and their religion came to the notice of outsiders. Some Sikhs had settled in Britain before the second world war, but the majority of the immigrants came during the 1950s and 1960s. A third of the South Asians who arrived from the Indian sub-continent and East Africa were Sikhs. The present population of over 300,000 probably exceeds the population of Hindus and in some areas such as Southall, Coventry and Smethwick Sikhs far outnumber members of other South Asian communities.

Despite this fact no university in Great Britain offers a course in Sikh Studies, although thanks to the efforts of Terry Thomas and Owen Cole respectively Sikhism is strongly represented in degree courses available at the Open University ('The Religious Quest') and the West Sussex Institute of Higher Education. More usually Sikhism is lucky to be allocated one or two lectures in the context of courses on world religions. Unfortunately the 1970s and 1980s have been a period of financial stringency for the universities and there are no signs of improvement. The possibility of a Chair or even a lectureship in Sikh Studies is as remote as ever. Plans underway in 1984 for a Centre for Sikh Studies in Selly Oak, Birmingham, came to nothing as the tragic events of that year diverted Sikh attention from such a project. This is ironic since in the years since 1984 the general public has become aware of Sikhs as never before because of frequent coverage in the news media of unrest in Punjab and Sikh 'terrorism'. The storming of the Golden Temple in 1984 by Indian troops and the violent repercussions have made Sikhs acutely aware of their identity and very sensitive to misrepresentation. During this period of intense religious and political activity among Sikhs in Britain there has been no increase in the academic facilities for the study of Sikhism.

Nevertheless the years 1970–90 have seen an unprecedented flow of publications in Great Britain on Sikhs and Sikhism. These range from illustrated books for infants to scholarly works. Both Sikhs and non-Sikhs have contributed to this output.

By Guru Nanak's quincentenary in 1969 many Sikh parents in Britain were realising that their children were growing up in virtual ignorance of the Punjabi language and the Sikh tradition. Born of this concern, the Sikh Missionary Society (UK) was inaugurated and began publishing a series of booklets in English on the Gurus and Sikhism. These proved helpful, not only to Sikh families but to the growing number of people, such as teachers, with a professional interest in the beliefs and religious practices of Sikhs.

Britain differs from India, Canada and the United States of America in that since the Education Act of 1944 schools have been legally required to provide religious education for all pupils unless they are exempted on religious grounds at their parents' wish. Syllabuses for religious education have since then been drawn up and agreed within each local education authority. Since 1975 most Local Agreed Syllabuses for religious education have stated that a major aim of the subject is to increase pupils' understanding of world faiths. This reflects the mounting concern of many religious educationalists to deepen and widen their pupils' understanding of world faiths, including Sikhism. Their concern paralleled the growing awareness that the whole curriculum should be less ethnocentric. The movement towards multicultural education in general and multi-faith RE in particular was a direct result of post-war immigration to Britain.

Recognition of the study of Sikhism in secondary schools was further formalised by the inclusion of Sikhism in some Religious Studies syllabuses for the General Certificate of Education (GCE). With one exception the Boards for the General Certificate of Secondary Education, which replaced both the Certificate of Secondary Education and GCE 'O' Level in 1988, offer a syllabus in Sikhism among their religious education options. At 'A' Level those Religious Studies candidates who are registered with the Joint

Matriculation Board and Cambridge Local Examinations Syndicate can sit papers on Sikhism. It remains to be seen how the place of Sikh Studies in the religious education provided by British schools is affected by the 1988 Education Reform Act which supplements the 1944 Act. Much may depend on parental pressure and the response of the local Standing Advisory Councils on Religious Education. It is possible that regional variations in the extent to which faiths other than Christianity are represented in the curriculum will increase.

Among the numerous books about Sikhs and their religion which have appeared since 1970, many are aimed at school children. Most abound in beautiful colour photographs. A favourite approach in books for primary school children especially is to introduce a Sikh child and focus on aspects of Sikh family life in Britain. A welcome recent development is the publication of illustrated books retelling traditional Sikh stories.

In the field of Sikh Studies in schools the major input and initiative has come from the partnership of Piara Singh Sambhi and Owen Cole. In 1969 in Leeds Owen Cole attended a celebration of Guru Nanak's quincentenary and embarked on a study of Sikhism which resulted in the co-authorship of what is now recognised as a standard work on Sikhism for pupils, teachers and undergraduates. This book, *The Sikhs: Their Religious Beliefs and Practices*, (London, 1976), subsequently translated into Polish and Japanese, has been followed by many more books and articles. By initiating the publication of a *Sikh Bulletin*, an annual collection of articles relevant to religious educationists, and by setting up a Sikh Studies Group in which matters of mutual interest to Sikhs and RE specialists are discussed, Owen Cole has endeavoured to bring more cohesion to otherwise scattered efforts in the area of Sikh Studies.

Serious study of Sikh history, religion and literature necessitates competence in the appropriate languages. Here, Christopher Shackle of the School of Oriental and African Studies in the University of London has made a special contribution to Sikh Studies by providing linguistic tools for people with little or no prior knowledge of Punjabi and related languages. Not only has he opened up the Sikhs' mother-tongue with *Punjabi* in the Teach Yourself Series (Norwich, 1972) and a Punjabi newspaper reader (*Punjabi Book II*, London: SOAS, n.d.) but he has facilitated study of the Sikh scriptures with *A Guru Nanak Glossary* (SOAS, 1981) and *An Introduction to the Sacred Language of the Sikhs* (1983). Among his numerous publications is a brief, but masterly account entitled *The Sikhs*, published by the Minority Rights Group (1986).

The extent of studies of the British Sikh diaspora is clear from Darshan Singh Tatla's and Eleanor Nesbitt's *Sikhs in Britain: An Annotated Bibliography*, (Warwick University, Centre for Research in Ethnic Relations, 1987). A decade after G. S. Aurora's *The New Frontiersmen: A Sociological Study of Indian Immigrants in the U.K.*, (Bombay, 1967), Roger and Catherine Ballard provided an analysis of the phases of Sikh settlement in Britain with their essay on 'The Sikhs: the development of South Asian settlements in Britain' (1977).[4] Since then studies of local Sikh communities, of their migration, settlement, employment, women, family and social life, language, literature, religion and politics in Britain have continued unabated.

In Britain and North America studies of the Sikh diaspora have flourished and are summarised by Buchignani as follows:

> Research activity has increased precipitously . . . since 1970. Since the beginning, studies of diaspora Sikhs done in the general metaphor of ethnicity and race have been prominent . . .
> Recently, the growth of Sikh studies has begun to shift this balance somewhat. Some researchers primarily interested in homeland Sikh cultural, religious and political development have extended their interests to the diaspora, and a few others long involved in diaspora studies have made an increasing commitment to understanding the specifically Sikh aspects of the diaspora equation. (p. 277)[5]

Conclusion

The future of Sikh Studies will depend upon Sikhs in India and the diaspora and upon non-Sikh scholars. The insights and conviction of Sikhs and the analytical discipline of western scholarship can be mutually enriching. On the other hand Sikh Studies will suffer immeasurably if insiders are hostile to critical method or outsiders are insensitive to religious sentiment. Those who are not brought up in an atmosphere of reverence for the Gurus and their teachings must recognise that: 'A significant range of understanding is bred in the bone and no amount of interest or diligence will ever confer it on the foreigner'. These are the words of Professor Hew McLeod, a scholar whose contribution to Sikh Studies, albeit controversial in some of its emphases, stands unsurpassed in the past three decades and whose painstakingly researched and lucidly expounded scholarship has run the gauntlet of insiders' suspicion.

Hew McLeod, a New Zealander, has lectured, and his works have been published, in India, North America and Britain. By applying the methodology of the historian and textual critic – in the western tradition of biblical scholarship – he has posed searching questions in tracing the development of Sikhism from Guru Nanak's religious antecedents to Sikh identity in the latter years of the twentieth century. His latest publication, *Who is a Sikh?*, (London, 1989) and his earlier works *Guru Nanak and the Sikh Religion* (London, 1968) followed by *The Evolution of the Sikh Community*, (Oxford, 1976), are well known. Some of the historical judgements reached by McLeod – the attribution of certain characteristics of the Sikh community to the influence of the Jat caste for example – have so far been met by Sikhs more often on the level of sensibility than of academic debate. In the years since these books appeared Sikh sensitivities have been heightened. There is a persistent danger of religious and political fervour constricting the scope of intellectual enquiry.

In 1980 McLeod published two works focusing on the *janamsakhis* (early accounts of Guru Nanak's life). These have been followed by studies of the Sikh codes of discipline (*rahit*), of the Sikh diaspora in New Zealand and the South Pacific. His *Textual Sources for the Study of Sikhism* (Manchester, 1984) provides students with excellent English renderings of an authoritative selection of scriptural, liturgical and sectarian material.

Sikh Studies have much to offer. An understanding of the dynamic at work in the evolution of the *panth* will enhance the understanding of Indian religious and political movements, the institutionalisation of religion as well as the relationship between religion and nationalism. With Sikhs dispersed as never before in five continents, there is a growing need for them to learn about their tradition and for non-Sikhs to develop an informed sympathy with particular faith communities, such as the Sikhs, of which multi-ethnic societies consist. With Sikhs concentrated as never before in the Indian state of Punjab and in some overseas areas such as Southall in West London, their interpretation of current political trauma and individuals' perplexity over identity can only benefit from historical study and a deeper grounding in the scriptures. This has implications for the relations between South Asian communities in Britain and elsewhere.

At a time of cuts in educational expenditure private funding will be critical for the continuance of Sikh Studies in Britain. Already at least one university department is exploring the possibility of running lectures in Sikh Studies funded by Sikh businessmen. In 1989 Indarjit

Singh, who is well known as a media spokesperson on Sikhism and who has edited two Sikh periodicals, was the first non-Christian to win a Templeton Project Award. This he plans to put towards establishing a national Sikh centre. Let us hope that these are small indications of future interaction, intellectual and financial, between Sikhs and non-Sikhs, which will enable Sikh Studies in Britain to realise its potential.

NOTES

[1] These early studies are examined in G. Khurana, *British Historiography on the Sikh Power in Punjab*, New Delhi: Allied Publishers, 1975.

[2] See for example S. K. Bajaj, 'British Historians of the Sikhs (Gordon, Bingley and Payne)', in *Punjab History Conference Proceedings* 8th Session, December 15–16, 1973, pp. 192–203.

[3] Harnam Singh Shan, *Scholarly Study of Sikhism*, Chandigarh: Department of Guru Nanak Studies, Panjab University, 1974.

[4] To be found in James L. Watson, ed., *Between Two Cultures*, Oxford: Blackwell, 1977, pp. 21–56.

[5] Norman Buchignani, 'Conceptions of Sikh Culture in the Development of a Comparative Analysis of the Sikh Diaspora', in Joseph T. O'Connell et al. (ed), *Sikh History and Religion in the Twentieth Century*, Toronto: University of Toronto Press, 1988, pp. 276–95.

SUGGESTED READING

N. Gerald Barrier, *The Sikhs and their Literature (A Guide to Tracts, Books and Periodicals 1849–1919)*, Delhi: Manohar Book Service, 1970.

W. Owen Cole, 'Sikhism: A World Religion' in *Studies in Sikhism and Comparative Religion*, II, 2, Oct. 1983, pp. 1–10.

Arthur W. Helweg, 'East Indians in England and North America', in P. J. F. Rosof et al. (eds) *Ethnic and Immigration Groups: The United States, Canada and England*, New York: The Institute for Research in History and the Haworth Press, Inc., 1983.

W. Hew McLeod, *Early Sikh Tradition*, Oxford: Clarendon Press, 1980.

G. S. Mansukhani, 'A Survey of Sikh Studies and Sikh Centres', in *Studies in Sikhism and Comparative Religion*, VI, 2, Oct. 1987, pp. 123–32.

E. M. Nesbitt, 'The Presentation of Sikhs in Recent Children's Literature in Britain' in J. T. O'Connell et al. (eds), *Sikh History and Religion in the Twentieth Century*, Centre for South Asian Studies: University of Toronto, 1988, pp. 376–87.

J. T. O'Connell, 'Sikh Studies and Studies of Sikhs in Canada', in *Studies in Sikhism and Comparative Religion*, V, 2, Oct. 1986, pp. 154–73.

Harbans Singh, *Berkeley Lectures on Sikhism*, New Delhi: Guru Nanak Foundation, 1983.

10. 'TRADITIONAL' AFRICAN RELIGIONS

Rosalind Shaw

How Traditional are 'Traditional' Religions?

When we describe religions as 'traditional', what do we mean? The word sets up certain oppositions. It suggests, for instance, that religions so termed are ancient rather than modern, static rather than changing, 'pure' rather than syncretic; yet the reverse is much more likely to be true. In practice, those African religious forms described as 'traditional' are usually those which have escaped classification as African Christianity, African Islam and new religious movements.

What are the alternatives? The term 'primitive religions' suggests a condition of arrested development which is totally inappropriate. 'Primal religions' sounds less derogatory, but again implies that which is basic in some way rather than complex contemporary African religions. 'Non-literate' religions brings a useful focus to the importance of the predominantly oral, rather than textual, character of such religious forms. But this would exclude, for example, the use of printed *Ifa* divination manuals among contemporary Yoruba diviners of south-western Nigeria, as well as the use of an indigenous African script called *nsibidi* in the cult associations of many south-eastern Nigerian peoples, which Robert F. Thompson has described for the Ejagham ('Emblems of prowess', in *Flash of the Spirit*, New York, 1983).

If we *must* use a general term at all, then, we are stuck with those which are artefacts of our need as academics to fill gaping holes in our own classification systems. Rather than denoting a specific 'type' of religion, we can only imply what such religious forms are not. We need to re-examine even the term 'religion' here, since the English word suggests thought-systems with written scriptures, explicit doctrines and centres of authority and knowledge. We are concerned here, however, with more implicit forms of knowledge, embedded in ritual practice, oral narratives, architecture and the organisation of everyday life.

Most studies of 'traditional' African religions have been conducted by social anthropologists rather than those in Religious Studies specifically. Historical studies have until recently been largely confined to African Christianity and African Islam, for which written records are more easily available. The ahistorical image of 'traditional' African religions thus perpetuated is highly misleading, but fortunately this is being rectified at the turning point at which we currently find ourselves, and which is outlined in the concluding section. The first part of this essay examines African Religious Studies, and the second part discusses anthropological studies of African religions.

I: African Religious Studies

Judeo-Christian Templates

The first serious studies of African religions were made in the course of Christian missionary work. Accordingly, certain aspects of religion were perceived as more significant – and more useful – than others. As John Peel has shown for the encounter between missionaries and *Ifa* diviners in nineteenth century Yorubaland ('The pastor and the *babalawo*', presented at the Colloquium on African Religion, Satterthwaite, 1987), missionary agendas depended upon the construction of homologies between Christianity and 'heathenism', in which certain elements could be retained and 'baptised' (such as God, prayer and the idea of a mediator), others replaced by parallel Christian forms (for example, blood sacrifice replaced by communion), and others still assimilated to the idea of Satan and rejected (such as practices defined as 'magic', as well as trickster deities such as the Yoruba god Esu). In the Yoruba case, the missionary encounter favoured the *Ifa* divination cult, which differed significantly from other aspects of Yoruba religion. Among other features, its hegemonic claims, its association with the Supreme Being and its male-dominated priesthood both distinguished it from other Yoruba cults and pre-adapted it, according to Peel, to mutually respectful interaction with Christian missions. The picture of African religious forms which were built up in early missionary studies were thus informed by the interests of those on both sides of the encounter, and shaped upon a Judeo-Christian template.

What is striking is how this kind of approach has endured in African Religious Studies. Research interests and strategies originally generated by missionary agendas were carried over into academic writing. A hundred years later, the construction of implicit or explicit homologies with Judeo-Christianity and the selection of elements which facilitate such homologies are still dominant features of a large number of volumes on African religions. Chapter sequences which themselves embody a normative view of the content and structure which religions 'ought' to have, which begin with 'The Supreme God', descend through 'The Lesser Deities' and 'The Ancestors', examine 'Prayer' and 'Sacrifice' and conclude with 'Magic', became the standard way to organise material on African religions, and are still found in recent works.

But the aims of those who studied and wrote about African religions, certainly by the 1950s and '60s, *had* changed significantly since the missionary era. More than anyone else at this time, it was Geoffrey Parrinder who set the new agenda: African religions, like other religions of the world, should be studied in their own right. In 1949 he published a work of regional comparison, *West African Religion*, and co-founded the first Department of Religious Studies at the University of Ibadan. The significance of Parrinder's work at Ibadan, at a time when Departments of Religious Studies did not exist in Britain, has been emphasised by Andrew Walls:

> Departments of Religious Studies as we now know them in Britain were born in West Africa, the product of conditions of a plural society where religion is a massive, unignorable, fact of life. And Geoffrey Parrinder found himself teaching what no-one had ever taught him – what, perhaps, no-one had ever taught at university level before: a course in the Indigenous Religious Beliefs of West Africa. ('A bag of needments for the road', *Religion* 10, 1980: 144)

As a result of these innovations, and of his prolific publication on African religions listed at the end of this volume, Parrinder gave African religions a much more central place within Religious Studies.

'Theological' Cultural Nationalism

From the 1950s and '60s onwards, the writings of African scholars on African religions gained increasing momentum. This was the era of Independence for most African nations, and these scholars were part of a much wider, pan-African movement usually termed Cultural Nationalism. Its aims were to bring about a parallel 'decolonisation' within scholarship and the arts, a reorientation in terms of Africa-centred rather than Euro-centric perspectives of history and culture. For African Religious Studies, the work of E. Bolaji Idowu was seminal.

Idowu came to be the spokesman for what had been called the 'theological' approach, the latter having dominated African Religious

Studies until very recently. Central to this approach is the definition of African religions as essentially monotheistic rather than polytheistic, an interpretation which Idowu applied to Yoruba religious ideas in his classic monograph, *Olódùmarè: God in Yoruba Belief* (London, 1962). Because, he argued, the supreme being Olédùmarè or Olórun is regarded as the ultimate source of the powers of all Yoruba divinities (just as the ministers in Yoruba kingdoms derive their authority from the king), Yoruba religion is a form of monotheism, which he characterised as 'diffused monotheism' (1962: 102, 204). Ten years later he published a textbook, *African Traditional Religion* (London, 1973), in which he claimed that 'diffused monotheism' was the only adequate description of *all* African belief systems (1973: 135). Moreover, because of what he asserted to be the 'identical concept' of God in all parts of Africa, he argued that 'we can speak of the religion of Africa in the singular' (1973: 104). Such claims, however, were asserted as articles of faith, statements about what African religious participants ideally *ought* to think, but which in practice, as he in fact conceded, they often do not (1973: 173).

It was important for Idowu that there should be a single and essentially monotheistic 'African Traditional Religion' with a well-developed sense of deity, to counter paternalistic European writing about 'withdrawn' African high gods. In this writing, African concepts of God were found wanting, since these were asserted to be ideas of a vague and remote deity. Idowu replied with a biting polemic which startled western Religious Studies into a new perception of African religions:

> Western scholars created an 'inferior' god or 'inferior' gods for the (to them) 'inferior' races of the world. It became complicated when he 'created' not just two gods – one for his race, and one for the collective batch of 'the primitives': he retained his own one god and gave his imagination the rein to overrun the world of 'the primitives' with 'high gods' of all descriptions. (1973: 65)

As far as Idowu was concerned, it was clearly *better* for African religions to be monotheistic than to be polytheistic, and to constitute a single, pan-African belief system comparable to Christianity itself than to be a multiplicity of diverse systems. Needless to say, the blow he struck for African religions by inventing a homogeneous 'African Traditional Religion' ironically entrenched yet further their description and assessment in terms of simplified Christian norms.

Idowu's work stimulated a massive output of 'theological' cultural nationalist writing in African Religious Studies, of which the most influential was that of the Kenyan scholar John Mbiti. Mbiti's major work, *Concepts of God in Africa* (London, 1970), is a collection of material about the high god from over two hundred and seventy African peoples, structured into chapters whose headings ('The Intrinsic Attributes of God', 'The Eternal Attributes of God', etc.) resemble those of a theology textbook. He does not claim to be compiling a single 'African concept of God', but his material, severed from the contexts from which it derives, is inevitably superficial, and his concern to find African equivalents to concepts from Christian theology results in the subordination of the former to the latter. He goes even further than Idowu, moreover, in elevating the 'diffused monotheism' interpretation to an article of faith. In his textbook, *African Religions and Philosophy* (London, 1969), he makes the extraordinary statement that 'God is the ultimate Recipient [of sacrifices and prayers to other deities] *whether or not the worshippers are aware of that*' (1969:58; my emphasis). In the context of the overwhelming concern in Religious Studies in the 1960s with scriptural religions, it was, however, inevitable that efforts to bring the study of African religions in from the margins should have involved their presentation in terms of normative Judeo-Christian forms.

Mbiti and Idowu thereby created an 'authorised' description of African religions which is still fairly common. Because their aims, and those of other 'theological' cultural nationalists who came after them, were to restore respect for African religions, criticism of their positions had been problematic since it has sometimes been construed as a denigration of African religions. A penetrating critique published in 1971, *African Religions in Western Scholarship* (Nairobi) by the Ugandan writer Okot P'Bitek (whose own cultural nationalist qualifications were impeccable), was greeted by a stony silence. As far as I know, there has not yet been a reply to his critique from 'theological' writers, but as a focus for those who are now challenging the authorised 'theological' description it may yet prove to be a turning point, almost twenty years after its publication.

Alternatives in Religious Studies

Not all writings on African religions in Religious Studies have followed the Idowu/Mbiti line, however. Benjamin Ray's useful textbook, *African Religions* (New Jersey, 1976) combines phenomenological, anthropological and historical perspectives. And recently, Jacob Olupona's research on Yoruba religion and Donatus Nwoga's work on Igbo religion have also broken new ground in African Religious Studies. Olupona's article with the social anthropologist Olatunde Lawuyi, 'Metaphoric associations and the conception of death' (*Journal of Religion in Africa* XVIII, 1988), for example, introduces an important emphasis on competition rather than homogeneity in the tension between male and female Yoruba religious perspectives. Nwoga's *The Supreme God as Stranger in Igbo Religious Thought* (Ekwereazu, Nigeria, 1984) probes the historical processes through which apparently 'traditional' Igbo religious ideas were produced. He argues on the basis of linguistic, historical and ethnographic material that the contemporary pre-eminence of the Igbo supreme god Chukwu, and the transformation of Igbo cosmology which accompanied this, are the outcome of earlier activities of powerful religious specialists who were firstly agents of the Arochukwu oracle and secondly Christian missionaries. These examples in particular place African Religious Studies at a new interdisciplinary turning point, which will hopefully develop further during the 1990s.

II: Social Anthropology and Religion in Africa

From Function to Meaning

Religious Studies and social anthropology have usually gone their separate ways in studies of African religions. They had different origins, articulated different concerns, and developed along different paths, although there is now increasing cross-fertilization between them. Whereas African Religious Studies developed primarily out of the missionary encounter, it was the colonial encounter which gave Africanist anthropology its major impetus, as Talal Asad's *Anthropology and the Colonial Encounter* (London, 1973) examines. Anthropologists were often employed in order to provide data to facilitate colonial rule, yet their attitude to this rule was not always positive, and many felt stronger sense of loyalty to the people among whom they conducted fieldwork. Although innovatory pieces of work which have subsequently become classics emerged from the contradictory conditions of their production, one of the hallmarks of such works was a highly artificial methodological convention known as 'the ethnographic present'. This usually involved taking a timeless 'snapshot' of a society, and examining the function fulfilled by that society's constituent parts: marriage, sacrifice, dispute settlement, gift-giving, and so on. These 'snapshots', however, were in practice of anything but the present, for the dislocations brought about by colonialism were typically left out of the picture, as if the writers were trying to distance themselves from the political circumstances which had brought them there. Out of this era came works which were often brilliant but ahistorical analyses of the 'functions' which specific aspects of religion were seen as performing in the societies to which they belonged, such as the release of social tensions via witchcraft accusations and confessions, the integration of the community through ritual, and the legitimation of elders' authority by ancestor cults (e.g., Jack Goody, *Death, Property and the Ancestors*, Stanford, 1962).

One consequence of the lack of communication between social anthropology and Religious Studies has been the persistence of outdated stereotypes about each other. The reductionist functional approach has remained the negative image which many in Religious Studies have of those engaged in anthropological studies of religion. Yet even during the functionalist era, which was in decline in the 1960s, certain classic analyses of African religions pursued much more interesting paths, inaugurating a shift from the study of function to that of meaning.

Evans-Pritchard's *Nuer Religion* (Oxford 1956), for instance, is outside the functionalist mould in emphasising the internal significance of Nuer ideas of deity, sacrifice and symbolism. A study of the Nuer's southern neighbours, the Dinka of the Sudan, by Evans-Pritchard's student Godfrey Lienhardt was again considerably ahead of its time. Entitled *Divinity and Experience* (Oxford, 1961), it focused on Dinka uses of myth, ritual and symbolism in controlling their own experience of the world. In the central place it gave to experience and in the active role it gave to the participants in generating and regenerating their view of the world through ritual, his analysis has only recently been equalled.

The third major voice in the turn towards meaning in Africanist anthropological studies has been that of Victor Turner, whose works have been central to the development of paradigms for wider comparison. From his study of initiation rituals among the Ndembu of Zambia, for example, he developed in his volume *The Ritual Process* (London, 1969) the concept of *communitas*, a state of being characterised by sacredness, a relative lack of structure, and close egalitarian human bonds. Common to such diverse phenomena as pilgrimage, Christian monastic orders and the liminal phase of initiation rituals, Turner saw *communitas* as vital to the constitution of human life.

Intellectualist and structuralist analyses

At the same time as semantic and symbolic interpretations such as those above were being explored, rather different lines of approach were unfolding. One of these was Robin Horton's intellectualist concern with religion as a system of explanation, prediction and control, which is best displayed in his famous piece of comparison, 'African Traditional Thought and Western Science' (*Africa* 37, 1967), and which he has developed over the past three decades in relation to ideas of the high god, conversion to Christianity and Islam and West African concepts of personhood. Like Victor Turner's work, Horton's writings have been of considerable influence in offering concepts for comparative study.

From the late 1960s and early 1970s, another kind of intellectualist perspective was being applied to African religious forms. Concepts from the structuralism of French writers such as Durkheim and, more recently, Lévi-Strauss, influenced the work of Mary Douglas, who has tried to demonstrate relationships between systems of classification, cosmology and social organisation in Africa and elsewhere (e.g. *Natural Symbols*, Harmondsworth, 1971). Lévi-Strauss' ideas were applied much more fully, however, to Luc de Heusch's regional study of founding myths of central African kingdoms, *The Drunken King* (Bloomington, 1982). Using structuralist concepts such as opposition and transformation, de Heusch charts the progress of certain common elements as they recur in various Bantu myths of the origin of the state, such as a king associated with the earth and the rainbow, and a rain-bringing hunter whom he opposes. On the basis of the recurrence of these elements in different combinations in several myths, de Heusch asserts that such myths are not 'about' actual historical events, but about the way the cosmos is conceived of.

Turning Towards Ontology

Anthropological studies of religion from the perspectives outlined above have often (though not always) been concerned to build up a picture of a usually rather static 'system', of which the people concerned may or (more often) may not be aware. Increasingly, however, there is concern to avoid imposing an external order, and instead to place more emphasis upon experience and ontology, especially in their mutual interaction with power as the *politics* of religious experience, *competing* subjectivities.[1] It has also become clear that such an agenda cannot be pursued outside the study of the historical context. Such an agenda is highly appropriate for the study of 'non-literate' African religions, which rarely receive historical treatment, and whose complexities and many voices cannot, without great distortion, be reduced to tidy, coherent 'systems'. For these reasons, it is worth going into some detail about a recent work, Wendy James' *The Listening Ebony* (Oxford, 1988), which is an exemplary representative of current anthropological concerns with ontology, power and history.

The Listening Ebony charts religious change among the Uduk of the Sudan. James prefers the term 'moral knowledge' when describing the implicit, fundamental forms of knowing which characterise Uduk understandings of themselves and the world, 'religion' having inappropriate connotations of explicit ideology. Uduk moral knowledge is informed by their historical experience – their hunter-gatherer origins, the depredations of slavery, their marginality in regional politics – and is likened by James to an 'archive' which Uduk draw upon in looking forward and responding to contemporary events. Closely linked to changing focii of political power in the region are competing forms of external religious authority – the religion of Nilotic prophets and of Islamic and Christian evangelism – which have waxed and waned among the Uduk, and continue to do so. Missionaries from each of these have tried to use the Uduk notion of *arum*, a spiritual power belonging to the body, to construct the concept of a high god fundamentally different to humankind. Uduk responses have typically consisted of the limited incorporation of such foreign ideas, through alliance with whatever religious affiliation is politically weakest against central authority.

Through this incorporation, however, they assimilate these new ideas to their own moral 'archive' in such a way as to transform them into a defence against future theistic incursions. As part of this defensive response, an acephalous, egalitarian 'order' of Ebony diviners has spread with spectacular success from the end of the nineteenth century onwards, and has brought the older 'archival' knowledge into a sharper, clearer focus, a focus through which Uduk are revitalising their existence:

The diviner kindles the [ebony] wand in the fire, and holds it over a gourd of water . . . It is the nature of ebony, people say, as it grows wild in the forest or bush, to 'hear' signals about what is going on in the human world, and it is these secrets which are revealed in the consultation. The ebony knows the grumblings and sufferings of the people; with its help, what is assumed to be a true picture of the people's condition is reflected back to them in the watery mirror ... The ebony can aid the people because it has *listened* to their voices. In strident contrast, spokesmen for the new religions loudly proclaim their prescriptions for faith, counting as their victory the silencing of others. None have noticed the quiet indications of the ebony, sensitive to the inner *arum*, the health of the Stomach, and integrity of the personal Genius. (1988: 10)

It is clear from James' book that religion and ontology – our major concerns – are not separable from power. We could not understand the significance of the 'listening ebony' for the Uduk without understanding how appropriate an image this is for a people who have not been listened to.

Conclusion: A Moving Together

After travelling on different trajectories, Religious Studies and social anthropology appear currently to be converging at very similar thresholds with regard to the study of African religions. Now that power has been incorporated into African Religious Studies in the form of competing perspectives, and ontology has been incorporated into anthropological analysis, cooperation between the two disciplines appears both more likely and more productive than ever before. In both cases, in fact, these thresholds have been reached through the dovetailing of different disciplines, especially that of history. Studies of 'traditional' African religions by historians appear, moreover, both to be gaining considerable momentum through innovative combinations of oral and archival material. Two recent examples are an article by Richard Shain on the development of colour symbolism and sacral kingship among the Etulo of Nigeria ('The Black and the White', *Journal of Religion in Africa* XVIII, 1988), and a study by Robert Baum of the encounter between French colonial and Djola understandings of witchcraft in Senegal ('Crimes of the Dream World: French trials of Djola witches', 1989, unpublished ms.). Both studies reflect, once again, a growing interest in historical dimensions of the interface between politics, religious meaning and experience.

It is ironic, therefore, that such potential for interdisciplinary collaboration should be reached at a point in time when Religious Studies, anthropology and history, as well as African studies, are suffering in Britain from devastating cuts due to government policy on higher education.

NOTE

[2] This emphasis on competing perspectives has received considerable impetus from feminist anthropology. However, apart from two very short but brilliant studies by Edwin Ardener (1975), there is as yet little published on gender and 'traditional' African religions.

SUGGESTED READING

Ardener, Edwin, 'Belief and the problem of women' and 'The "problem" revisited', in S. Ardener (ed.), *Perceiving Women*. London: Dent, 1975, pp. 1–17, 19–27.

Heusch, Luc de, 'What shall we do with the drunken king?', *Africa* 45, 1975, pp. 363–72.

Horton, Robin, 'Judeo-Christian spectacles: boon or bane to the study of African religions?', *Cahiers d'Etudes Africaines* 96, 1984, pp. 391–436.

James, Wendy, *The Listening Ebony. Moral knowledge, religion, and power among the Uduk of Sudan*. Oxford: Clarendon Press, 1988.

Lawuyi, Olatunde B., and Olupona, J. K., 'Metaphoric associations and the conception of death: analysis of a Yoruba world-view', *Journal of Religion in Africa* XVIII, 1988, pp. 2–14.

Lienhardt, Godfrey, *Divinity and Experience. The religion of the Dinka*. Oxford: Clarendon Press, 1961.

Ray, Benjamin, *African Religions. Symbol, ritual, community*. Prentice-Hall, 1976.

Turner, Victor W., *The Ritual Process*. London: Routledge and Kegan Paul, 1969.

11. AFRICAN NEW RELIGIOUS MOVEMENTS

Rosalind I. J. Hackett

Geoffrey Parrinder was one of the first to write on new religious movements in West Africa. In his useful 1953 survey of religion in Ibadan, Nigeria (*Religion in an African City*, London, 1953, repr. Westport/Conn., 1972) – one of the earliest studies of religious pluralism in Africa – he identified seventeen distinct 'separatist churches'. He defined them as 'sects which have split away from, or sprung up in relative independence of, the older mission churches', with the observation that, given their growing importance, they were surprisingly absent in missiological literature. Parrinder had already encountered several of these movements in the course of his missionary work in neighbouring Dahomey (now the Republic of Benin) and he was familiar with the landmark study of separatist churches in South Africa by Bengt Sundkler – *Bantu Prophets in South Africa* – which had appeared in London in 1948.

Religious Independency on the Rise

However, even Geoffrey Parrinder, with his early field experience, could not have anticipated the veritable explosion of African new religious movements that would occur over the next forty years. In Ibadan itself, now the largest metropolis in black Africa with an estimated population of over four million, there are scores of movements with hundreds of branches. They are not all Christian-related either, some are Islamic, others trace their roots to India or California. The majority of movements have arisen in sub-Saharan Africa; by 1968 it was estimated that there were around 5,000 independent and 1,000 semi-autonomous Christian-related movements.[1] Later estimates suggest that there may be over 10,000 movements with between 10–12 million active members and twice that involved in a broader spectrum of religious movements.[2] With their dynamic rituals and innovatory structures, these movements have spawned numerous theories regarding their genesis and stimulated comment on their potential as agents of change and protest. Above all they have emerged as the vanguards of indigenization, of religious self-determination – creators of meaningful religious worlds for Africans.

My concern in this essay is less with the earlier, well-documented phase of Africa's new religious movements, that is to say the colonial and post-independence periods (see Turner 1977 and 1979). However, I shall use Parrinder's description and typology of these movements in the Ibadan context as a springboard for examining the changes that have occurred in the field.[3] There have been some interesting new developments in the last decade or so, namely an observable 'internationalization' of many of the movements as they seek global connections and evangelize beyond African shores. I shall address the challenges these pose to our discourse on the subject as well as the significance and comparative interest of these newer movements. My discussion is based primarily upon my work on Nigerian religious movements, with relevant examples drawn from other contexts.

Parrinder, along with many other observers, such as Sundkler, Barrett and Turner, attributed the emergence of these movements to the encounter with western culture, more specifically western Christianity. He distinguished three types of movements in Ibadan: the first, the 'orthodox' separatists or 'African Churches' (such as the United Native African Church and the African Church), so named because they seceded from their parent bodies (namely the Anglican, Baptist and Methodist Churches) over a 'desire for independence' and disagreements regarding church polity and polygamy and yet differed little in terms of liturgy and doctrine.[4] This type of separatist church had already been identified in South Africa by Sundkler as the 'Ethiopian' type.[5] The second type is the prayer-healing church, which approximates that of the 'Zionist' Church in South Africa, according to Sundkler's classification. Parrinder describes these churches, such as the Christ Apostolic Church and the Sacred Cherubim and Seraphim Society, as laying particular emphasis upon healing by prayer and faith, hence their generic term, *aladura* or 'owners of prayer'.[6] He links their emergence to revivalist activity (several renowned local evangelists, such as Babalola and Odubanjo were emerging at that time) and prayer groups within the churches, inspired in part by overseas pentecostal churches such as the Faith Tabernacle of Pennsylvania and the (British) Apostolic Church. Today, these churches, which Parrinder was then describing in their nascent phase, are the dominant variety of new religious movement in Nigeria and the rest of sub-Saharan Africa. Sometimes referred to as spiritual churches, they are characterized by their predilection for dreams and visions, prophetism, prayer, healing and spirit possession.

In keeping with his criterion of orthodoxy as a tool for

classification, Parrinder's third category is the syncretist church. This refers to those movements that seek a fusion of Christian and non-Christian elements. A well-known example in Ibadan at the time was the movement known as Orunmlaism (Orunmila being the Yoruba god of divination), which sought to demonstrate the Yoruba roots of Christianity. Parrinder also mentions here those healing homes which draw upon a variety of traditional African, Muslim and western occult sources. It is significant that in the late 1940s, such religious specialists were already drawing on and incorporating international sources. A number of these healing homes expanded into movements, adopting the church model. Orunmlaism, now known as Ijo Orunmila (the Church of Orunmila), has a successful following in south-western Nigeria and produces a newsletter which reaches some interested African-Americans in the United States.

Prophetic movements centred around revitalized high god or spirit mediumship cults do not appear in Parrinder's account since they emerged as a form of protest against colonial hegemony in East and Southern Africa in the late nineteenth and early twentieth centuries. Renowned leaders were Kinjikitile, who led a millennialist movement known as the Maji-Maji rebellion in German East Africa and Nongqause, a prophetess in the great Xhosa cattle-killing sacrifice of 1856–57. These neo-traditional movements lent themselves to historical and political interpretations. Several of the early African Christian prophets, such as Simon Kimbangu (1889–1951) and William Wade Harris (c. 1865–1929), provoked government repression in the form of imprisonment and exile. Ironically, the primary concerns of these movements were healing and conversion, but their ability to mobilize the masses was viewed as destabilizing and subversive by some missionaries and colonialists. Today, nearly forty years after Kimbangu's death in 1951, the Kimbanguist Church is one of the three churches officially recognized by the Zairean government.

Four Decades of Change

From the numerous studies conducted on new religious movements, it is apparent that they flourish in urban contexts, such as Ibadan. With their emphasis on problem-solving and 'practical Christianity' (the motto of one of eastern Nigeria's largest movements, the Brotherhood of the Cross and Star), they draw a large clientele, both casual and regular. Among the social functions they provide are employment, education, welfare, counselling, healing, marriage guidance, entertainment. This has led several observers, both in academia and the media, to downplay or even question the religious orientation of these movements, viewing them rather as adjustment cults or as proto-political movements. These observations fail to understand how such religious communities construct a viable order of signs and practices in order to cope with, even transform, the forces which surround and dominate them.

The common denominator of the movements described above is their quest for religious self-determination. This indigenous religious intitiative may be manifested through new leadership structures, increased lay participation, greater roles for women, use of indigenous music and dance, doctrinal or ritual innovation, rejection of Western practices such as the use of bio-medicine and endorsement of traditional forms of religious experience. The motto of the African Orthodox Church conveys the sentiments and aspirations of many independent church leaders: 'A Church, of the Africans, governed by the Africans, and for the Africans, to make daily supplications to Almighty God led by priests who have the welfare of Africans at heart.'[7] We think also of Isaiah Shembe's Nazaretha Church as an extension of, and reconstruction of, the Zulu nation with its Zulu rituals, music and dance. The Celestial Church of Christ was founded by Samuel Bileou Oschoffa in 1947 in Dahomey, West Africa, as a church where Africans would find the necessary salvation and not need to resort to alternative (traditional) means. The Africa Israel Church Nineveh and the Church of Christ in Africa, two well known East African independent churches, are the subjects of a book by Welbourn and Ogot, significantly entitled *A Place to Feel at Home*.[8] The many Cherubim and Seraphim churches in Nigeria have developed an elaborate hierarchy which they believe reflects the spiritual orientation of their movement.

An interesting feature of Africa's new religious movements is their structural mobility and rapid growth. A movement such as the Brotherhood of the Cross and Star, for example, began as a healing home in Olumba Olumba Obu's compound in Calabar, eastern Nigeria, in 1956. Today it is an international organization with branches in several West African countries, the United Kingdom, the United States, and many hundreds of branches in Nigeria itself. The Brotherhood has its own printing press, transport fleet, bookshop, hotel, trading company and spiritual hospitals. The Kimbanguist

Church in Zaire, one of Africa's largest and most well known movements, has a university and a theological seminary and was appointed to the World Council of Churches in 1970. Some churches never make the transition from compound to cathedral. They prefer the intimacy of the house church model or do not have the resources to expand. At the death of the founder or leader, a movement may disintegrate and disappear into insignificance, as was the case with the Lumpa Church of Alice Lenshina in Zambia in the 1960s. The fissiparous tendencies and perceived structural instability of many of the movements are linked not just to the leadership struggles which occur at the moment of succession but are also attributable to the charismatic orientation of many of the movements.

It is precisely those features outlined above – rapid expansion, increased contact with other religious groups, pragmatic spirituality, freedom from external authority and the encrustations of tradition, confidence to choose and innovate which stems from independency – which have given rise to a new breed of new religious movement. It is tempting to employ the terminology of the Japanese context – 'new new religious movements', which distinguishes between the earlier and later new religious movements. It is not that the newer African movements are radically different, but rather that their new emphases and growing predominance constitute a new phase in the history of Africa's new religious movements. They are characterized by an orientation and outreach which is global, rather than African alone or linked to some specific ethnic group. While of African initiative, these movements draw upon an international repertoire of beliefs and practices, whether in the form of occultism, metaphysics, pentecostalism or fundamentalism. They are not necessarily founded in Africa; there are several cases known to this author of movements founded by expatriate Africans in the United States and then brought back to Africa (see Hackett 1989: 112–13). These are not just movements having branches in London for their expatriates as was the case with many of the early Aladura churches. These movements engage in international evangelism; their leaders have received training in Britain, the US or India, and make available to their members or clients resources which come from the world over. From their African headquarters these movements liaise with associates and branches in various countries; the pentecostalists and fundamentalists especially have an elaborate network of cooperation for preaching, crusades and revivals.

A good example of this new type of religious movement is the

Truth and Life Ministries founded in Calabar by a breakaway group from the Apostolic Church in 1978. Rev Dr A. O. Akwaowo, who is the current leader, traces the emergence of the church to a crusade led by the American pentecostal preacher, T. L. Osborn, in Calabar in 1976. In just over ten years, Akwaowo, formerly a government secretary, has built up a revivalist organization with an expanding international outreach. Akwaowo has associates in India, Britain and the US and goes there to conduct revivals. Initially he drew heavily on literature from the Osborn ministry, but now has established his own television, radio, cassette and literature ministry in Calabar. He has links with a number of similar evangelists and organizations in Nigeria and Ghana.

Also in Nigeria is the Church of God Mission, a religious organization well known to Nigerians and many others because of its very charismatic and controversial founder and leader – Benson Idahosa.[9] Following training by the All Nations for Christ Bible Institute, Idahosa set up his own ministry. With assistance from the PTL Ministry of Jim and Tammy Bakker, he established Nigeria's first religious broadcasting station at Benin City. (It has not broadcast to date, due to the ban on religious broadcasting.) Idahosa leads mass crusades in a number of countries, as far away as Australia. His flamboyant preaching addresses local needs and aspirations, couched in well-honed revivalist techniques. The Deliverance Church, probably one of the largest independent and indigenous pentecostal churches in Kenya, with several branches in Uganda, in association with the Morris Cerrullo Ministries in California, has plans to establish direct satellite links with a number of countries worldwide to broadcast their revivals. Some of the older movements have been influenced by this internationalization process as is often reflected in their titles: Celestial Church of Christ Worldwide, Cross of Christ World Ministry, etc. The Brotherhood of the Cross and Star embarks on annual overseas evangelism to Britain and the US, publicizing their meetings with church leaders and civic dignitaries. The founder of the Cross of Christ World Ministry in Ibadan, Dr V. Oluwo, informed me that he aspires for his church to become like the Cathedral of Tomorrow of Rex Humbard in Akron, Ohio.

Developments and Transformations

As stated earlier, American and British pentecostalist churches were influential in the formation of some of the first Aladura churches in Nigeria, such as the Christ Apostolic Church; Alexander Dowie's Church of Zion provided a model for the South African Zionist churches. One scholar even maintains that the essential elements of all independent churches are taken from the heritage of pentecostal and revival movements from the USA or Europe.[10] In this essay I have tried to show that these influences and links are being used and reshaped by the new type of religious movement. Their appeal lies in the type of multi-media religion they provide – camp meetings, revivals, crusades, inspirational literature, radio and television ministries, door-to-door, ferry, ship and bus evangelism. This assures reception of the message by different social groups. It also demonstrates an ability to appeal to both individual experience through personal conversion and soteriological discourse, as well as collective experience through the mass media and the mass revival. Aside from the form and techniques of this type of religious expression, the this-worldly, pragmatic content (success, healing, miracles, blessings) lends itself to an urban population, notably its aspiring youth. The latter are particularly drawn by the 'modern' and international orientation of the movements and the opportunities for travel, training and upward mobility. Another important factor is the inter-denominational or non-denominational emphasis of many of the movements and the ecumenical cooperation they demonstrate – shared preachers, literature, music, etc. This is significant given the perceived factionalism of Christianity.

Critics of these movements see them as manifestations of American religious and cultural imperialism and as bearing little continuity with African tradition. Their gospel of prosperity and miracles of materialism are heavily criticized by many of the mainline churches. Governments view their capacity to mobilize the masses and commandeer the air waves with growing concern (in Uganda, for example, there has been a curtailing of the activities of many evangelists). The media ridicule the multiplication of movements and the charlatanism of the protagonists.

In considering the implications of Africa's new religious movements in general, it is important to view them not just as agents of indigenization or enculturation – interpretations favoured by theologians and many historians of religion. They must also be seen as religious communities emerging from the interface between global and indigenous forces at the fringes of the modern world system. They are not 'halfway houses' between traditional religion and

Christianity, but conscious and concerted attempts to reinterpret and reconstruct, through religious symbols and practices, the world which surrounds them. In the same vein, it is important to situate the newer African movements within such global religious trends as religious trans-nationalism. By this is understood religious movements which are not confined to or defined by national boundaries and which vigorously promote and cultivate religious internationalism. We have increasing evidence of links being developed between African movements and similar organizations in the United States, India and Europe, as well as with the new religions of Japan or the Unification Church, for example. This obviously constitutes a challenge to the earlier notion of an African new religious movement as autochthonous and hostile to external forces. The sheer diversity and complexity of new religious movements in Africa today defies the use of simple definitions, typologies and explanations. Geoffrey Parrinder's early interest in these movements and in African religion in general has served as an inspiration for many. It is our responsibility to continue to meet the challenge provided by the data on Africa's new religious movements to our understanding of the complexities of religion and society and their inter-relationship in the modern world.

NOTES

[1] D. B. Barrett, *Schism and Renewal in Africa: an Analysis of Six Thousand Contemporary Movements* (Nairobi: Oxford University Press, 1968).

[2] J. W. Fernandez, 'African Religious Movements', *Annual Review of Anthropology* 7 (Winter 1978), p. 195.

[3] My choice of the Ibadan context is also determined by the fact that, as a postgraduate student at the University of London, I retraced many of Parrinder's steps in conducting fieldwork on the Aladura churches from 1975–79 in Ibadan, Lagos and the neighbouring Republic of Benin (formerly Dahomey).

[4] Parrinder, *Religion in an African City*, London, 1953, p. 113.

[5] For alternative typologies of new religious movements in Africa, see J. W. Fernandez, 'African Religious Movements: Types and Dynamics' *Journal of Modern African Studies* 2, 4 (1964), pp. 531–549; H. W. Turner, 'A Typology for African Religious Movements', *Journal of Religion in Africa* I, 1 (1967), pp. 1–34; R. I. J. Hackett, ed. *New Religious Movements in Nigeria* Lewiston, NY: Edwin Mellen Press, 1987, p. 12.

[6] Parrinder, *Religion in an African City*, p. 115.

[7] F. W. Welbourn, *East African Rebels*, London: SCM, 1961, p. 148.

[8] London: Oxford University Press, 1966. See also Jules-Rosette, *The New Religions of Africa*, Norwood INJ, 1979, p. 222.

[9] See R. Garlock, *Fire in his Bones*, Plainfield, NJ: Logos International, 1981.

[10] T. Ranger, 'Religion, Development and African Christian Identity', *Neue Zeitschrift für Missionswissenschaft* 42, 1 (1986), pp. 44–68.

SUGGESTED READING

J. Comaroff, *Body of Power, Spirit of Resistance*, Chicago: University of Chicago Press, 1985.

R. I. J. Hackett, ed., *New Religious Movements in Nigeria*, Lewiston/NY: Edwin Mellen Press, 1987.

——, *Religion in Calabar: the Religious Life and History of a Nigerian Town*, Berlin: Mouton de Gruyter, 1989.

B. Jules-Rosette, ed., *The New Religions of Africa*, Norwood/NJ: Ablex, 1979.

J. A. Omoyajowo, *Cherubim and Seraphim: the History of an African Independent Church*, New York: Nok, 1982.

H. W. Turner, *New Religious Movements*, vol. I *Black Africa*, Boston: G. K. Hall, 1977.

——, *Religious Innovation in Africa: Collected Essays on New Religious Movements*, Boston: G. K. Hall, 1979.

12. CHRISTIANITY IN AFRICA

Adrian Hastings

When, some fifty years ago, Geoffrey Parrinder first went to work in West Africa as a young man, there was really very little at all he could have read on the subject of African Christianity. He could turn to some books on the subject of African religion and society by Edwin Smith and others, and he could read through a small library of missionary biographies of varying quality, the most interesting probably being those concerned with that eminent Victorian, David Livingstone. He could read books about education in Africa, such as the Phelps-Stokes Reports which were indeed largely about church schools, their impact and development. But between the missionary, his beliefs and institutions upon the one hand and traditional religion upon the other, there was nothing seen really to exist or to write about – beyond a paragraph or two on 'native agency'.

The Missionary Inheritance

The major works of the 1950s remained for the most part essentially missionary orientated. These were the carefully planned and at the time very useful four volumes of C. P. Groves, *The Planting of Christianity in Africa* (London, 1948–58), Roland Oliver's highly influential *The Missionary Factor in East Africa* (London, 1952) with its extensive use of archival material and sensitive relating of missionary achievement to other 'factors' political and economic, and Ruth Slade's *English-Speaking Missions in the Congo Independent State* (Brussels, 1959). However, three other books of this period were in their way probably more creative and indicative of a coming change of direction. Bengt Sundkler's *Bantu Prophets in South Africa* (London) first appeared in 1949, George Shepperson and Thomas Price, *Independent African* (Edinburgh) in 1958. Here for the first time were major and highly imaginative works of scholarship focussed upon African Christians. It was in a way with these two works that a new reality fully worthy of study was seen to exist – 'African Christianity'.

It is, of course, noticeable that these two books concerned African Christians who had rejected a missionary church and become, instead, leaders in churches of their own. Sundkler's truly seminal and wide-ranging work, though he has subsequently much revised it and in *Zulu Zion and Some Swazi Zionists* (London, 1976) notably modified many of its original judgements, established nevertheless a model typology for African religious independency still largely made use of. Shepperson and Price, on the other hand, concentrated upon the single figure of John Chilembwe, the Malawian minister and rebel. While Sundkler's themes were more symbolic and ritual, Shepperson and Price were demonstrating by the meticulous examination of one case study the interaction of Christian radicalism and proto-nationalist politics. To some extent the latter proved a red herring in encouraging half a generation of secular historians to interpret religious independency in overly political terms.

Could something genuinely describable as 'African Christianity' only then be found where missionary control had been formally rejected? Many then and later have tended to believe that the answer to this question could only be 'yes'. To the contrary, however, our third work of this period, John Taylor's *The Growth of the Church in Buganda* (London, 1958) described a third generation Ganda Anglicanism which was certainly Christianity but, equally certainly, African. The missionaries had largely withdrawn, at least at village level, but they had never been evicted. This was a church subject to a missionary bishop but in which the process of Africanisation, inculturation, or whatever you like to call it, had gone very far. Christianity was being reshaped for good or ill by continual interaction in the minds of villagers and the practices of village society with traditional religion and custom.

1960 was the 'Year of Africa' in which Nigeria, Zaire and many other countries became politically independent. It was the year in which the *Journal of African History* began. In every side of life, secular and religious, intellectual and institutional, a rapid movement gained momentum over the next years concerned to reaffirm and re-evaluate what was distinctively African rather than what appeared as a colonial importation. In reality, of course, the movement itself could be seen as a further step in westernization of a more sophisticated kind. If universities and schools grew immensely in number and size during the 1960s, they and the books they produced or made use of were expressions of current western convention: 'modernisation', the principal goal of every new government and social elite, permitted no other underlying model. Yet Christianity, in so far as it had been imported and was still controlled by white missionaries, seemed particularly open to attack, precisely because it did not appear theoretically as a necessary part of modernisation at all. The western missionary could be denounced as at once an anti-modernist in a secularly dominated world and as an arch anti-traditionalist in terms of African society. It was pleasing that he could be denounced on both counts. However, he remained, in point of fact, a very useful person to have around. He was seldom evicted, but undoubtedly in the field of religion more than almost anywhere else the pursuit of African identity in the 1960s meant a belabouring of the ideas of the white man and a preoccupation with what could be seen as authentically African.

It was, however, quite impossible to go back on the large-scale conversion to Christianity of many African societies. Instead the academic strategy was rather to concentrate upon alternative, non-missionary strands of the existing tradition. On the historical side this was possible whenever an African Christian Church had in point of fact existed for some generations, and especially on the coast of West Africa. Two major works by Nigerian historians should here be mentioned: Jacob Ajayi, *Christian Missions in Nigeria 1841–1891: The making of a new elite* (London, 1965), a particularly distinguished work, and Emmanuel Ayandele, *The Missionary Impact on Modern Nigeria, 1842–1914* (London, 1966). These and a number of other books, while admittedly based predominantly upon missionary archives and still unified by a concern for the missions as the dominant institution within the story, were able to focus across the missionary lens upon the African Christian community developing vigorously enough from the second half of the nineteenth century in the coastal towns and countryside from Freetown to the Niger and led by figures like Samuel Ajayi Crowther, James Johnson and Mojola Agbebi. James Webster in *The African Churches among the Yoruba, 1888–1922* (London, 1964) showed how much of this society moved into religious independency, but already the mission church/independent church divide could be seen as something within African Christianity rather than as, necessarily, something separating African Christianity from missionary Christianity. The most balanced of 1960s books is the symposium *Christianity in Tropical Africa* (London) edited by Christian Baeta from the proceedings of a 1965 international scholarly conference held in Accra and published in 1968. Stronger on the historical than on the contemporary side, it nevertheless straddles most of the frontiers and points the way forward for research in many fields.

The Independent Churches

While historical, often rather critical, studies of the missionary movement in nineteenth-century Africa continued to multiply, the focus of later 1960s scholarship was undoubtedly, however, upon the Independent Churches as a twentieth-century contemporary phenomenon. If African Christians had on occasion begun to separate themselves from missionary control already in the 1890s, and if there had been a great wave of African prophet movements in Nigeria, South Africa and elsewhere beginning about 1914, there was a third wave of religious independency (meaning Christian movements, or churches from which foreign and missionary control has been excluded), building upon those earlier foundations, which coincided with the coming of political independence around 1960. The scholar (generally still white) looking for an interesting research topic in the field of African religion at that time could hardly fail to be attracted by one of the almost innumerable new churches springing into vibrant existence in Zaire, Kenya, Zambia or Ghana in those years. This surely was a second turning point: 'African Christianity' was now, suddenly, a popular subject indeed but almost entirely in terms of the independent churches. The 'mission churches', despite the move to replace their white bishops by black, were easily dismissed as unadapted to the new situation and certainly uninteresting. Very little extensive research was done in their field while a considerable number of exciting and important studies were published in the other: Fred Welbourn and B. Ogot's *A Place to Feel at Home*: a study of two independent churches in Western Kenya (London, 1966) was an early example which provided in its title a theme which would be returned to again and again – here in an independent church an African Christian could really feel at home. It was followed the next year by Harold Turner's two massive volumes, *African Independent Church* (Oxford, 1967), providing for the first time a minutely detailed study of the history, teaching and rituals of a single body, in this case the Church of the Lord (Aladura). The following year saw the publication of John Peel's *Aladura* (London, 1968) and David Barrett's *Schism and Renewal in Africa*: an analysis of six thousand contemporary movements (Nairobi, 1968). These are but the best known and most widely used of a far larger number of publications continuing into the mid 1970s with Marie-Louise Martin's *Kimbangu* (Oxford, 1975) and the three vast volumes of Martinus Daneel's *Old and New in Southern Shona Independent Churches* (The Hague, beginning in 1971).

By 1975 there was absolutely no shortage of published material for the study of African Christianity but it was overwhelmingly concerned with independency and written by either liberal-minded missiologists or at least equally sympathetic sociologists absorbed by fascinating material, but little disposed to relate it with comparable sympathy to a study of the main-line churches. Perhaps Benetta Jules-Rosette's highly imaginative and participant study of the Vapostori: *African Apostles. Ritual and conversion in the church of John Maranke* (Ithaca, 1975) represents the climax of this movement. By 1975 anyway it was clear enough that while religious independency had certainly not run out of steam, it had not continued to escalate with the vibrancy of the early sixties. On the contrary, the main-line, mission-founded churches continued to hold the loyalty of the vast majority of African Christians. There was, indeed, a very real danger that the exciting new opening of the 1960s would in terms of scholarship produce a quite unbalanced and one-sided picture of the subject as a whole, and especially for the less observant reader at a distance who would only too easily be nourished on a menu of Barrett, Welbourn, Turner and Sundkler and not unnaturally take *pars pro toto*.

Modern African Christianity

The 1970s witnessed a not wholly adequate effort to redress the balance. Fifteen years or so after the coming of political independence it was time enough to examine the way in which the main churches of Africa – Roman Catholic, Anglican, Lutheran, Methodist or Presbyterian – had responded to the challenge of the post-colonial era. In many of them a missionary presence had sharply declined, whilst indigenous clergy had increased. All of them were continuing to grow. Some of them were closely intertwined with the central political life and struggles of the era of independence. In the colonial ethos the mission churches had been institutionally central, the independent churches socially marginal. It seemed at times in the early sixties that this pattern might, partially at least, be reversed. By the mid-seventies that had proved not to be the case, with one or two possible exceptions. But while the public allegiance of the elite to the mission-founded churches had hardly diminished and at a high level the ecclesiastical structure had changed rather little (a black archbishop now residing where formerly lived a white, just as a black president had replaced a white governor), at the level of popular village and township religion things were definitely different. Here the number of church adherents had greatly multiplied and the framework of pastoral discipline established by the early missionaries, but already under great strain by the 1950s, had considerably collapsed. The integration in belief, piety, the care of the sick and the performance of rites of passage of the Christian and the traditional had proceeded apace and ever more publicly within the lives of churchgoers. Much that was formerly hidden was now acknowledged quite openly. The Christian life of many a local church community, Catholic or Protestant, was far less different from that of many an independent church than on paper might seem possible.

The academic or religious observer concerned to understand African Christianity in the 1970s was conscious of a need to reintegrate a good many diverse strands. The preoccupation with independency was not to be abandoned, but it had to be reined in within a wider interpretative whole. It had flourished especially with a phenomenological approach which had been rather weak in terms of history and the wider context of politics and economics. From this point of view it had for the most part lacked a good deal of the detached objectivity and social contextualisation which the latter-day school of mission history had achieved. An early collaborative fruit of this renewed resolve to integrate history and contemporary observation, mission and independency, within a single framework is to be found in the symposium edited by Terence Ranger and John Weller, *Themes in the Christian History of Central Africa* (London, 1975).

The same year a large international conference was held in Jos, Nigeria, (September 1975) to re-examine modern African Christianity as a whole. It was the follow-up to a considerable series of seminars which had been held over the previous two years at the School of Oriental and African Studies, London, and elsewhere. The publication of a selection of its papers in a 600-page volume, *Christianity in Independent Africa*, ed. Edward Fashole-Luke, Richard Gray and others (London, 1978) provided a massive source book, an almost adequate collection of materials for the examination at undergraduate level of contemporary African Christianity. As I was very closely involved in the organisation of this three-year programme both at SOAS and at Jos, it was suggested that I should write a more unitive approach to the subject. This I did, rapidly and thematically, in *African Christianity* (London, 1976) and, more slowly and chronologically, in *A History of African Christianity 1950–75* (Cambridge, 1979). At much the same time, John McCracken's *Politics and Christianity in Malawi 1875–1940* (Cambridge, 1977) achieved for a single area and the pre-second world war period what the Jos conference was attempting for the post-independence era: a resolute overcoming of the temptation to study African independent churches or, wider still, 'New Religious Movements' within a sort of ecclesiastical, religious and even secular vacuum; equally to go on writing any sort of mission history at all. African Christian history had, and has, instead to be treated as a single study, including on the one side prophets, healers and their followers, on the other the continuing impact of some foreign missionaries, but focussing above all upon what is central to the larger churches and society as a whole.

All this (and, of course, far more has been published than can be referred to here: the pages of the *Journal of Religion in Africa*, begun in 1967, reveal a great deal of work of the last twenty years) was still only a beginning which needed a great deal of detailed follow-up in regional studies. Unfortunately, on the contrary, the 1980s have seen a considerable falling away in major published work in this as in most other sides of Africanist scholarship. Conditions for field research are often simply too difficult; money is far harder to come by; almost all interested departments in African universities are under great strain and suffering from both a continuing brain drain and the absence of at all adequate funding for their libraries. While quite a number of very interesting PhD theses have in fact been written in this period, publishers are much less interested in works in this field than they were fifteen years ago and therefore research remains mostly unpublished. Hence while there has been a recognisable advance in both interest and publication in this field in South Africa (which, until recently, lagged intellectually well behind in terms of a concern for what is African rather than for the missionary), elsewhere there has been too little observable progress since 1980.

Recent Developments

If African Christianity is being less written about, it is not being the less lived. On the contrary. The numerical and even institutional growth of the churches (as of Islam) responding to the overall growth of the general population and the increasing disappearance of pockets of 'pure' traditional religion, continues unabated. In Africa south of the equator (and in many areas north of the equator too) Christianity is almost everywhere, apart from the high Muslim density of much of the east coast, now in some sense a majority religion. Countries like Zaire, Zambia and Zimbabwe are essentially Christian countries. This is not a matter, primarily, of personal conversion or norms of behaviour, but of the public reference points and self-identity of a society and its culture. This massive social conversion has certainly been made easier by the way in which Christianity was largely able to take over (or indeed may be taken over by) traditional religion. In the minds of many people there are undoubtedly deep conflicts engendered by perceived differences of belief and moral permissibility, but still more important are the continuities, less formally presented but undoubtedly there, even if at times they may be continuities of misunderstanding. Black Africa today is totally inconceivable apart from the presence of Christianity, a presence which a couple of generations ago could still be not unreasonably dismissed as fundamentally marginal and a mere subsidiary aspect of colonialism.

All this means that the subject of African Christianity is an immensely important one, both for the understanding of the present and future of modern Africa and for an understanding of the world Christian Church today in which its African branch is becoming one of the most lively and prolific, while the specifically Religious Studies dimension of its appeal lies in the exploration of a range of ambiguities in relationship between two large traditions. This makes the scarcity of major publications or even large research projects since 1980 all the more serious (Nigeria remains the principal exception). It is painful how often work published fresh today actually turns out to be based on research done more than a decade ago, and symposia published as new volumes consist of articles themselves largely published many years ago. This is by no means a characteristic of African religious scholarship only, but is in large measure true of almost every side of African social research; nor is it only true for Africa – the research opportunities and resources have almost everywhere diminished. The 1960s were a golden age for the venturesome academic; the 1980s were not. Nevertheless the effect of this on the study and understanding of African Christianity can be particularly serious as it was so very much a new study and of a largely new phenomenon, a study only just getting healthily under way when it was so considerably cut short. Hence there is in fact a poverty of adequate published literature, especially of literature which had absorbed the implications of the advance in perception of the subject as a whole, partially achieved in the 1970s.

Perhaps the most weighty contribution made principally by outsiders in the 1980s is a number of studies of the contemporary, or near contemporary, political dimension of the subject. Much of this has been done, or at least guided, by Scandinavians. One can think here of David Westerlund's *Ujamaa na Dini* (Stockholm, 1980), Per Frostin's *Liberation Theology in Tanzania and South Africa* (Lund, 1988) and *Church and State in Zimbabwe*, ed Carl Hallencreutz and Ambrose Moyo (Zimbabwe, 1988) among others. Of course these major academic studies simply reflect the fact that the relationship of Christianity and politics, church and state in a wide sense, is now central to the subject of African Christianity as it is to that of African politics. A key document here, and by far the best known single expression of African Christianity of recent years, is the *Kairos* document produced by a group of South African theologians in 1985.

Still more significant is the increase of published works of a more theological kind deriving from African Christians, books such as F Eboussi Boulaga, *Christianity Without Fetishes* (New York, 1984), Emmanuel Milingo, *The World in between* (London, 1984), Charles Nyamiti, *Christ as our Ancestor* (Zimbabwe, 1984) and Jean-Marc Ela *My Faith as an African* (New York and London, 1988). Most of these writers are Catholic priests and such books, providing a far more extensive available interpretation of the African Christian predicament by Africans than existed previously, must come to constitute a large part of our subject. But here again, as with the church-state studies, the focus has moved away from Independency and back to the life and problems of the main-line churches, the Roman Catholic particularly.

It would, however, be a mistake to think that further historical study and research is not greatly needed over a very wide range of areas.

What is most required at present seems to be a serious of new publications based on archival research, personal experience and field work and focussing, regionally or locally, on mission-founded Christian churches in the periods 1920–50 and 1970–90. Nearly all the best histories of the early years tail off around the first world war when – for most of the continent – the Christian churches were still extremely small if they existed at all outside the missionary's immediate circle. The years before 1950 were in many ways formative, but extraordinarily little has been written about them. Again while – as we have seen – there was a good deal of writing in the decade following the coming of political independence, research has declined since 1970 while the subject has burgeoned. Scholarship and publication may be seen as luxuries which a church going through what may well be described as a long 'dark tunnel' (as I have suggested to be the case in my recently published *African Catholicism,* London, 1989) can barely afford, it may also be claimed that they are necessities which a thoughtful church must afford. But scholars are unwise to trust in the patronage of bishops. The excitement of the subject of African Christianity and the complexity of interactions between two religious traditions is simply well worth exploring in itself. It cannot be done without a good sense of history, a good deal of sympathy alike for white missionaries and black converts and clergy, a common human predicament in which the blind are leading the lame, if in the most well-intentioned way. Above all it cannot be done without a considerable grip both upon the flexible subtleties of African cosmologies and upon the hardly less flexible subtleties of Christian theology. Without a sense of both, for instance, the work and trials of Archbishop Milingo for one cannot begin to be understood.

As published scholarship, then, this is a subject which has grown almost from nothing in the last 35 years. It has expanded, turned this way and that, matured a great deal but come also to a considerable extent, and largely for extraneous reasons, to a partial impasse. We look forward to Bengt Sundkler's *opus magnum,* a history of Christianity in Africa over almost two thousand years to be published by Cambridge University Press in a year or two and finally to replace Groves' work of the 1950s. That should certainly be a help in charting an overall map of our subject, but it will be a map with many empty spaces waiting to be filled by a new generation of African scholars, able in the 1990s to probe both the vast growth of the twentieth century and the many still unexplored roots of earlier years.

SUGGESTED READING

D. Barrett, *Schism and Renewal in Africa,* Nairobi: OUP, 1968.

E. Fashole-Luke, R. Gray et al, eds, *Christianity in Independent Africa,* London: Rex Collings, 1978.

P. Frostin, *Liberation Theology in Tanzania and Sout Africa,* Lund: Lund University Press, 1988.

A. Hastings, *A History of African Christianity 1950–75,* Cambridge: CUP, 1979.

——, *African Catholicism,* London: SCM, 1989.

B. Sundkler, *Zulu Sion and some Swazi Zionists,* London: OUP, 1976.

13. ISLAM IN SUB-SAHARAN AFRICA

Peter B. Clarke

Background: Islam's Recent Development

By comparison with its previous long history there of over one thousand years Islam has made rapid progress in sub-Saharan Africa during the twentieth century and particularly during the past quarter of a century. In Eastern Africa where at the beginning of this century it was largely confined to the coastal areas and to Arab and Persian traders, Islam has penetrated inland and secured an ever increasing following, especially in Tanzania. In Western Africa also where for many centuries it was the religion of court and commerce and of the inhabitants of the towns, leaving the rural areas virtually untouched, Islam has made great strides in recent times in the hinterland.

Moreover, areas once classified by colonial regimes as 'pagan' and/or non-Muslim, such as the southern region of the Ivory coast, had a sizeable Muslim presence by the end of the second world war and growth has continued since. And Nigerian towns such as Lagos and Ibadan, whose populations are to be numbered in millions, are now predominantly Muslim. Although the pace of development has been variable, there is no country in either Eastern or Western Africa where Islam has not made progress during the past thirty years and this is true also of the Nilotic Sudan, Malawi and South Africa.

With this brief sketch of its progress as background we can consider the headway made in the study of Islam in sub-Saharan Africa during the period since independence, *c.* 1960–to the present. The field is vast and much of what follows is necessarily selective, being derived largely from the writer's own limited field of interest and enquiry. There are more wide-ranging surveys available which can be consulted.[1]

Source material

Much valuable scholarly work on African Islam had been carried out prior to independence, including P. Marty's many regional studies, the largest and most informative being his several volume work *Études sur L'Islam et les Tribus du Soudan* (Leroux: 1922). There was also the first and some would say the finest of J. S. Trimingham's important regional studies, *Islam in the Sudan* which appeared in London in 1949, the same year as Geoffrey Parrinder's seemingly timeless *West African Religion* (London, 1949). While these and numerous other works provided a great deal of the inspiration and the references for much of the scholarship that followed over the next half century, we can look back to the late 1950s and the 1960s as a turning point in its own right in the study of Islam in sub-Saharan Africa. It was then that scholars and academic institutions began to give systematic attention to the collection of source material in Arabic and indigenous African languages which has facilitated much of the interesting work on African Islam that has been done during the past thirty years.

This kind of initiative dictated that much of the research on Muslim societies in Africa in the past thirty years would be carried out by social historians and linguists and we can point, albeit selectively for reasons as previously given, to some of the important advances begun during the late fifties and early sixties in this area so vital to any worthwhile study in these fields. Confining the discussion of source material to West Africa, both anglophone and francophone, there are numerous examples of invaluable work in the area of providing new data for the study of African Islam, and not only data but also directions that future scholars were to pursue to great effect.

On the anglophone side the contribution of the late Thomas Hodgkin was outstanding in both respects. In the early 1960s Hodgkin, as director of the Institute of African Studies at the University of Ghana, gathered around him in a collaborative effort researchers both Muslim and non-Muslim, European, American and African and started to build up a collection of documents on African Islam in Arabic, Hausa and a number of other local languages. Ivor Wilk's 'The Transmission of Islamic Learning in the Western Sudan' (in J. Goody, ed., *Literacy in Traditional Societies*, Cambridge, 1968) is but one example of such collaborative, inspirational and widely influential work based on source materials, both Arabic and indigenous, to come from the Hodgkin initiative.

Almost simultaneously the same kind of activity had begun to take place in Nigeria, at the newly founded (1964) Centre for Arabic Documentation at the Institute of African Studies, University of Ibadan. It should be noted that W. Kensale of the University of Ibadan library had begun this work in the 1950s and Professor

Abdullahi (H. F. C.) Smith of the history department at Ibadan did much to promote it. Smith, like Hodgkin, opened up so many avenues of research and encouraged and assisted so many younger scholars to probe and test the waters. Indeed both of these men did more; they held the ladder for others to climb.

Among the most fruitful of Hodgkin's proposals for further research was that much more should be done on seventeenth and eighteenth century African Islam and much more in the way of comparative work on French and British approaches to Islam. While a great deal of value has been done on the first of these two suggestions, the second is still somewhat neglected. Smith broke new ground more than once and here we will simply refer to his seminal article in 1961 on that 'neglected theme', as he rightly expressed it, of Western African Islamic studies, the jihads.[2] From this one article much valuable research has since appeared on the causes, aims, and effects of the Islamic reform movements in West Africa in the nineteenth century.

More generally it can be said that as a result of Smith's endeavours in this area, there is a much clearer picture of the theological and intellectual side of West African Islam. And while on the question of reform movements, the work of the American scholar Curtin also deserves mention for showing how such movements belong to a longer and wider tradition of jihad spanning several centuries.[3]

In 1964 Smith moved to Zaria in Northern Nigeria and there with the Sudanese Muslim scholar Muhammad al-Hajj among others began the Northern History Research scheme which has made a significant contribution to the collection of Arabic manuscripts now at the disposal of the historian of African Islam. Other Nigerian centres of documentation started in this period include Arewa House in Kaduna, which Smith was also instrumental in establishing. Another collection of Arabic documents at the Jos Museum, for which Alhaji Coomasie and A. D. Bivar were initially responsible, was started a little earlier in the 1950s.

In addition to the Arabic sources a rich literature has also been built up since the late fifties and early sixties in a number of indigenous languages, particularly in Hausa where Hiskett's contributions have been significant, among them his *History of Islamic Hausa Verse* (London, School of Oriental and African Studies, 1975).

What has been said so far concerns anglophone Africa and we can now turn to francophone territory for a brief survey of the developments there in terms of collation of documentary sources during the same period beginning with Mauritania, the cultural pipeline between the Maghrib and West Africa. Here special mention must be made of the work of Adam Heymowski at the Royal Library in Stockholm. Heymowski, with the invaluable assistance of such Mauritanian scholars as Shaykh Mukhtar ould Hamidun, has spent many years cataloguing materials in the numerous private libraries of Mauritania, some of them examined previously by Massignon, and many of them in nomadic or semi-nomadic encampments.

Professor Charles Stewart of the University of Illinois (Urbana/Champaign) has also made valuable contributions to the study of Mauritanian Islam. In addition to his *Islam and Social Order in Mauritania* (Oxford, 1973) these include the microfilming of the private library of Shaykh Sidia at Boutilimit. Other efforts in this direction have come from the University of Tübingen which in collaboration with the government of Mauritania has placed on microfilm materials in Arabic and African languages used by Muslims in this region.

The contribution of archaeologists in Mauritania, and the Sahel, has been impressive. Three names can be mentioned here among others: Jacques-Meunié on Mauritanian cities, Lhote on the Tuareg and Mauny on the Sahel (1961). While thinking of archaeological contributions to our understanding of Islamic civilization in Africa, reference should also be made to the work during the 1980s of the McIntoshes in the Niger Bend region. Turning for the moment from individual scholars to institutions, it is undoubtedly the case that the research initiated and guided by the Institut Fondamental d'Afrique Noire (IFAN) in Dakar merits special mention in any discussion of the sources for the study of African Islam. IFAN's contribution in this field will have to be limited to a very brief mention of one of its many achievements under the directorship of Vincent Monteil (1958–69) who was responsible for the creation in 1965 of a special section for the study of Islam in Africa. In that year IFAN published a catalogue of manuscripts in Arabic and African languages, particularly Fulfulde, and thus made available for scholarly research a rich collection of sources.

In addition to IFAN in Dakar and its several branches in other West African states, other documentation centres have been established in recent times including the important Centre Ahmad Baba de Documentation et Recherches at Timbuktu for the collection of Arabic materials relating to Islam in Mali. Also important for the study of Islam in Mali was the publication of the *Fonds Archinard* in 1985. A much older centre exists in Niger, the Centre Nigérien de Recherches en Sciences Humaines founded in 1960 which publishes a series of monographs in the *Études Nigériennes*.

Other important documentary and specialist studies relating to Mauritanian Islam include Norris's *Saharan Myth and Saga* (Oxford 1972), and P. F. de Moraes Farias's work on the early history of the Almoravid movement (Dakar: Bull. IFAN XXIX, ser B 3–4: 1967). Also on the thorny question of the impact of the Almoravid movement on West African Islam the Fisher and Conrad questioning of the alleged Almoravid Conquest of the Old Kingdom of Ghana in 1067 is of considerable importance. By making effective use of both Arabic sources and oral tradition it mounted the most serious challenge to date to the time-honoured opinions on Almoravid-West African relations based on what it saw as misleading interpretations of the Arabic material. Furthermore, this study makes an important contribution to our understanding not only of the early development, but also of the character of Islam in West Africa.[4]

The work of building up the sources continues, as does the equally important work of publishing the source material. Publishing projects are many, among them the *Fontes Historiae Africanae* which publishes Arabic texts and translations of relevance to Islam in sub-Saharan Africa. This was under the direction of John Hunwick for many years and the same scholar is editor of the important publication *A Bulletin of Information* (begun in 1975) which publishes translations of documents in Arabic relating to sub-Saharan African Islam. Other translations of note include the *Corpus of Early Arabic Sources for West African History* translated by J. F. Hopkins and edited and annotated by N. Levtzion and J. F. Hopkins (Cambridge, 1981) and J. Cuoq's *Recueil des Sources Arabes* (Paris, 1975).

The list of useful translations is getting longer by the day and we can simply note one outstanding recent work of this kind: J. O. Hunwick's edition, translation and commentary on the North African Muslim scholar Al-Maghili's *The Replies* (Oxford, 1974). This, along with H. I. Gwarzo's doctoral thesis 'The Life and Teachings of Al-Maghili, with particular reference to the Saharan Jewish Community' (University of London, 1972) is indispensable reading for anyone interested in the development of the reformist tradition in Western African Islam.

So far we have given some indication of the advances made in terms of the collection of source materials in Arabic and indigenous languages for the study of Islam in West Africa since the late 1950s and early 1960s. There are still, of course, many gaps and these are particularly evident when we move beyond West Africa to parts of the Sudan, for example in the Eastern region of that country. Although the work of scholars such as Fadl Hassan, O'Fahey, Lange, Lavers and Spaulding among others has helped to improve this situation.

Not only is more source material needed for the Eastern Sudan, but also for parts of the Horn of Africa, an area dominated by the works of I. M. Lewis and B. W. Andrezejewski, East Africa – Uganda Kenya, Madagascar and Tanzania – and also Central and Southern Africa – Malawi and South Africa itself. There has been little by way of a systematic attempt to establish a body of source material for the study of Islam in South Africa.

Specialist and General Studies

From the late 1950s, then, a body of source materials began to be assembled and despite its limitations, some of which have been noted, within a decade was providing historians and linguists with the tools to produce solid and interesting work on African Islam both medieval and modern.

Some of the specialist studies have already been mentioned and there is no space here to list the many works of scholarship of the past twenty-five years. Of course, it is not only the specialist studies that have been important. Others where the focus has not been exclusively on Islam have contributed enormously to an understanding of sub-Saharan African Islam stimulating researchers to think along lines they perhaps otherwise would not have entertained. J. Goody's *Literacy in Traditional Societies* (Cambridge, 1968) is an example, as are J. Nicholaisen's *Ecology and Culture of the Pastoral Tuareg* (Copenhagen, 1963) and H. Lhote's *Les Tuaregs du Hoggar* (Paris: Bulletin de l'Institut Francais d'Afrique Noire, B, XVII, 1955 pp. 334–70).

Clearly, there are several specialist studies in the field of history that have stood the test of time and become classics. Among these not already mentioned is P. M. Holts's *The Mahdist State in the Sudan* (Oxford, 1958). While the quality of the research is not always as high as Holts', other works have been important in advancing the study of a particular aspect of African Islam which, until they appeared, received very little serious attention. Abun Nasr's study of the *Tijaniyaa: a Sufi Order in the Modern World* (Oxford, 1965) comes into this category.

Political scientists – among them Coulon at Bordeaux, Copans at Paris, Paden at George Mason and Cruise-O'Brien at London – have been among the forerunners in opening up the study of African Islam in recent times raising for research and discussion questions of the nature of charismatic authority in Islam, Islam and economic and social stratification, Islam and secular authority and the place of the shari'a in the thinking of African communities. A number of these topics are taken up in D. Cruise-O'Brien and C. Coulon (eds) *Charisma and Brotherhood in African Islam* (Oxford, 1989).

Another area which until relatively recently received little mention and even less serious attention, but which constitutes a turning point, at least in this writer's opinion, in the study of African Islam, is the research done on Muslim communities in what are traditionally regarded as the non-Muslim areas. N. Levtzion's *Muslims and Chiefs* (Oxford, 1968) is an important landmark here. Other studies include *The Growth of Islam among the Yoruba* by T. O. Gbadamosi (London, 1978).

This emphasis on Muslim communities, also seen in J. Paden's study of *Religion and Political Culture in Kano* (Berkeley, 1973), is an important countertheme to the many studies that have tended to imagine an ideal Islamic community somewhere out there in empty space to use it as the exemplary centre with which all Muslim communities in Africa had to be compared and contrasted. One of the consequences of the latter approach was that little or nothing was said or understood about the logic or desirability of local interpretations of Muslim belief and practice, the emphasis in research being on whether this community which professed to be Islamic was really so according to the model.

Another consequence was the lack of interest in 'local theological' opinion, legal and educational practices and other important aspects of the religious life of Muslim communities. Of course, this is to generalize and forgets to mention that very interesting research which Professor Parrinder among others encouraged on the interaction between the different religious traditions of Africa. H. J. Fisher and Robin Horton have done as much as anyone to examine this question during the past decade and in doing so have inspired a great deal of fruitful debate on that most difficult and intractable of issues – conversion.[5]

To summarise briefly: What is available is some excellent work on sub-Saharan African Islam from the medieval times to the present, and this is the achievement of an international body of researchers. It should now be possible to produce a worthwhile general history. In practice, however, both the wealth of the material available and the gaps, some of which have been noted, make this an extremely demanding and difficult task. It is worth mentioning here that the gaps will undoubtedly be much fewer from the early 1990s when the multi-volume biographical and bibliographical work *Arabic Literature in Africa*, to be produced jointly by J. O. Hunwick at Northwestern University and R. O'Fahey at Bergen, become available. Meanwhile a periodical Bulletin is available from the former in which the preliminary findings of these two scholars are published.

Of the general works available the volume edited by I. M. Lewis, *Islam in Tropical Africa* (London, 1980, 2nd edition), is the most valuable. This is a work which is of considerable interest not only in terms of its content but also its methodology as it provides an excellent example of how one might set about studying Islam in Africa as part of larger process of social and cultural change.

Conclusion: Further Research

In terms of a change in the general orientation of research we can do no better than to echo Professor Hunwick who has rightly pleaded on more than one occasion for a more Muslim community-centred rather than Islam-centred focus; it should deal, he suggests, with living communities of believers rather than constructs however valuable these may be.[6]   As to those aspects of Muslim community life which might receive more attention, L. Brenner in London has not only singled out many of these, but also has already mounted an ambitious research project which promises to provide very interesting material on Muslim education, law, and medicine in the Western African setting.

But no one researcher or team can take on all that requires to be done. With regard to more in-depth study in addition to that already under way, a thorough study of the theological and social roots of contemporary forms of fundamentalism in a number of Muslim communities, and more comparative research on Muslim-Christian relations, would certainly meet a need. With regard to the latter area R. Deniel's *Croyances Religieuses et Vie Quotidienne. Islam et*

Christianisme à Ouagadougou (Paris, 1970) which covers Burkina Faso, formerly Upper Volta, stands virtually alone.

There is need, furthermore, to get away from treating knowledge about Islam as if it were the preserve of the shaykhs, and also for more study of Muslims from below. There is treatise after treatise on the ulama, the scholars, and little on the life and thoughts of the ordinary Muslim. Why does Sufism seem to exercise such a strong attraction for Muslims? Moreover, next to nothing has been done on Islam in Africa's social gospel.

Gender is another equally important subject that has been sadly neglected. Research on Muslim women in particular is required. Some work has already been carried out on Muslim women and deserves to be mentioned. We can point first of all to I. M. Lewis's treatment in his *Ecstatic Religion* (London, 1988, 2nd edition) and *Religion in Context* (Cambridge, 1987) of Muslim women in the context of the female possession cult known as 'zar', which is widely practised in Somalia, the Sudan and elsewhere in Northern Africa and the Middle East. Other important works on Muslim women include M. Smith's *Baba of Karo, A Woman of the Muslim Hausa* (London, 1954), A. Cloudsley's *Women of Omdurman. Life, Love and the Cult of Virginity* (London, 1983) and J. Boyd's recent biography of Uthman b. Fudi's daughter *Nana Asma'u (1793–1865), Teacher, Poet and Islamic Leader* (London, 1989) which might well prove to be something of a landmark, shedding new light on the role of African Muslim women in a world which, according to virtually everything else we read, was dominated by men. Finally, do Muslim communities in Africa have a distinctive attitude to ecological and environmental issues, to moral issues arising from developments in modern medical science, to secularisation, and to modernisation in general? All of these are matters about which we know almost nothing at all and which invite further research.

NOTES

[1] See for example J. O. Hunwick's 'The Study of Muslim Africa: Retrospect and Prospect' in C. Fyfe, ed., *African Studies since 1945; a tribute to Basil Davidson*, London: Longman, 1976, pp. 136–55.

[2] H. F. C. Smith 'A Neglected Theme of West African History: The Islamic revolutions of the Nineteenth Century', *Journal of the Historical Society of Nigeria*, 212, 1961, p. 77.

[3] P. Curtin 'Jihad in West Africa: early phases and interrelations in Mauritania and Senegal', *Journal of African History*, XII/I, 1971, pp. 11–24.

[4] D. Conrad and H. J. Fisher, 'The Conquest that Never Was: Ghana and the

Almoravids, 1076.I, The External Arab Sources', *History of Africa*, vol. 9, 1982: pp. 21–59; 'II, The Local Oral Sources', *History in Africa*, vol. 10, 1983: pp. 53–78.

[5] See R. Horton, 'On the Rationality of Conversion', *Africa* 45, 1975, pp. 219–35, and H. J. Fisher, 'Conversion reconsidered: some historical aspects of religious conversion in Black Africa', *Africa* 43, 1973, pp. 27–40.

[6] J. O. Hunwick, op. cit.

SUGGESTED READING

J. Boyd, *Nana Asma'au (1783–1865), Teacher, Poet and Islamic Leader*, London: Frank Cass, 1989.

D. Cruise O'Brien and C. Coulon, eds, *Charisma and Brotherhood in African Islam*, Oxford: Clarendon Press, 1989.

P. M. Holt, *The Mahdist State in the Sudan*, Oxford: Clarendon Press, 1958.

J. F. Hopkins and N. Levtzion, *Corpus of Early Arabic Sources for West African History*, Cambridge: Cambridge University Press, 1981.

J. O. Hunwick, 'Islam in Tropical Africa to c. 1900' in S. R. Sutherland et al., eds, *The World's Religions*, London: Routledge, 1988, pp. 470–97.

I. M. Lewis, *Islam in Tropical Africa*, London: Hutchinson, 1980 (second edition).

14. THE STUDY OF TRUTH AND DIALOGUE IN RELIGION

Keith Ward

Philosophy and the Religious Traditions

Philosophy is an important part of Religious Studies because it is concerned with questions of meaning and truth. The two main philosophical questions are, 'What does it mean?' and 'How do you know it is true?' Since most religions have beliefs as part of their content, we do need to know what those beliefs mean, and how anyone could set about discovering that they were true, or how anyone can be justified in claiming that they are true. Philosophers do not have to concern themselves with religion; there are many other sorts of belief worth serious critical attention. And there can be hostility between some religious attitudes, which resent critical study or analysis, and the Socratic questioning of grand claims to universal knowledge. Yet truth can only be advanced by clear understanding and the preparedness to justify one's beliefs as far as possible; so the philosophical study of religious beliefs is important both to religion and to philosophy.

The practice of philosophy in this sense has mostly developed within a Christian context. Though there have been major Jewish and Muslim philosophers, the theoretical analysis of beliefs has been of less interest in those traditions than the interpretation of the religious law. Christianity, with its very theoretical and Platonically influenced doctrines of the Trinity and Incarnation, has always had a strong inclination towards philosophical speculation, though it has been less receptive to the sort of critical questioning espoused by Socrates and by most post-Cartesian philosophers. Thus the philosophy of religion has mostly in practice been the philosophy of Christianity.

In the nineteenth century Hegel did write a large work in which he attempted to deal systematically with all the world religions; but the main impetus for this was to show the inherent superiority of Hegel's version of the (Protestant) Christian faith over all other religions. In general, 'other religions' were regarded either as masses of superstition or as inferior precursors of liberal Christianity, and so not worth serious philosophical treatment. In the hey-day of German-influenced Idealism, religion tended to be seen as a mythical or pictorial expression of truths about the ultimate reality of one Absolute Spirit, which could be better expressed in philosophical terms. Because it increasingly saw this, and was prepared to renounce old sacramental superstitions in favour of a more austere ethical monotheism, liberal Christianity was seen as the supreme form of religion.

It is only within the last century that, with a growth in the knowledge of world scriptures in their original languages and a rediscovery of important medieval philosophical works in Islam, Hinduism and Buddhism especially, it has come to be thought that even liberal Christians may have something to learn from other religious traditions. As the techniques of historical and literary scholarship seemed to undermine claims to biblical infallibility, and as philosophical criticism seemed to cast doubt on human ability to prove the existence of God, so it began to seem that historical Christianity was not, after all, on a much stronger rational footing than many other faiths. Indeed, the Hegelian philosophy itself was in many ways nearer to Vedantic Hinduism than it was to traditional Christianity. So the way was open to look again at the great religious traditions of the world, and to extend philosophical questions about meaning and justification to all those traditions, instead of confining them to the Christian.

Problems of Religious Truth

It soon became apparent that in many religious traditions similar claims to spiritual experience are made; similar reverence is given to the moral heroism and asceticism of the saints; and similar appeals to the authority of outstanding religious teachers are made. It began to seem arrogant to claim that one set of religious beliefs was absolutely true while all others were false − a position that has been termed 'exclusivism'. This view has been held by a number of influential Christian theologians, of whom Karl Barth and Emil Brunner are probably the best known. They simply assert that there is no way of knowing God except through Jesus Christ, so that all other religions are in error. But since other religions can say that they have the absolute and sole truth just as bluntly, there does not seem to be much to choose between them, as far as justification goes.

But it seems not much less arrogant to claim in Hegelian fashion that one's own beliefs are superior to all others, though the others might contain lesser approximations to the truth. What was soon called the 'inclusivist' view began to seem like simple prejudice in favour of one's own beliefs. Thus the Roman Catholic theologian Karl Rahner held that sincere believers in other faiths could be called 'anonymous Christians', slightly inferior versions of real, explicit Christians. This seems to be as misguided as calling Catholics 'anonymous Muslims', and this version of inclusivism has not found widespread favour.

However, since the faiths differ from each other on so many points, it hardly seems possible to say that they are all true, as they stand. Thus a serious philosophical problem is created as soon as one acknowledges that there are many diverse religious traditions, none of which has a clearly superior justification. It is not the philosophers' job to defend any particular set of religious truths; but they are concerned with the sorts of justification that can be offered for religious beliefs. Now if many differing beliefs can be justified on equally strong grounds, this creates a problem about the concept of truth in religion, since the concept of truth is closely connected with the idea of having some method of coming to agreement, at least in principle, about what is true. If there is no such method, there is a strong argument for saying that the notion of truth does not apply, that it must be renounced. One could, like many early anthropologists of religion, hold that virtually all religious beliefs are false; that, as Sir James Frazer put it, the religious history of humanity is 'a melancholy record of human error and folly' (*The Golden Bough*; abridged ed., London, 1941, p. 711). But some philosophers have gone even further, and declared that religion is not so much false as irredeemably irrational or even meaningless. The course of English-speaking philosophy of religion in this century was set by A. J. Ayer's provocative dismissal of religious talk as meaningless, in his beautifully lucid book, *Language, Truth and Logic*, of 1936. According to him, believers were literally talking nonsense, since their beliefs could not be verified by appeal to any available sense-experiences.

Of course, Ayer never seriously asked religious believers what they meant. He applied a ruthless test to religious beliefs – could any observations show them to be true? – which he thought they all failed. But his rather high-handed approach stimulated other philosophers to concentrate on the question of whether religious assertions do refer to observable matters of fact or not. It seemed to many that they do not do so in a very straightforward way, if at all.

Non-Cognitivist Accounts of Belief

Three different approaches to this question have existed, and still exist, in English-speaking philosophy; and they suggest rather different answers to the question of how different religions are to regard one another. First, philosophers like R. B. Braithwaite (*An Empiricist's View of the Nature of Religious Belief*, Cambridge, 1955) and Don Cupitt (cf. *Taking Leave of God*, London, 1980) hold that religious beliefs do not refer to observable matters of fact at all. They are stories or myths which recommend commitments to act in a loving way, or which evoke helpful psychological attitudes. Religion is not about the facts; it is about ways of life, attitudes and moral policies. Now if one takes that view, different religions will just be different sets of stories recommending forms of life which may be different in detail, but may be very similar for all that. For most religions try to encourage lives of love and compassion, of self-renunciation and inner peace – at least in theory. So this view encourages us to look beyond the boundaries of any one tradition of faith and see all the great traditions as culturally influenced patterns for particular forms of human life. It offers a great degree of tolerance between religions; for we can learn to appreciate them all, much as we can learn to appreciate different styles of music.

However, it must be said that, in another way, it is not a very tolerant view, because it says that all religious beliefs about happenings in history or about supernatural beings (like God) are not true; or at least that their truth is irrelevant to the real business of religion. This does not appeal much to most religious believers, who tend to think their beliefs are true. These philosophers – the non-cognitivists – have to say that such believers (the vast majority, probably) are just wrong; and that is not so tolerant after all! So when Don Cupitt argues that Christianity and Buddhism can come together in a fruitful alliance, what he means is that their stories, which are literally false, outline helpfully complementary ways of life. And that does not please most Christians and Buddhists very much. These views seem very helpful to religious dialogue; but only on their own terms, after all.

Religions as Forms of Life

A second sort of interpretation of religious beliefs is provided by thinkers like Ian Ramsey (cf. *Religious Language*, London, 1957) and D. Z. Phillips, utilising some of the later work of Wittgenstein. On this view, one must not try to make the meaning of religious assertions conform to some *a priori* criterion of meaning like Ayer's verification principle. The meaning of an assertion or class of assertions is to be discovered by seeing how such assertions are actually used, within various forms of human life. Religion can be seen as a specific form of life, including ritual activity, worship and prayer; and religious language has a specific use or function within such forms of life. This function is to be neither straightforwardly fact-stating nor wholly prescriptive. Religious terms are cognitive; they do state facts of a sort; but not empirical facts.

So Ramsey proposes that religious language is rooted in certain sorts of situation, which it tries to express and evoke in others. He calls these 'disclosure-situations', and describes them as situations in which, as well as all the observable features one can apprehend, there is an indescribable 'more', a sense of an inexpressible reality which evokes in us a total commitment to respond by living in a certain way. When we say, 'God is Love', we mean that in situations of human love, we may come to apprehend a depth and significance which is cosmic in scope, and draws from us a commitment to love in response. We are not saying that there is some metaphysical being, God, who has a set of properties including that of being loving. We are saying that a sense of the inexpressible is conveyed to us which evokes love from us, as an appropriate response to the complex reality which we confront in all our experience. Even to try to describe it in these words changes the meaning subtly; and really the only way to see what sort of reality this is, is to use religious language. The language is untranslatable into any other terms; it means what it means; and to know what that is, is to participate in a particular religious form of life.

D. Z. Phillips amplifies this account, stressing that there is no way of justifying religious language in factual, metaphysical or even non-religious moral terms. To understand the meaning, we have to understand the use; and we cannot do that without participating in the appropriate form of life. There is a cognitive dimension here, but it cannot be put in the quasi-scientific terminology of traditional metaphysics. To take a clear example, when Christians speak of 'eternal life', they do not in practice mean that they will exist after they have died – that, he says, would be absurd. They mean that they participate in a form of life which can only be properly understood from within, and which can be characterised as living in the light of eternal values, whatever happens.

It is clearly possible that Buddhists, in speaking of Nirvana, for example, are using language in a similar way, or with a similar function. So on this view, the different great religious traditions become culturally conditioned ways of responding to a reality which is not adequately describable in terms of scientific language, and which makes its own distinctive and irreducible sort of claim upon us. There is no way in which we can call one tradition 'true', and all the others 'false'. Truth is a concept which only operates within the language-games, the concepts and forms of thought which are defined by particular forms of thought. Metaphysical speculation is the great enemy of true religion, on this view, even though it often threatens to hijack faith and turn it into pseudo-science. Believers do not actually use their language to construct large-scale theories about the nature of the universe. They use it to cope effectively with selfishness, despair and loss, and to discern structures of meaning in experience which give their lives depth and coherence.

On this view, it is silly to try to say that one set of religious beliefs is true and all the others false, or to compare religions for truth against some supposed external reality which we can never match against our language. On the other hand, it is doubtful to what extent we can ever really understand a very different religious tradition; since we cannot participate in many very different religious forms of life at the same time. The 'exclusive' view that I am right and everyone else is wrong becomes impossible. But neither can I say that everyone is right. I must simply say that I cannot fully understand many religious beliefs and pictures; I do not use them; they have no significance for me. I can be committed to one tradition if it grasps me by the power of its evocative language, but I am not entitled to denigrate other traditions which do not regulate my life. A gap of understanding opens up between the faiths, and I can no longer say that they are false, precisely because I do not grasp their meaning.

Nor can I say, like Ayer, that they are meaningless; for they are successfully used, and there are criteria, internal to them, for proper and improper use. So religious assertions are not purely regulative or practical; they are also disclosive of something that cannot be put in any other way. Holding such a view of religious language, I cannot assert that only my beliefs are true. But I must assert that many others are unintelligible to me, and offer alternative patterns of disclosure and commitment.

The great danger of this view is that religions seem to enter ghettoes of intelligibility, closed to outsiders. And they become divorced to a large extent from other areas of human activity and interest, like science and philosophical speculation. Many religious believers do make factual assertions about the world – that they will live after death; or that there will be a final moral consummation of the universe; or that there is a cosmic law of moral cause and effect which ensures that good and evil will be rewarded or punished. The disclosure view cannot cope with such beliefs, and so it seems to apply only to a radically revised form of religious belief. That would be very ironic, since it began by seeking to ask how religious language is actually used, and it ends by asserting, no less than Ayer, that most believers are misusing their language, or at the very least are grossly mistaken when they come to give a reflective account of it. It seems that religious believers are only to be trusted when they are actually praying or worshipping; one cannot take them seriously when they come to give an account of what they are doing when they pray. This view, too, is not as tolerant as at first it may appear to be.

Realism in Religion

The third main type of response to the verification challenge is to meet it head on and say that religious assertions are fact-stating, even though not establishable as true by presently available techniques of observation. Richard Swinburne and John Hick (cf. *An Interpretation of Religion*, London, 1989) can be taken as major representatives of this view, both defending the necessity of metaphysics for religious faith. The word 'metaphysics' can be very misleading, and it is worth taking a moment to clear away some possible misconceptions. The word itself came into use when the editors of Aristotle's works wanted a title for some lectures that came after his lectures on physics, a subject that he virtually invented. Aristotle seemed to call the notes in question 'theology' – reflections about *theos*, or God. But they simply called them *meta ta physica* – the lectures after the ones on physics. The word stuck; and for many years it was taken to mean part of what Aristotle was talking about in those lectures, the first principles of being, or the ultimate character of the things which exist. P. F. Strawson was therefore right when he called any sort of thinking about the most basic character of the set of concepts we use to talk about the world 'descriptive metaphysics'. If you say that the world consists of material things causally interacting, simple and obvious though it seems, that is a form of descriptive metaphysics. And if you ask whether 'God' is one of the sorts of things which exists (whether there is a God), that is a metaphysical question.

It is in this sense that many religious beliefs depend upon metaphysical beliefs – they depend on saying that there is a God, or that there is an ending of sorrow, or that there is a Self of all. Part of the trouble with the word 'metaphysics' has been that people have thought it refers to some flighty and abstract speculation about realities 'beyond the physical'; so that to do metaphysics is to pretend to know a lot about supernatural realities of one sort or another. That is completely wrong; for any statement about what sorts of things exist – that there is a God; that there is not a God; that humans are free; that they are not; that there is life after death; or that we all die and that's the end of us for ever – all these are metaphysical assertions. We just cannot escape metaphysics, if we think at all. The only question is what sort of metaphysical views we have.

Swinburne and Hick have both defended the necessity of metaphysics to religion; and such questions are factual, even if we cannot decisively settle them now. Any realist view of truth – that some assertions really are true, whether we believe them or not – must accept that there could be factual assertions which humans, with their limited cognitive faculties, cannot settle. Hick has proposed that there will be an 'eschatalogical verification' of such claims – that after death the experience of being fully conscious of God would verify God's existence and nature. It may seem, therefore, that he must assert one religious tradition to be true, and the others false. Instead he has proposed 'the pluralist hypothesis': that the great religious traditions agree in positing the existence of one transcendent reality, and offering ways of overcoming egoism and relating to this reality in a life-fulfilling way. They thus offer authentic experiences of 'the Real' and valid ways of salvation. Where they differ, they either offer partial and complementary assertions about a reality that transcends all our concepts; or they differ on points irrelevant to the real business of religion, which is salvation by relation to a reality of supreme objective value.

Hick sometimes puts these points too strongly, as it hardly seems possible that all religious beliefs could be *equally* authentic when they differ so much. But he seems entirely right in saying that no tradition can justifiably claim an obvious superiority in truth over all others, and that all traditions fail to state the truth about ultimate reality completely or incorrigibly in all respects. Thus the question of truth in religion becomes closely connected with the existence of dialogue between religions, wherein each can learn from the perspectives of others and help to correct inadequacies in its own presentation of truth by being open to critical and constructive opposition. The great traditions all stress the ineffability of the supremely real, and the primacy of a practical commitment to compassion and selflessness. Where our most basic religious beliefs are bound to be more or less inadequate to the reality they seek to express, there is a necessity for dialogue which may lead to a mutual transformation of belief, as each seeks more adequate forms of expression.

The Need for Dialogue

In this respect, the work of Ninian Smart and Cantwell Smith is of major importance, in bringing us to see each set of religious truth-claims in the context of a wider global vision. Perhaps, as Cantwell Smith (cf. *The Meaning and End of Religion*, London, 1978) argues, the very word 'religion', when used to create opposed totalities of exclusive belief, is fundamentally misleading. We might rather speak of personal faith, as expressed and worked out within a variety of cultural forms and traditions, which are constantly changing and interacting in very fluid ways. A growing-point for the philosophical study of religion in this new context is analysis of the ways in which practical commitment and theoretical belief interact; of the very complex nature of metaphorical and symbolic language in religion; and the deconstruction of 'religions' as exclusive totalities locked in immutable opposition.

The philosophy of religion has come a long way since the terse three pages in which Ayer dispensed with the whole subject in 1936, and even Ayer more recently conceded that religions do propose *prima facie* meaningful explanatory hypotheses (though he still thought that they turned out to be empty on inspection). Meaning, justification and truth remain its central concerns; and I think it has become clear that if truth does not necessitate attainable agreement, it at least requires a self-critical and open dialogue between a multiplicity of differing perspectives which seem to be equally justifiable. In such a dialogue, one must be prepared for much change; and this is made easier by a knowledge of history which shows how much change has already taken place within each tradition of faith. It is also made easier by a practice of philosophy which shows how precarious and fallible our claims to truth are, and how ambiguous and multi-layered the meanings of religious assertions are. If this proves worrying for certain forms of dogmatic belief, it is wholly compatible with a firm commitment to the search for truth and goodness, to the demand to renounce self in love and compassion, which comes in response to our discernments of the supreme reality though the filter of our own cultures and systems of belief.

Religious Studies is good for philosophy, since it keeps alive the questions of ultimate meaning and value which are its lifeblood. Philosophy is good for Religious Studies, since it keeps alive the questions of truth and justification which preserve religion from complacent dogmatism. The discipline of Religious Studies now offers to philosophers a much wider and more informed base for the investigation of questions of meaning and truth in religion; and the most fruitful results are to be expected from the increasingly inter-disciplinary approach which is being adopted in British Universities. It may even be that forms of religious faith will change as believers take seriously the question of what it means to believe and of how such beliefs can be justified. Yet to the extent that religious belief is seriously concerned with truth, it has nothing to fear and much to gain in the way of tolerance and understanding from supporting such scholarly study of the whole phenomenon of religion.

SUGGESTED READING

W. Cantwell Smith, *The Meaning and End of Religion*, London: Sheldon Press, 1978.

J. Hick, *An Interpretation of Religion*, London: Macmillan, 1989.

D. Z. Phillips, *Faith after Foundationalism*, London: Routledge, 1989.

I. T. Ramsey, *Religious Language*, London: SCM Press, 1957.

N. Smart, *Beyond Ideology: Religion and the Future of Western Civilisation*, San Francisco: Harper and Row, 1981.

R. Swinburne, *The Existence of God*, Oxford: Clarendon Press, 1979.

K. Ward, *Images of Eternity*, London: Darton, Longman and Todd, 1988.

15. SCIENTISTS AND THE REDISCOVERY OF RELIGIOUS EXPERIENCE

David Hay

For a brief moment in New England, at the turn of the present century, a group of students appeared (including E. D. Starbuck, Stanley Hall, A. H. Daniels, James Leuba and William James) who believed it was possible to make a scientific study of religious experience. The school was headed by James and given credence by his Gifford lectures, presented at Edinburgh University and published as *The Varieties of Religious Experience* (New York, 1902).

When the movement finally collapsed in the 1930s, it did so in a welter of ontological confusion. The range of opinion on the nature of religious experience was, and continues to be, so great that it is hardly a parody to describe the poles of the debate as 'Insight into Ultimate Reality v. Insanity'. For the remainder of the century this has led to considerable problems in the matter of devising an acceptable methodology for the study of religious experience, especially amongst those of us who fancy ourselves as (somehow or other) working in the field of science.

Nevertheless, the work of the New England school presaged developments which have led to a change in the attitude of a number of contemporary scientists towards religious experience. In this chapter I will attempt to sketch an argument to show that the source of both the Victorian initiative and the current recovery of interest lies in the reclamation of a psychological perspective to be found in the traditions of Puritanism and more especially, German Pietism. The significance of this as a turning point is that the empirical data gathered cast doubt on the plausibility of a number of reductionist hypotheses about the nature of religious experience.

Subjectivity and Objectivity

As Clifford Geertz once remarked, one of the major problems in trying to write scientifically about religion is to transcend the tone of an argument between a village preacher and a village atheist. Pierre Janet, whose sympathetic but sceptical contribution to the study of religious experience in his book *De l'Angoisse à l'Extase* (Paris, 1926) has been overshadowed by the work of Freud, commented critically on what he perceived to be a lack of integrity on the part of religious people in their discussion of these questions. Freud himself once made the remark that where questions of religion are concerned, people are guilty of every possible kind of insincerity and intellectual misdemeanour. I am certain that he had in mind what he conceived to be the self deceptions of religious people.

But this problem afflicts secularist students of religion as well as believers. The world view of all investigators, their basic notions of what human beings are, 'have a way of combining with methodological and epistemic factors to determine what empirical data are sought, and how they are interpreted' (Peter Bertocci, 1971). Bertocci points out what may well be associated with this, the fact that Freud in his descriptions of religious experience hardly ever goes beyond what is necessary to prove his point, and therefore misses aspects which would be considered highly relevant to a believer. Thus, in his famous paper of 1907, in which he compares religious ritual with the ritualistic behaviour of obsessional neurotics, he asserts that, 'In all believers ... the motives which impel them to religious practices are unknown to them or are represented in consciousness by others which are advanced in their place.' This statement implies ignorance of, or perhaps simple disbelief in the consciously adopted purpose of ritual in assisting the increase of awareness, something which has been more widely realised in the West as Yogic practices have become better known.

There is probably also an affective component to be considered if one is to take an wholistic view of scholars as human beings with their own set of personal conundrums and private sufferings, rather than as disembodied 'objective intellects'. Taking the example to hand, although he had an extreme personal distaste for religion, Freud nevertheless continued to be interested in the psychodynamics of religious belief until the end of his life. His last major book, *Moses and Monotheism* (1938) is a strange and awkwardly written culmination of this, often interpreted as a work produced when he was entering senility. Nevertheless, its intensity and oddity has also appeared to some authors to signal the bizarre reappearance of a repressed religiosity in this great striver after the objective truth at the heart of human subjectivity.

It is the unquestioning belief in the objective correctness of their scientific preconceptions that strikes a reader who consults the works of secular critics of religious experience. Such a lack of fear and trembling may look very grand, but I find myself suspecting that it is more likely to be a masquerade concealing blindness. As Hans–Georg Gadamer has pointed out in his book *Truth and Method* (Sheed & Ward, 1975: 324),

> A person who imagines he is free of prejudices, basing his knowledge on the objectivity of his procedures and denying that he is himself influenced by his historical circumstances, experiences the power of the prejudices that unconsciously dominate him as a *vis a tergo*. A person who does not accept that he is dominated by prejudices will fail to see what is shown by their light.

Underlying this kind of obtuseness in critics of the notion of religious experience there is a grievous difficulty for believers, contained in the mainstream of the European philosophical tradition. This emerged most sharply in the eighteenth century with Kant's assertion of a distinction between theoretical and practical reason. Henceforth, the beleaguered student of supposed religious experience was faced with the notion that, almost by definition, there cannot be a 'something' available to be studied and possibly labelled as 'religious experience'. Roger Williams in his book *Schleiermacher the Theologian* (Philadelphia, 1978: 2) notes that,

> Kant is a major contributor to the dualism pervading Western culture, between the cognitive and the non–cognitive, between reality and non–reality. Reality has virtually come to mean that which is researched and experimented with in the natural sciences and knowledge is patterned after the experimental methods of the empirical sciences. Anything not an object in the physical sense is not real. Examples of such 'unrealities' include the humanities, man as an ethico–religious being, the transcendent . . .

By definition, the *noumenon* had become unattainable in human experience and hence the notion of religious experience became incredible.

Puritanism, Pietism and Phenomenology

The religious objection to this came, not surprisingly, from members of the German Pietist community, where the pivotal role of the conversion experience in the culture made it difficult to ignore the challenge (though one must note, paradoxically, that Kant himself was reared in the Pietist tradition). They were bound to protest about a claim which amounted to saying that God has no knowable reality beyond or apart from an ethico–religious postulation. Such a statement sounds but a short step away from Feuerbach's assertion that God is nothing but a projection of the ethico–religious consciousness.

At first the Pietist response, as for example in the writing of F. H. Jacobi (1743–1819), amounted to a bare insistence on the reality of personal religious experience which Kant had failed to respect, a claim for direct 'religious awareness' as an empirical basis for belief. Following Jacobi, Schleiermacher attempted the first full-scale defence of religion on the basis of direct experience, in opposition to the theological abstractions of the Englightenment which culminated in Kant.

It is not possible to enter into the detail of Schleiermacher's systematic exposition of his theology, but I take it that in essence his contention was that religious feeling, like all human feeling, is an original, pre-theoretical consciousness of reality. According to Williams, what Schleiermacher is claiming implicitly is that in making his propositions about religious consciousness, he is performing what would nowadays be called Husserl's phenomenological reduction. The starting point of Husserl's phenomenology is the human being in its pre-theoretical, pre- reflective intentionality, and if Williams is right, there must be a fairly clear line of succession from the pietism of Schleiermacher, via Dilthey, Husserl and Schutz to modern ethnomethodology, which by-passes or rejects the reductionism implied in post-Enlightenment science.

At the end of the century which began with Schleiermacher's defence of religious experience, Puritan New England produced another defender. William James' radical empiricism asserted that everything real must be experienceable and that every kind of thing experienced must somewhere be real. Contemporary students who are benignly disposed to James sometimes see his examination of the varieties of religious experience as a phenomenological exercise, an attempt to probe towards its essence by analysis of what it means for an individual to have such an experience. Again, it can be seen as a fore-runner of Husserl's advice to phenomenologists to examine the *Lebenswelt*, the world of immediate experience as given to unreflecting consciousness, in other words the bedrock out of which all sophisticated reflection and philosophising about the world takes its origin. Bruce Wilshire (1968: 179) notes that for James,

> the psychical event . . . is specifiable only in terms of that which is known by it, or at the most basic level imaginable, of the whole lived world. . . . To lose the sense of the *Lebenswelt* as the founding level of meaning would be disastrous for psychology, for James surely implies that psychology without the *Lebenswelt* has no valid basic conceptions with which to begin.

A second route-way to the modern phenomenological approach to religious experience also takes its origin from Schleiermacher, via Ernst

Troeltsch (1865–1923), Rudolf Otto (1869–1937) and the rise of the German sociologists of religion. Otto's teaching was to influence crucially the thought of several European scholars who, by their decision to live in the United States, brought about a direct physical representation of that tradition in America. One such was Joachim Wach (1898–1955) who had his scholarly roots in the ideas of Husserl, Troeltsch and Max Weber as well as Otto. His academic career in Germany was brought to an end by the advent of Nazism and in 1935 he settled in America, eventually becoming professor of the History of Religions in Chicago. Wach's influence in the United States was to add weight to the perspective which sees public religion as the social expression of a personal experience of the 'sacred' or 'holy'. Following Otto, he claimed that the most workable definition of religion is that it,

> is the experience of the Holy. This concept of religion stresses the objective character of religious experience in contrast to psychological theories of its purely subjective (illusionary) nature which are so commonly held amongst anthropologists. We agree with MacMurray that a great deal of our modern study of religion attempts to give an account of a response without any reference to the stimulus. . . . The basic genuine experience which we call 'religious' tends to express or objectify itself in various ways. We need a phenomenology of the expressions of religious experience, a 'grammar' of religious language, based on a comprehensive empirical, phenomenological and comparative study (Wach 1944: 13, 14, 15 *passim*).

Religious experience, according to Wach, is mistakenly taken to be a dependent variable, another form of cultural expression. Figuratively speaking religion (the experience of the Holy) is 'not a branch', but 'the trunk of the tree'.

In re-opening a perspective which permits the phenomenon of religious experience to be taken seriously as an independent variable, Wach recovered an American link with the Pietist and Puritan tradition which had been expressed and then seemingly lost with the declining influence of William James and his school. My contention is that the effect of contemporary phenomenology has been to re-legitimise the tradition of empirical enquiry into religious experience pioneered by this group.

The Methodology of Physical Science

The criticism by phenomenologists of the wholesale use of the methodology of the physical sciences is that the application of it to the human sciences engaged people in a spurious search for objectivity. Thus, Aaron Gurwitsch (1974: 80) writes,

> Contemporary psychology emulates the example of the exact natural sciences, especially atomistic physics. It dissects or decomposes psychic and mental life into well defined last elements, and, by means of hypotheses and inferences, endeavours to establish causal connections between them and to construct a thoroughgoing causal context which transcends what is given in immediate experience. According to Dilthey, such a procedure is fully justified and even necessary in the natural sciences, because the facts of nature as encountered in external experience are given as *partes extra partes* in spatial disconnectedness and separation, so that the connection between them – precisely because it is not directly experienced – must be established in a constructive way. This procedure, however, is utterly inadequate where psychology and the human sciences are concerned. In inner experience, mental life is directly and immediately given as a thoroughgoing context.

This distinction is surely correct, but subjectivity is inextricably bound up with the physical sciences as well. The philosopher Peter Koestenbaum has examined this question by comparing how we confirm public and private facts. He instances the following example. When I call a colleague into my laboratory to confirm that I do see what I think I see in an experiment, my belief that he has the same experiences as me when he looks at it, or that he, likes me, is a person, are reasonable enough inferences. But, says Koestenbaum, suppose my colleague has a surge of anxiety or a stomach ache whilst he is in my laboratory; though I cannot share his private pain or fear, I can explore my own experience for facets that correspond to the evocative words induced by his unhappiness. So, in practice, I infer that fact of his pain in a way similar to the way I infer that his experiences in looking at the experiment are like mine. Koestenbaum (1966: 312) continues thus,

> the difference between public and private facts is not absolute. Both contain an element of first person experience and of inference and construction. From this it follows that first person private facts, properly delineated and used, are facts in a perfectly legitimate and scientific sense and are open to the operations characteristic of the scientific method. If we condemn first people or private facts (a typical characterisation of phenomenological descriptions) as 'too subjective' to have any scientific significance, we *pari passu* condemn public facts. Conversely, if we accept public facts as *bona fide* facts, we are equally committed to acknowledge the existence and usefulness of first person facts.

Modern Empirical Research

So far I have attempted, very briefly, to trace one major root of contemporary phenomenology back to its source in the religious intuitions of Pietists and Puritans. My sense is that in important respects the influence of phenomenology has been to revivify and give legitimacy to a tradition of empirical enquiry into religious experience which itself finds its original motivation in the Pietist and Puritan branches of European religion. It now becomes conceivable that a researcher released from unnecessary constraints by this perspective could set about building up a cumulative set of accounts of religious experience. As they accumulate, it may begin to become clear that these experiences are not random, but are found to be amenable to classification and to have patterned relationships to other phenomena, including demographic variables and personality factors.

Something like this has indeed been emerging during the past two decades. It would be wrong to claim that most, or even a majority of those engaged in the revival of research into religious experience over the past twenty years or so have a sophisticated understanding of phenomenology. But the groundswell of the movement has, so to speak, loosened some of the rigid fences separating public and private 'facts' and permitted the broadening of the empirical realm to represent something like James' radical vision.

One of the component influences on this recent change of fortune is the work of the late Alister Hardy and of the Centre he set up in Oxford (Hardy, 1966, 1979). With his biological background (he had been Head of the Zoology Department at Oxford University), Hardy was personally convinced that religious awareness is natural to the human species and has evolved because it has survival value to the individual. This starkly functional way of referring to religious experience could be construed as reductionist. Such was not Hardy's intention; he was a deeply religious man and his views on the matter were not too far removed from those of Teilhard de Chardin, though he was critical of what he took to be Teilhard's failure to understand the scientific method.

The interest of Hardy's conjecture is apparent to those of us with a schooling in empirical science, because of the dictum of Karl Popper that whilst it is not possible to prove the correctness of a scientific hypothesis by the accumulation of data, it can be refuted by data that contradict it. Hardy's claim that religious experience has a positive biological function conflicts directly with the view of religion which sees it as a mistake, or as Feuerbach puts it, an 'esoteric pathology'. What has happened, almost by mistake, during attempts at the Alister Hardy Research Centre (A.H.R.C.) to examine the nature, function and frequency of reports of religious experience is the amassing of a body of evidence that must be at least contributory to a refutation of the 'pathology' hypothesis.

Here in briefest summary are some of the recent findings. A more detailed exposition is available elsewhere (Hay, 1987).

1. Theorists of secularisation sometimes assert that the steep drop in the numerical strength of the religious institutions in many western countries during this century is a true index of the decline of religion. Proponents of religion themselves are inclined to act as if this is so and, in relation to religious experience, feel that it is an abnormal, marginal phenomenon, something that used to happen a lot amongst medievals but is so infrequent today as to be insignificant.

The research evidence gathered over the past twenty years strongly contradicts this assumption; large scale surveys in Britain, the United States and Australia repeatedly come up with figures of between 35 per cent and 50 per cent of national samples claiming to have had such experience. In three in-depth surveys carried out with smaller samples by A.H.R.C., positive response rates have all been over the 60 per cent mark. The indications are that the considerable rise in the latter case is due to the greater rapport which is possible with people during a lengthy interview. They are more able to talk about what is a highly taboo subject; taboo because of the stereotype of people reporting religious experience as stupid or mentally unbalanced.

2. The anxiety of many people that their religious experience may be interpreted as symptomatic of mental illness has a sound basis in psychiatric literature. The American *Diagnostic and Statistical Manual of Mental Disorders* (American Psychiatric Association, 1987) includes amongst the criteria for diagnosing certain phases of schizophrenia, claims by an individual that they have felt aware of a presence, or that they feel they are being guided by God. There is however an uncomfortable ambiguity, underlined by remarks in the preface to the latest edition of the manual, where it is indicated that when such symptoms are reported by members of religious groups which sanction religious experience, they are not normally to be interpreted as diagnostic of pathology. To put it crudely, if it happens to people inside such a group, that is normal; outside, the matter needs psychiatric attention.

There is no need to debate the obvious proposition that mental illness can on occasion take religious forms. But again, the data from large scale surveys in Britain and the United States contradict the received wisdom. Particularly in Britain, where formal religious adherence is in any case relatively infrequent, a majority of those reporting religious experience will not belong to religious groups emphasising experience (such as Pentecostalists, Charismatics etc.). Yet the association between report of religious experience and good mental health is statistically significant both in Britain and the United States. Furthermore those reporting experience are on the whole better educated, personally happier, less materialistic, more concerned about social issues and probably less racist than those not reporting such experience.

3. Durkheim's theory of religious experience assumes it to be the 'effervescence' that occurs in crowded religious gatherings. It is debatable whether Durkheim has a truly reductionist intention, but at any rate his thesis is easily testable, since on his terms one would hardly expect religious experience to be reported very commonly in solitude. The evidence overwhelmingly contradicts this prediction; around 70 per cent of all accounts come from situations when the person reporting it was alone.

4. Deprivation theorists interpret religion as a compensation for suffering caused by some kind of personal lack. The most eloquent exponent of this view is of course Marx with his reference to religion as the 'sigh of the oppressed creature, the heart of a heartless world, just as it is the spirit of a spiritless situation. It is the *opium* of the people'. There is a benevolent interpretation of this famous aphorism, but taken in its usual sense it implies that the illusion of religion (and hence the greater illusion of religious experience) will be found especially strongly in the deprived sectors of society.

Once more, the statistical data contradict this interpretation. In Britain, the United States and Australia, it is amongst the poor and the badly educated that religious experience is least likely to be reported.

Conclusion

The figures quoted above refer only to three wealthy, western-style industrialised countries. A different story might be told for other nations, though secularisation theory would not lead one to predict less religious experience elsewhere. At any rate the data indicate that the major reductionist hypotheses tested are too sweeping and simplistic. When they are subjected to the straightforward test provided by a large-scale survey, which brackets out reductionist presuppositions and simply asks people to describe their human experience, the conjectures begin to look rather thin.

I hope that in my discussion of the re-emergence of a longstanding religious perspective in modern form, I have succeeded in working in the light of my prejudices rather than concealing them from myself or my readers. My bias leads me to suggest that the importance of this turning point in the study of religious experience is twofold. Firstly, it may help to clear away an unhelpful taboo that prevents people from integrating what appears to be perfectly normal human experience with the rest of their lives. Secondly, the data gathered, whilst they make the pathology hypothesis distinctly less plausible, do not make any statement about ultimate reality. But because religion is so often criticised on the secondary issue that it is disfunctional, it may be easier to set aside this distraction and get at the primary question of its truth claims.

SUGGESTED READING

A. Gurwitsch, *Phenomenology and the Theory of Science* (Ed. by Lester Embree), Evanston: Northwestern University Press, 1974.

A. Hardy, *The Divine Flame*, London: Collins, 1966.

———, *The Spiritual Nature of Man*, Oxford: Clarendon Press, 1979.

D. Hay, *Exploring Inner Space: Scientists and Religious Experience*, Oxford: Mowbrays, 1987.

P. Koestenbaum, 'Phenomenological Foundations for the Behavioural Sciences: the nature of facts', *Journal of Existentialism*, vol. 6, 1966, pp. 305–41.

J. Wach, *Sociology of Religion*, Chicago: The University of Chicago Press, 1944.

B. Wilshire, *William James and Phenomenology: A Study of the 'Principles of Psychology'*, Bloomington: Indiana University Press, 1968, pp. 179–180.

16. MYSTICISM AND RELIGIOUS EXPERIENCE

Peter Moore

The study of mysticism and religious experience has, over the last thirty years or so, established itself as a rich and important theme across the whole field of Religious Studies. This of course reflects the role religious experience has played in religious life and history as well as in debates about religious truth that have taken place within, between and outside religions. Few religions could have arisen or continued to flourish without the stimulus of some kind of religious experience, much of their authority deriving from the paradigmatic experiences of founders, saints and leaders. Many ordinary people report experiences of religious emotion or illumination, while some pursue practices associated with more specialized states of consciousness. It is worth emphasizing, however, that religious experiences also occur outside traditional religious contexts, and are reported by people with no formal religious beliefs or adherence.

There are several overlapping varieties of 'religious experience', the best known, and arguably the most important, being 'mystical experience'. This may be characterized, very broadly and in its own terms, as a brief episode or more prolonged state of direct contact or unity with a transcendental reality, experienced as the source or subject of a profound metaphysical knowledge or insight. Any more precise characterization risks presenting such experience in terms of this or that type of religious doctrine. In fact mystical experience is linked with many different types of religious doctrine, admits of a greater variety of detail than any general definition could suggest, and may well comprise significantly different types. While some would classify any intense religious experience as mystical, most have given this term a more restricted reference. Ninian Smart, for example, has insisted on the importance, especially for understanding different strands of religious thought, of the contrast between the 'mystical' or 'contemplative' type of experience and the 'numinous' or 'prophetic' type, the latter involving a sense of awe and creaturely distinction in the face of an overwhelming divine reality (see, for example, his *The Yogi and the Devotee*, London, 1968).

'Mysticism' refers to mystical experience viewed in the context of the ideas, symbols, practices, texts and institutions associated with it. For most scholars nowadays, neither their etymological roots in ancient Greek religion nor the evolution of their modern usage within

Christian theology prevents the use of 'mystic', 'mystical' and 'mysticism' as neutral descriptive terms equally applicable to all religions. If anything, mysticism still tends to be identified with eastern rather than western religions, and in more popular contexts (in many bookshops, for example) it is also linked with occultism and fringe science (not altogether inappropriately given the connotations of hidden knowledge and initiatic secrecy attaching to the ancient Greek terminology).

The Sources and Earlier Development of the Modern Study of Mysticism

The study of mysticism and religious experience established itself within the developing academic study of religion from three main traditions of scholarship – Christian theology, oriental studies, and psychology. Of these the theological tradition is clearly the oldest, in so far as mystics and scholars, in Christianity as in other religions, have taken an intellectual as well as a personal interest in religious experience and in the claims based upon it. Such interest, however, has naturally been defined by religious goals and values, not by the ideal of objective scholarship to which modern academic studies aspire. The study of religious experience in this specifically modern sense began around the turn of the present century, as part of a new psychological and anthropological interest in religion. Of the new generation of psychologically based studies the most influential was undoubtedly William James's *The Varieties of Religious Experience* (1902). Sub-titled 'A study in human nature', this book set a whole agenda for the psychological and philosophical study of religious experience.

The new scientific and psychological approach grew up within as well as alongside the traditions of theological study; continental Roman Catholic treatises such as A. Farges' *Mystical Phenomena* (trans. London, 1926) or A. Poulain's *The Graces of Interior Prayer* (trans. London, 1910) paid as much attention to the psychological details of religious experience as did secular studies like J. B. Pratt's *The Religious Consciousness* (New York, 1920) or J.H. Leuba's *The Psychology of Religious Mysticism* (London and Boston, 1925). Moreover, the authors of the new scientific studies, whatever their personal beliefs, could hardly avoid being under the sway of Christian preconceptions about mysticism and religious experience. Quite apart from the Christian ancestry of much of the terminology they used, their whole approach was based on ideas about the value of individual, subjective experience that owed something to Protestant piety as well as to the priorities of rational empiricism. At the same time the more free-thinking Christian authors adapted to their own purposes concepts and insights derived from the new science of psychology. A good example is Evelyn Underhill's *Mysticism: A Study in the Nature and Development of Man's Spiritual Consciousness* (London, 1911).

What the earliest psychological studies also had in common with theological studies was that both were based largely on Christian texts, which as well as being culturally more familiar were far more accessible than the texts of other religions. Where taken into account, non-Christian traditions tended to be assimilated to Christian models, even where the interests of the author clearly extended beyond Christianity, as did Underhill's for instance. In fact orientalists had been preparing editions and translations of non-Christian mystical texts, and writing about the traditions from which texts emanated, from at least the mid-nineteenth century; and as this work grew in volume it became increasingly difficult for even the most traditional writers on Christian mysticism to ignore the mysticism of other traditions. In fact it was often through their mystical traditions that non-Christian religions first made an impact on Christian theological studies. But the orientalists and historians of religion writing about the mysticism of Hinduism, Buddhism and Islam not only provided source material for those concerned with mysticism at a more general or theoretical level; they also worked the ideas and observations of theologians, philosophers and psychologists into their own more textually oriented studies.

The integration of theological, psychological and orientalist approaches can be seen in a new generation of works on comparative mysticism, such as Margaret Smith's *Studies in Early Mysticism in the Near and Middle East* (London, 1931), and Rudolf Otto's *Mysticism East and West* (trans. New York, 1932). The latter in particular is an important landmark in the development of the study of mysticism. Substitled 'A comparative analysis of the nature of mysticism', it attempts to formulate general conclusions about mysticism through a systematic comparison between the mysticism of the Hindu Shankara and that of the Christian Meister Eckhart. Not only comparative studies but also those dealing with particular types or contexts of religious experience, such as Mircea Eliade's *Shamanism: Archaic Techniques of Ecstasy* (1951; trans. Princeton, NJ, 1964) and *Yoga: Immortality and Freedom* (1954; trans. London, 1958), could hardly avoid relating their subject matter to general themes in the study of mysticism. J. de Marquette's *An Introduction to Comparative Mysticism* (New York, 1949) was an early attempt to give an overview of a subject now no longer automatically identified with Christianity.

Broader Perspectives and New Approaches

No other books have ever stirred up as much interest in mysticism as R. C. Zaehner's *Mysticism Sacred and Profane* (Oxford, 1957) and W. T. Stace's *Mysticism and Philosophy* (Philadelphia, 1960). Declared, without exaggeration, to be of comparable importance to William James's classic study, these two books were to dominate the academic study of mysticism for the next three decades. Each offered a complete theory of mysticism, based on a comparative study of texts from a wide range of sources. In their methods and conclusions, however, they were very different. Zaehner emphasized the variety of mysticism, offering an eclectic Christian interpretation, while Stace argued for the unity of mysticism, developing a new metaphysics of pantheistic paradox. Zaehner's book, despite its theological leanings, belonged in a tradition of comparative religion based on the detailed analysis of texts, whereas Stace's book was primarily a study in the philosophy of religion, its conclusion resting on abstract logical argument and metaphysical theorizing. Zaehner's comparative religion proved too tendentiously Christian for some and his theology of mysticism too syncretistic for others, so that the book's very real merits were not always recognized. Reactions to Stace were more positive, his overall approach and general conclusions finding favour even though his arguments were seen to be shaky and their textual support rather flimsy – perhaps because the book seemed more in tune with the spirit of the times. Stace's checklist of the main features of mystical consciousness would be widely adopted (often quite uncritically) as an authoritative criterion for distinguishing the essence of a mystical experience from its accidents, and a mystical type of experience from a non-mystical type.

Zaehner identifies three distinct (and for him progressively more valuable) types of mysticism: a 'panenhenic' mysticism of oneness with nature, an impersonal 'monistic' mysticism of the soul's own interior unity, and a mysticism of the soul's loving union with a personal God. For Stace on the other hand the evidence points to a single universal type, an 'introvertive' mysticism of paradoxically full but empty unity, though he does also distinguish an incomplete, 'extrovertive' type of the same experience. In so far as they agree that beneath the variety of mystical interpretations one or more identical types of uninterpreted experience can be discovered, and accept the distinction between an uninterpreted core of experience and a subsequently imposed correct or incorrect interpretation, Stace and Zaehner share what might be called an 'essentialist' view of mysticism. Their disagreements are about which elements in a given account represent the core and which the subsequently imposed interpretation, and hence about how many cores, or basic types, do in fact exist. For Zaehner, Stace and many other authors the task of determining how many basic types of mysticism there are must clearly be settled before one can use mystical experience as a basis for confirming or constructing any all-embracing theology or metaphysics.

The work of Zaehner and Stace formed a watershed in the study of mysticism; in the years following, few studies of the subject would fail to make reference to them. Their books were also among the last which attempted to address the whole field of mysticism in one grand theory. From now on the trend was towards more specialized and methodologically sophisticated studies, in line with the increasing speccialization taking place within Religious Studies as a whole. The volume of information and range of texts now available demanded, and made demanding, the writing of comprehensive surveys. The first comprehensive historical survey was Sydney Spencer's *Mysticism in World Religion* (Harmondsworth, 1963), which remained the only work of its kind until Geoffrey Parrinder's *Mysticism in the World's Religions* (London, 1976). In the long-established field of Islamic studies there eventually appeared the first overall historical and phenomenological account of Sufism: Annemarie Schimmel's *Mystical Dimensions of Islam* (Chapel Hill, NC, 1975). There also emerged a new generation of detailed comparative studies of mysticism, some conducted from the neutral standpoint of the history and phenomenology of religion, others (such as William Johnston's work on Zen and Christian mysticism) from a more confessional standpoint. But interest in mysticism and religious experience, although it remained concentrated in the twin fields of theology and Religious Studies, was increasingly evident in a variety of other disciplines too. I. M. Lewis' *Ecstatic Religion: An Anthropological Study of Spirit Possession and Shamanism* (Harmondsworth, 1971) impressively tackled the neglect religious experience had suffered in the social sciences.

It is easily forgotten that historical and theoretical studies of religious experience are based not directly upon the experiences themselves but upon the published accounts of such experience (and even where writers draw upon their own experiences these must in effect be turned into written accounts if their work is to be open to critical discussion). Published accounts have taken the form of traditional religious texts, modern autobiographical literature, and material gathered from surveys and questionnaires. Questionnaire techniques had been used in some of the earliest psychological studies, and over the years these techniques have been refined and applied within an ever greater range of contexts. Noteworthy examples of questionnaire-based studies from more recent years include Marghanita Laski's *Ecstasy: A Study of Some Secular and Religious Experiences* (London, 1961), Michael Paffard's *Inglorious Wordsworths: A Study of Some Transcendental Experiences in Childhood and Adolescence* (London, 1973), and Sir Alister Hardy's *The Spiritual Nature of Man: A Study of Contemporary Religious Experience* (Oxford, 1979). The last of these was one of a number of studies based on material from the Religious Experience Research Unit (now renamed The Alister Hardy Research Centre), set up in 1969 by Sir Alister Hardy for the purpose of collecting and analyzing contemporary accounts of religious experience from all sections of the population. The mere accumulation of accounts, however detailed, can never in itself answer the philosophical and theological questions such accounts raise, and not surprisingly some of the most valuable findings of questionnaire-based studies have been of a cultural or sociological kind.

Most types of religious experience occur unpredictably and apparently spontaneously, or to individuals following specialized religious disciplines in monastic settings, all of which hardly makes such experience amenable to close scientific scrutiny. For most types of religious experience, therefore, questionnaire techniques offer perhaps the nearest approach to any kind of systematic scientific investigation. In the 1960s and 1970s, however, scientific attention became focused on two types of experience – both closely associated with the youth culture of the times and both falling within the broad category of religious experience – over which experimenters, or their subjects, could exercise a degree of real control: some of the experiences induced by psychedelic drugs, and the states of mind brought about through meditation techniques.

Claims that some at least of the experiences induced by psychedelic drugs were akin to, if not identical with, the kind of mystical states described in traditional religious sources or in modern accounts were taken seriously by a number of scholars. Zaehner had categorized these experiences, along with nature mysticism and certain psychotic states, as instances of an inferior, 'profane' type of mysticism. Other scholars took a more positive view, comparing them with the more mythologically elaborate forms of experience associated with the ritual use of drugs in shamanic cultures. A number of experiments certainly demonstrated that, particularly in favourable surroundings, individuals taking psychedelic drugs could have intense religious feelings and would in some cases report vivid mental images of a specifically religious kind; but whether such experiences deserved classification as mystical states was more doubtful. The doubts were perhaps confirmed by the fact that the interest in psychedelic drugs was relatively short-lived.

Far more lasting has been the interest aroused by meditation, on which an enormous literature, both popular and scholarly, has accumulated during the last twenty years or so. In earlier years knowledge about eastern religions had been based largely on books written by western scholars interested more in the ideas than in the practices of these religions. But when teachers from eastern religious movements began establishing centres in the West, a range of practices loosely referred to as meditation techniques started to be practised and studied. For scholars and scientists as well as for aspiring practitioners, the attraction of meditation lay in its practical rather than its theoretical aspects. The states of mind induced through meditiation techniques, unlike spontaneous religious states, were susceptible to control and experimentation; their various physical and physiological accompaniments could be measured and compared with those of other known states. The claims made on behalf of meditation, though less exalted than those made in connection with mysticism, were nevertheless substantial. A good idea of the range of scientific research in the field of meditation if given in Patricia Carrington's *Freedom in Meditation* (Garden City, N.Y, 1977) and in *Meditation: Classic and Contemporary Perspectives* (New York, 1984), edited by Deane H. Shapiro Jr and Roger N. Walsh.

The term 'meditation' is somewhat misleading as a general term, blurring the distinction between two significantly different, though obviously related types of practice: on the one hand meditation properly so-called, which involves the systematic application of the discursive and imaginative functions of the mind to a chosen religious theme, and on the other hand contemplation, a state of unwavering attention in which the discursive and imaginative functions are suspended. Here again two terms developed within the Christian tradition are also acceptable as neutral descriptive terms within the study of religions. While many people have understood or practised meditation as something without religious or mystical associations, the fact remains that meditation techniques are historically inseparable from religion and mysticism, whatever the uses to which meditation techniques have been put in modern times. Their traditional and modern uses are usefully described in surveys such as Daniel Goleman's *The Varieties of the Meditative Experience* (London, 1977) or Willard Johnson's *Riding the Ox Home* (London, 1982), the latter being 'A History of Meditation from Shamanism to Science'. Winston L. King's *Theravada Meditation: The Buddhist Transformation of Yoga* (University Park, Pa., 1980) is an example of the more specialized studies of individual traditions that grew out of the general interest in meditation. The initial interest mainly in eastern meditation led on to a renewed interest in the neglected western traditions of meditation, and hence to comparisons between the various eastern and western meditation systems.

More recently a considerable body of literature has been generated by the study of the 'near-death experience', a type of experience involving both psychical and mystical elements which is quite commonly reported by individuals revived after having almost or apparently died. Although records of similar experiences can be found in various cultures and historical periods, the main impetus for the modern interest has come from medical scholarship, largely as a result of advances in medical technology. The nature of the near-death experience and of its implications for mysticism and religion are well surveyed in Kenneth Ring's *Life at Death: A Scientific Investigation of the Near-death Experience* (New York, 1980), while its historical and anthropological dimensions are explored in Carol Zaleski's *Otherworld Journeys: Accounts of Near-death Experience in Mediaeval and Modern Times* (New York, 1987). Research into the connections between mysticism and parasychology has been a fallow area in recent decades, partly following the decline of the old-style psychology of religion (William James, for one, was certainly interested in parapsychology) and partly because widespread prejudices against parapsychology as a scientific discipline have denied the subject much of an academic base. Two interesting attempts to interpret a variety of psychic and mystical experiences within one overall theory were R. C. Johnson's *The Imprisoned Splendour* (London, 1953) and Robert Crookall's *The Interpretation of Cosmic and Mystical Experience* (Cambridge, 1969).

The new sociological surveys and experimentally based scientific studies tended to subsume mystical, meditative and other religious states within the much broader category of 'altered stated of consciousness' which includes types of experience by no means necessarily described as having any transcendental content or religious significance: trance and hypnotic states, aesthetic and 'peak' experiences, drug-induced states, manic and schizophrenic states, and so on. Many new insights and theories emerged from the study of mysticism and religious experience within this wider perspective, which also helped rid the subject of some of the prejudices surrounding it. But the inclusion of religious states within so broad a category tended to obsure their distinctively transcendental elements and also led to somewhat exaggerated claims being made about the more mundane types of experience.

The demystification of mysticism at the hands of scientists and sociologists was sometimes echoed by scholars working in more traditional fields. There was a long tradition of regarding mystical experience as intrinsically incapable of rational investigation, a view voiced sometimes by those hostile to the subject and sometimes by those seeking to protect it from profane analysis. In *Exploring Mysticism* (Harmondsworth, 1975) the indologist Fritz Staal presented a sharp critique of several theories of mysticism and methods of studying it, arguing that mystical states are no less susceptible to rational inquiry than any other human experience, provided one is prepared to study them at first-hand. This book, with its two main sections entitled 'How to study mysticism' and 'How not to study mysticism', illustrates how complex and methodologically self-conscious the study of mysticism had become in the two decades following Zaehner and Stace. What was most significant, however, was that mysticism could now be approached as a subject in its own right. Robert S. Ellwood's *Mysticism and Religion* (Englewood Cliffs, N. J., 1980) has the distinction of being the first general text-book on the study of mysticism, attempting a rounded picture of the subject in relation to the various dimensions of religion. Of similar significance is the inclusion in a series on 'Issues in Religious Studies' of a volume devoted exclusively to religious experience: Peter Donovan's *Interpreting Religious Experience* (London, 1979).

Recent Developments in the Study of Mysticism

A new phase in the study of mysticism was marked by the

publication of two volumes edited by Steven Katz: *Mysticism and Philosophical Analysis* (London, 1978), and *Mysticism and Religious Traditions* (Oxford, 1983). These essays, although contributed by scholars from a variety of disciplines, embody an impressive critical consensus against the 'essentialist' view of mysticism, expressing in its place a more sophisticated 'contextualist' view. At its most basic the 'contextualist' view is that mystical experiences cannot be detached in any simple way from their doctrinal and cultural contexts, since such experiences, like any others, are mediated by doctrinal and cultural factors. Consequently the mysticism of one religion will inevitably differ from the mysticism of any other tradition, not just in the way it is interpreted but even in the way it is experienced. That a direct knowledge of God would nevertheless be a 'mediated' knowledge had long been argued by some philosophers of religion, notably by John E. Smith in his *Experience and God* (New York, 1968). Katz and his collaborators were now expressing this idea in the wider context of comparative mysticism, and in relation to every aspect of mysticism.

Just as earlier studies of mysticism had to take account of the theories of Zaehner and Stace, so in more recent studies scholars have had to respond to the ideas of Katz and his contributors. The great merit of the new contextualist emphasis is that it re-directs attention to the particularities of mysticism which some of the more theoretical studies had tended to dismiss as accidental to the main subject. In so doing it has strengthened the links between formally separate disciplines such as textual studies, history of religions and philosophy of religion. A perfect example of this, as suggested by its title, is Paul J. Griffiths' *On Being Mindless: Buddhist Meditation and the Mind-Body Problem* (La Salle, Ill., 1986).

The search for a universal essence of mysticism beyond the accidents of culture and history had gradually given way to an emphasis on the diversity of mystical experience and its interpretations, not least within the same tradition. This is not because there are no common elements within the different forms of mysticism (as clearly there must be for this word to have meaning) or no similar types across different cultures, but because it is only when set within its historically particular contexts that mysticism can be properly understood and appreciated.

The 'contextualist' view, although logically allowing for the autonomy of mystical experience, easily slips into the more radical claim that mystical experiences are actually the *products* of doctrinal and cultural factors. This more radical position is for some scholars all the more attractive in that it takes mysticism seriously as a cultural phenomenon, while absolving them of the need to consider the existential and cognitive claims traditionally raised by religious experience, and especially by mystical experience. To all but proponents of the most radical versions of 'contextualism', however, these claims must continue to impress themselves as trans–culturally coherent and important, even though they can no longer be examined independently of the contexts in which they arise, in the way many philosophers have tended to do in the past. The extent to which in recent years philosophers of religion interested in the evidential status of religious experience have responded to the more sophisticated phenomenological analyses of such experience now customary and to the far greater range of relevant textual and historical material now available is well illustrated in Caroline Franks Davis, *The Evidential Force of Religious Experience* (Oxford & New York, 1989).

The importance of viewing religious experience in the context of the doctrines, symbols, techniques and institutions historically associated with it is now widely accepted by scholars working in this area of Religious Studies, regardless of the degree to which their work is informed by specifically 'contextualist' theories. For the range of methods and materials now available not only allows one, but positively invites one, to take a wider view. But this wider view inevitably raises questions about the whole concept of religious experience on which so many academic studies have been based, as well as reminding us what mystics, theologians and other have so often insisted upon: the mysticism and the religious life are not just about individuals having 'experiences', but about changes in the whole structure of experience in relation to a religious goal. The intellectual sources of the idea of religious experience, and the implications of its uses in academic studies, are investigated in Wayne Proudfoot's *Religious Experience* (Berkeley, Calif., 1985). This fine book, fruitfully combining insights from psychology, philosophy and the history of ideas, explores questions about the nature and interpretation of religious experience in relation to more fundamental questions concerning the nature and interpretation of human experience as such.

SUGGESTED READING

Robert S. Ellwood *Mysticism and Religion*, Englewood Cliffs, NJ: Prentice-Hall, 1980.

R. K. C. Forman (ed.), *The Problem of Pure Consciousness: Mysticism and Philosophy*, New York & Oxford, Oxford University Press, 1990.

I. M. Lewis *Ecstatic Religion: A Study of Shamanism and Spirit Possession*, 2nd ed., London & New York: Routledge, 1989.

Geoffrey Parrinder, *Mysticism in the World's Religions*, London: Sheldon Press, 1976 and New York: Oxford University Press, 1976.

Wayne Proudfoot, *Religious Experience*, Berkeley, Calif.: University of California Press, 1985.

Frits Staal, *Exploring Mysticism: A Methodological Essay*, Berkeley: University of California Press, 1975.

William J. Wainwright, *Mysticism: A Study of its Nature, Cognitive Value and Moral Implications*, Brighton (UK): Harvester Press, 1981.

Richard Woods (ed.), *Understanding Mysticism*, Garden City, NY: Doubleday, 1980 and London: Athlone Press, 1981.

R. C. Zaehner, *Mysticism Sacred and Profane: An Inquiry into Some Varieties of Praeternatural Experience*, London & New York: Oxford University Press, 1961.

Part III

POINTERS TO NEW DIRECTIONS

17. RELIGION AND THE ARTS

John R. Hinnells

Introduction

Over the millennia the great majority of the world's religious people have been illiterate. Mass literacy is a relatively modern and still mainly a 'western' phenomenon. Many religions in various parts of the world include many non-literate people, the rural populations of India and Iran are but two examples of reasonably developed countries where this is still the case, quite apart from people in so-called 'primal' societies. Within the literate 'developed' societies numerous practitioners remain non-literate, notably the children. Only a hundred years ago literacy was not common in much of the known world. The implication is that if the study of religions focuses on textual sources, then it is 'plugging in' to a level of religion which most of the practitioners are not, or have not been, engaged in. Religious people commonly learn their religion not by studying texts but by practising it, not so much in terms of ethical practices but through various art forms such as the dance and drama of ritual, the emotional experiences of music and the inspiration of the visual arts. If that is how religions are transmitted, then surely the study of religions should have the arts not as a peripheral, but rather as a central concern. Historically arts are the earliest, or primary, means of religious communication since the palaeolithic cave paintings and artefacts long predate any scriptural sources. What I am suggesting here is that they are also primary in the sense that the arts represent a major form of religious expression in modern times as well.

I have to admit to a decided bias in that my original career was in art, specifically the visual arts of drawing, painting and sculpture, first as a student, then a teacher and as 'producer' on a free lance basis. Much of what follows, it must be said, is a personal and subjective approach to Religious Studies. It seems to me that the almost exclusive attention given to literary sources in scholarly studies of religions is ignoring the position of the practitioner in favour of the scholar's own intellectual bias. It is noticeable that in courses on religions the arts play virtually no role, only occasionally appearing as a single lecture in a total course on, say, Hinduism, Christianity or

Islam. It is my contention that such an emphasis necessarily leads to a distorted picture of the living reality of the religion concerned.

If blame is to be apportioned for this academic narrow-mindedness, then some must also be laid at the door of the art historians. Studies of art typically emphasise stylistic techniques, composition, use of colour, influences etc. It is rare for attention to be given to the function for which the work of art was produced. Only in relatively recent times, and again mainly in western circles, have works of art been produced for the emotionally antiseptic environment of museums and art galleries. Similarly the production of artefacts simply for decorative purposes (as opposed to decorations on functional objects) is relatively modern and mainly western. It is not, for example, normal in the great diversity of African arts. Many great works of art were produced to be used in religion, mainly in rituals, and I suggest they cannot be understood adequately without a study of that context. Can a Buddha image be appreciated apart from the meditative practices for which it was made and in particular the process of visualisation?

Some Definitions

Some thought has to be given to what is meant by the term 'arts'. It is here used in a very broad sense to include the performing arts (dance, drama and music) as well as the visual arts. In the study of religion architecture is also commonly important. It is obvious that literature is also a major art form, not least poetry. Whether it is the *Psalms* in the Hebrew Bible, the beauty of the Arabic of the *Qur'an* or the verse of the Zoroastrian prophet Zarathushtra, poetry has been a prominent element in the literature of most religions. One practical reason for this is that it aids the memory in a non-literate society. It also helps to integrate the literature with music. But in what follows little attention is paid to it because it has often been considered within scholarly studies.

The distinction between 'art' and 'folk culture' is for present purposes invalid. One must study all 'levels' of art, regardless of whether an individual, or academic, convention considers it to be 'good' art. Thus in western terms attention should be focused not only on the works of the great artists, such as Leonardo, but also on the statues and paintings popular among the majority of practitioners. Whatever a scholar's aesthetic judgement of the 'Bleeding Hearts of

Jesus', or the 'chocolate box' pictures of the young (white, Anglo Saxon) Jesus found in countless Sunday Schools, these commonly express or stimulate popular devotion; they are potent visual images for millions of the faithful. The subjective tastes of the academic should not lead him or her to neglect the art forms which have been widely used as a part of living religion. What is true of western traditions is equally true elsewhere. Classical Indian art has a beauty which can appeal to many, even without a knowledge of the historical and cultural background. But an appreciation of Hinduism, as it exists in practice in the sub-continent, must embrace the decorated stones and trees, the portable shrines at local festivals, the image in the ordinary home shrine, the crudely made carvings, as well as the splendid art of the great temples.

What precisely makes a work of art a religious work of art? Is, for example, Leonardo's painting of 'the Virgin of the Rocks' to be classified as religious art because of the names he attached to the women and children depicted? It is a masterpiece of composition and that was perhaps the focus of the painter's interest in producing the work. If an artist has little or no interest in the religious implications of his work, does that exclude the piece from the category of religious art? Could it be argued that Picasso's work 'Guernica' is in some sense more of a religious work, despite the artist's lack of religious commitment, because of the nature of the message he was seeking to communicate about the horrors of war? Or is the artist's intention basically irrelevant? Here a personal example serves to illustrate the point. During my time as an art student I produced one painting the subject matter of which was a couple walking down a dark path with a street light casting dark shadows and giving bright highlights. I was fascinated by the patterns of light and shade which were so stark and yet intricate that, for me, the work was essentially an abstract composition. A critic commenting on the painting, however, saw it as having essentially a religious message of people striving for the light at the end of a dark tunnel. Who was I, a young insignificant student, to argue with a critic? Thereafter the painting was seen as essentially being of a religious nature suitable for use in a church. It is, perhaps, the use that is made of a work of art that defines it as religious rather than the intention of the artist, and not the subject matter.

On one occasions I was given a commission to produce a painting for a retreat centre. No directions were given on subject matter, only the brief to do something which I felt would help create an atmosphere suitable for a room in which to meditate. I therefore spent some time in a place which I found conducive to tranquillity, then painted a semi-abstract interpretation of the scene trying to convey something of the sense of peace. Although there was nothing whatsoever in the subject matter which could possibly be described as religious, perhaps the function which the painting served made it a religious work of art. Might it then be suggested that a painting, such as Leonardo's, could be considered religious when used in one setting, say as a focus of worship in a church, but not when it hangs on the walls of an art gallery?'

Symbolism

There are numerous and fundamental issues which cannot be included in a short essay, for example the meaning and various uses of the word 'symbol'. As a starting point I would suggest that symbolism is the use of an empirical motif to express or point to something beyond itself. With the use of a symbol ordinary objects assume religious significance. It is common to distinguish between at least three types of symbols, the iconic, those with a likeness to what is depicted, for example a crucifix; aniconic, without likeness to what is depicted, for example the simple cross without a figure depicted, and multivalent, that is the use of one symbol with many levels of interpretation at one and the same time. The multivalent symbol is best illustrated from the field of Roman Mithraism where the motif of the lion can symbolise either the fourth grade of initiation, the sun, the astrological sign Leo, the guardian spirit of the sanctuary and is part of a complex theology depicted on the main cult relief.

A major problem with the interpretation of symbols is that their meaning is opaque to the outsider but suggestive to the believer, for 'symbols' are commonly produced by faith for faith, i.e. a sort of visual short hand or code. Where there is little or no accompanying literature to interpret the art, outsiders can easily misinterpret the message. The common Christian symbol of a sheep waving a red flag conveys little if the viewer does not know the doctrine of the paschal lamb! Difficulties can be compounded when one reflects on the schematisation of symbols. The Christian cross provides a good example: the 'T' cross; the Maltese cross; a cross with rubies in key points to allude to the blood shed by Jesus and so on. Many religions are as sophisticated in their symbolism as Christianity. Perhaps the most obvious use of aniconic symbolism is in early Buddhist art. It was thought that since Gotama, the Buddha, had passed beyond a state which human beings can comprehend, it was inappropriate to portray him in human form. He, or better his work, is, therefore, represented in art by a wheel to symbolise the doctrine; a footprint to represent his mission; a tree to represent the knowledge gained under the *bodhi* tree or a throne. Buddhism is a very literate religion and so one can find elucidations of these symbols. Such elucidation is not always available, especially in the artistically prolific but non-literate traditions of such regions as West Africa and the Pacific. It is too easy to assume that because we do not have any written explanations of religious symbols, no sophisticated explanations have or do exist. The danger which all too obviously confronts the scholar is that without internal elucidations the field of interpreting religious symbols is one in which academic imagination can run riot and wild theorising become the norm.

The problems of interpreting religious symbols are made yet more complex by the fact that the understanding of a symbol can grow and change within the religion, and indeed can be different within a religion at any one time either from one region, period or person to another. The Gothic church provides an obvious example. Scholars debate the question of whether or not the cosmic symbolism attached to it was intended by its original designers. But does it matter what the original intention was for an appreciation of the part the symbolism in fact came to play within Christian emotion and worship? Symbolism is something which develops. It therefore follows that even if the scholar is confident (s)he has identified what it conveys in one place at one time (s)he cannot necessarily extrapolate from that to a global assertion about that symbol in the religion as a whole. Although my overall argument is that the study of religious arts has to be more central in Comparative Religion than it has ever been, it would be foolish to underestimate the difficulties involved.

The Functions of Arts in Religions

The theme I wish to focus on here is the diversity of roles which the arts play in a religion. Perhaps the most obvious one is the didactic. In non-literate societies and among non-literate members of religions (e.g. children), the arts are commonly used for instruction. The most vivid forms may be the dance and drama performed by groups such as the Kathakali dancers in India or, at an immeasurably less sophisticated level, the Christmas play in English schools. Not only 'folk art', but also much of the 'great art' was produced for didactic purposes. Statues and paintings, such as those of Giotto in the Arena Chapel at Padua, are commonly there to teach the faithful the stories of the religion.

But the teaching work is not only at the level of narrative, it is also a matter of conditioning attitudes. Art rarely merely reproduces, it commonly interprets. Few religions are as anthropomorphic as Christianity, at least in its popular form. In part the anthropomorphism stems from the biblical teaching that human beings are made in God's image and the doctrine of the incarnation tends to underline the point (though logically it need not have done so). This anthropomorphic trend has undoubtedly been reinforced in western Christianity by the countless artists who have depicted God as an old man with a long white beard. The image of God has, for many, been fixed by such artists as Michaelangelo and Blake as much as by theologians. Western artists have represented and reinforced a perspective on the Ultimate which is dramatically different from that found in many cultures. Reference has already been made to the aniconic element in early Buddhist art. There are many other examples. The Hindu conviction that God is beyond human form is expressed by showing the gods with many heads or arms to emphasise their wisdom and power or by a mixture of human and animal forms, as in the case of the elephant headed Ganesha, reflecting the belief that there is a unity behind diverse forms of life.

The Zoroastrian tradition has a very different approach to representing God. Here the focal point (in earthly terms) of worship is the fire. In part this draws on ancient Indo-Iranian life styles on the Asian steppes where the fire was that which provided protection for the nomads from marauding animals; it was part of the process of providing food in cooking; it was associated with the warmth of life rather than the coldness of death; it was associated with justice through the ordeal by fire and it was the earthly manifestation of that heavenly source of life, the sun. These ancient traditions have, in modern times, been blended with other ideas, notably the common Parsi saying, 'what better symbol is there of He who is pure undefiled light than the pure flame of the fire'. To many Zoroastrians the fire is the formless living icon, and for many it represents the very presence of God, the source of light and life. Within Zoroastrianism there is not only less inherent anthropomorphism, it is also the case that any such potential trend received no support from the potent conditioning of the artistic tradition. In the West, in contrast, artists have reinforced and popularised what is inherent in the theology. In short the arts function not only as purveyors of stories, but also as conditioners of perceptions and attitudes, even on ultimate issues.

A second function to be noted is what might be called the 'transformatory role' of religious arts. Within the secular world we are accustomed to the idea of dress, itself an important art form, expressing the transformation of an individual person into a functionary of a different order. So in the English legal system a judge has his or her own personal identity submerged or cloaked in the traditional symbols of legal authority with the wig and robe. It is no longer John Jones who passes judgement but My Lord, Mr Justice Jones, the embodiment of the legal system at that moment and place. The transformation from an ordinary person into the holder of an office is portrayed and expressed in visual form. This transformatory role is particularly prominent in religious art. One obvious example are the priestly vestments in the Catholic and Orthodox churches which make visible and public the belief that this is not an ordinary human being, or individual personality, celebrating the Mass, but the representative of the church, a sacral person who is at this moment set apart. Another good example of this transformatory role is the use of masks in various North American Indian, African and Pacific communities. Functionally their use is not dissimilar from that of vestments, submerging the individual personality and making explicit the mediation of the supra-human source of spiritual power. It is not the art forms in and of themselves which effect this change but rather that they communicate and give force to the transformation.

The physical representation of the holy can sometimes be thought to throw a cloak of religious protection around an object or person, often by showing an eye, or by the use of religious motifs, for example Quranic quotations or Hindu holy figures on Afghan lorries, or a St Christopher medallion for travellers. Thus the artefact, the charm, the amulet, can itself be invested with religious potency, the visual art form thereby not only publicising, but actually itself becoming part of the sacred. The simple description of this phenomenon in art histories as 'magic' explains nothing, partly because of the ambiguity of the word and partly because of the emotive overtones involved. The holy power of art is well illustrated by the Eastern Orthodox beliefs in icons as sacramental means of making visible and accessible to the worshipper the heavenly forces they represent.

A third role of arts in religion which merits emphasis is as stimulators of emotion. One of my Manchester theological colleagues once commented that 'religion is concerned with concepts'. That I would dispute. It may be the concern of religious intellectuals, and has undoubtedly been the more or less exclusive focus of scholarly studies, but I doubt if that is true of the mass of religious people in any culture. People typically practise their religion because it makes them feel better. The emotive dimension of religion can, of course, be found in literature, but it is more commonly experienced through one or more of the other art forms; through the moving music of the church organ; through the stirring experience of the liturgical drama in temple, mosque or synagogue; the divine is apprehended in the reverential awe with which a Hindu sees with the eye of experience the image in the shrine where deity dwells; the soaring spirit or contrite heart is communicated through song and chant. This experiential dimension is what commonly makes a religion live for most of its adherents, rather than any intellectual assent to a set of teachings. If that is so, then an appreciation of the emotive dimension of religion is best gained through a study of the appropriate art forms.

Doctrinal formulations are typically codified by, and significant for, merely a thoughtful few. The art forms, I contend, are expressive of the religion experienced by the many, and there is commonly a contrast, if not a gulf, between the two. This contrast between the theoretical ideal of a religion and its living reality is exemplified by two uses of sacred space: the Gothic church and the Hindu temple. Theoretically one might have expected the emphasis of Christian worship to have been on the closeness of the worshipper and God because of the doctrine of the incarnation and the saying 'where two or three are gathered together in my name, there am I in the midst of them'. But in European Christianity the reverse is commonly the case. The Gothic church was part of a technological revolution. Thick walls and massive pillars were no longer necessary, instead slim columns, large window filled spaces were possible. Consequently one part of Gothic symbolism is of walls of light representing the light coming into the world. But there is another emotion engendered by Gothic architecture. The typical reaction of people entering a Gothic church is to whisper. The high pointed arches sweeping up to the distant vaulted roof make people feel small in the presence of a remote God, awe inspiring in his abode above. Whatever the theory, the emotion inspired by Gothic architecture is not so much the closeness of the worshipper and God, but rather the sense of human lowliness and humility.

Just as the emotional reality of much European Christian worship is evidenced by its architecture rather than by theological treatises, so is that of Hinduism. Numerous popular text books on Hinduism give the impression that it is an austere, ascetic religion. Accounts of teachings on rebirth often suggest that belief in the spiritual self being bound in the material world implies a negative attitude to earthly life. This is a distortion of the attitude of the majority of Hindus. The buoyant note of religious happiness typical of Hinduism is well expressed by the atmosphere of temple worship. A fundamental understanding of Hindu worship is the relationship between guest and host. In the home shrine the devotee is the host and treats God as the honoured guest. In the temple God is the host and the worshipper the guest so that the worshipper takes gifts of fruit and flowers, rings the bell on arrival to announce his or her presence and then enters the shrine to see God and receive divine grace. Colour, sound, gaiety, bustle – these are the characteristics of daily Hindu worship. It is, I suggest, in the emotive environment created by architecture, and through the drama of the ritual that the living spirit of a religion is encountered.

Art and Theology

It is important to ask precisely whose theology it is that is reflected in the arts. I was once asked by a theologian to do a painting of the Trinity. When a preliminary design was produced, the comment was made 'well, yes, I like the composition and so on, but unfortunately it is heretical because . . .', a comment which was repeated with my second, third, fourth, fifth and countless others drafts. Whose religious perspective did the work finally reflect? It was certainly not the painter's! The role of the patron is very powerful in most cultures. The artist rarely works as a free agent. Within the Indian tradition, at least until recent times and before western influence, an artist did not sign his work because it was not seen as a personal production. The bulk of Indian art has always been produced for religious purposes and the manner of its production is determined by official texts, the *Agamas* and the *Shastras*. They determine the posture, the gestures, even the proportions of the figures, indeed they lay down the canon of beauty. The reason is that these texts are thought to relate the visions of the gods experienced by holy men in trances and it is they who are the appropriate guides on how to depict the gods. Because in classical Indian art it is believed that the gods only dwell where there is beauty, a shrine or image must conform to the divinely revealed canons of beauty if the gods are graciously to abide there. The artist is, therefore, seen as standing within a religious tradition, hence he should prepare for his task, as should the dancer, in meditation. It is a modern and largely western assumption that the artist is a free agent. Within some societies, notably North American Indian, African and Pacific religions, there is a little or no concept of a separate role of the 'artist' because life is not divided into religious and secular realms, nor are roles of holy man and artist necessarily distinguished.

How, it may be asked, do these remarks on the importance of the patron relate to the earlier observations that the arts provide effective guides or introductions to the living popular religion of the people? The answer lies in the role of the artist as a communicator with the 'ordinary' worshippers. The great thinkers, be they western theologians, Hindu philosophers or Chinese sages, may be the great intellectual pioneers, but the profundity of their teaching is not easy for the mass of religious people to grasp. Through the medium of their art, I suggest, the artists make ideas more accessible. A good example of this is the work of Giotto. Prior to the Renaissance it had been the strict European convention that religious figures such as Jesus, Mary, and the saints could not be depicted in an earthly setting, but only against a gold background, the emblem of heaven. In part this was a reflection of contemporary theological emphasis on the divinity of Jesus. With the Renaissance came the philosophical elevation of the human spirit and the humanity of Jesus came back into focus. So in his work Giotto placed Jesus firmly in an ordinary (Italian) landscape of hills, trees and houses. He showed the form and solidity of the body with light and shade and the folds of drapery. He also emphasised the humanity of his figures by showing the emotions of joy or despair, fear or thoughtfulness on their faces, indeed by their very poses. Giotto did not supply the original philosophical inspiration for this intellectual movement, but I suggest that his paintings, and those of his contemporaries and followers, were effective ways in which the new theological insights were communicated from the theologians to the ordinary people. In one sense, therefore, the artist functions rather like the narrow waist of the hour-glass or egg-timer: the sand from the top is filtered through it and is reshaped into the form below. The artist sums up the spirit of the times (sometimes, of course, he or she may add his own reflections) and through them the tradition is passed on, but in a manner people can share in emotively. The arts can, thus, be effective communicators of the official or developing theology, through the influences of the ecclesiastical patron. This 'communications role' of the arts is probably expanding rather than shrinking in the twentieth century because of the wider accessibility of the arts through mass reproduction of pictures and statues as well as through radio and television presentation of drama.

The arts can also reflect a popular theology or a perspective which may be at variance with formal theological logic. This can be illustrated by the use of the symbol of the nude in western Christianity and in classical Indian art. Not only does this illustrate contrasting uses of the same theme, it also shows how a symbol can develop in exactly the opposite way from that which one might expect.

The nude is one of the subjects most favoured by artists in many cultures. From a secular (western) artist's point of view the human form is perhaps the most beautiful of all forms; it is the most difficult and demanding of subjects, the most varied and the most complex. No two models, no two poses, are the same. It has often been considered the great test of an artist's ability as well as one of the most powerful sources of inspiration. The nude form can represent a far greater range of emotions than any clothing or inanimate object. By posture, muscle tension, by position, by bodily and facial expression, as well as through overall composition, colour and texture, the artist can vividly convey ecstasy or fear, joy or despair, tension or tranquillity, tenderness or agony, pride or despondency, dignity or degradation.

Within Christian art one might have expected the nude to be the classic symbol of God. In historical terms Christian art is largely based on Greek and Roman art where the nude is typically the symbol of perfection, particularly the male nude. In theological terms one might have had the same expectation. In modern thought the biblical teaching that human beings were made in God's image may not be taken literally, but it almost certainly has been by the great majority of Christians over the centuries. Further, the doctrine of the incarnation, that God could be thought to assume normal male form, might be expected to encourage such a symbolic use of the male body. In practice the nude is used in an entirely different way in Christian art.

One of the two most common uses of the nude in Christian art is to represent the state of Adam and Eve after the Fall, when they are seen in a state of sin. Within these portrayals the body is generally made to look ugly. Eve, for example, has a pear shape body with large hips, small shrunken breasts, skinny legs and shoulders. It is also rare for Adam and Even to be shown completely nude. A falling fig leaf, a convenient branch or protective hand usually cover the genitals. The second main use of the nude is in scenes of the flagellation, crucifixion and deposition from the cross or of saintly martyrs. In short the nude is used to depict ideas of sin, shame and humiliation. It is not used as a symbol of purity or holiness, even though there are subjects where it would, from an artistic point of view, be natural, for example the mother and child studies. The infant Jesus may be naked, but rarely is Mary so depicted. Adults are rarely nude. Despite its undoubted lack of historicity a loin cloth almost invariably drapes the figures. Normally the only figures shown completely naked are pre-puberty cherubs and figures from classical Greek and Roman mythology. Nudity is rarely found in 'Christian' art. That is not to say that sexuality is a theme entirely absent, for it may lay hidden beneath the surface, and not necessarily in a 'healthy' form. If an artist were to focus his studies of the nude on slim young men in bondage being whipped and tortured, questions may be asked about the boundary between art and pornography. Perhaps that question needs asking more often of some Christian art! But the main point here is the absence of the nude as a symbol of the divine, or of purity, in western Christian art. There are very few examples of a 'good' person both happy and nude.

The symbolic use of the nude in Indian art is entirely different. For various reasons one might have expected the body to have been a symbol of bondage or corruption. One is the belief in rebirth as a process where the individual's spiritual dimension, or soul, is encased in a material body through successive lives until liberation, *moksha*, is achieved. Another factor is that the ultimate state is rarely thought of in physical terms, so for example there is no traditional Indian belief in the resurrection of the body as there is in Christianity. But in practice the nude often appears in Indian art as a symbol of the holy. On temple reliefs, in paintings and sculptures, healthy, happy, nubile maidens are used to portray the soul's yearning for the ecstasy of union with God. In accord with the scriptural canons of beauty mentioned earlier, their narrow waists and broad chests represent the power of the life-giving spirit. Especially in South India there are explicit scenes of ecstasy in sexual intercourse representing the bliss of

union with the Absolute. Unlike western Christian art there is no
attempt to conceal the genitalia. The spirit filled maidens may well
wear necklaces, belts, buckles, and sometimes a lower garment, but
there is no reluctance to show them entirely naked. Throughout
India in the temples of Shiva the most common motif in the sanctuary
is the stylised, but unmistakable, representations of the male and
female generative organs, the *lingam* and the *yoni*. Whereas the means
of birth might have been associated with what is undesirable – rebirth
– they are in fact considered to be the most potent symbol for
conveying the sense of the overpowering love of God for man and
for divine creative energy.

The almost unbridgeable gulf between the European Christian and
Hindu attitudes to such symbols is encapsulated in the comments of
an Anglican missionary in India who commented on Hinduism: 'of
that fearful system it may with truth be said that the corrupt heart of
man, under Satanic influence, elaborated it out of the depths of its
own depravity and set up as objects of worship the personification of
its own vices.' (Quoted in E. J. Sharpe, *Not to Destroy but to Fulfil*,
Uppsala, 1965, p. 27). The cultural conditioning of the missionary
erected an intellectual (or emotional) barrier which prevented
understanding. In each case the religion has in practice used the
symbol in the opposite way to that which one might expect. The
explanation as to why this should be, is complicated. Muslim and
later western influences may be factors, but it may also be as mundane
a cause as the weather – where the climate makes nudity
uncomfortable, it is seen as abnormal and therefore taken as
significant. Whatever the causes for this contrasting use of a symbol,
there is no doubt that social conditioning determines the use of artistic
motifs and religious symbols as much, if not more, than do theological
concerns. Symbols can, therefore, be used in a manner at apparent
variance with the inherent logic of the tradition, and one motif can
take on contrasting meaning in different environments.

So far the emphasis in this essay has been on the creative
relationships between arts and religions, but that is only one side of
the story. Religious leaders have been not only patrons, but also
persecutors of the artist. The obvious example is in Europe after the
Reformation when countless works of art were destroyed. Religious
restrictions of the artist are not, however, confined to the Christian
world. Islam has a luxuriant artistic tradition, but only within clear
parameters. The magnificence of its architecture, the beauty of its
calligraphy, geometric and stylised plant forms represent, in my

opinion, a pinnacle of certain types of art forms, but the painter and especially the sculptor have been typically castigated (the tradition of Persian and Indian miniature painting being exceptional.) In particular the depiction of the human form, in common with Judaism, is forbidden because of the commandment forbidding the use of 'graven images'. Further, Muslims and Christians have both undertaken wholesale destructions of the artistic and cultural heritage of those they have conquered. In short, religions have suppressed as well as supported the arts.

But despite the religious persecutions of artists, despite the complexity of the fine entangled web of relationships between religions and the arts, or the enormous difficulties involved in scholarly interpretation, I would still wish to stress the fundamental role of the study of the arts in any attempt to understand religions. The bias of university, college and school syllabuses requires not merely a 'tinkering' with questions of emphasis, but fairly dramatic reassessment of focus. If the arts are commonly what makes a religion live for its adherents, then they should be at the centre of Religious Studies and not merely an odd chapter in a book on, say, Hinduism. Similarly, art historians are wrong to exclude the study of religion which so often gave birth to the art.

After stressing the dangers of wild speculation in the subject I wish to end with a speculative suggestion. There are, obviously, numerous possible motives for the production of a work of art. Since the artist has to live, money is an obvious basic drive. Some works of art are produced for decorative purposes. Some art is produced simply for personal satisfaction. Rarely perhaps, but in my opinion occasionally, art is produced to express a message that cannot be put into words. The story is told of a famous ballerina who after the performance of her life was asked by a critic, 'Tell me, exactly what were you trying to say?' To which she replied that if she could have put it into words, she would not have gone to the exhausting effort of a dance lasting hours! What in such cases, is the distinction between the religious and the artistic experience? Is it the case that some people sometimes use religious language to communicate an experience which others may choose to express through dance, or music or another form of the arts? Another personal reference can be used to illustrate the point. My first visit to the Shah mosque in Isfahan was an unforgettable experience. I stood transfixed, literally for hours. The harmony of the symmetrical architecture, the exquisite detailed work and overall balance of the omnipresent coloured tilework, the ethereal atmosphere created by the merging of the blue of the tilework into the sky all combined to inspire an overpowering sense of wonder at such splendour and beauty, a feeling of both ecstasy and peace. For the Muslim the mosque is the place where one meets God. Was this experience a religious or an artistic one? Or is that an inappropriate distinction? Religious experience can take many forms. So, too, can the artistic one. Are there times when the two merge? We cannot, I suggest, gain an insight into a religion without a feeling for the forms in which it is experienced by its followers. Those forms such as music, dance, the inspiration of sacred architecture and the visual arts are the media through which many experience what is beyond words. If courses and books on the various religions do not include a study of the arts as a central, not peripheral, theme then, in my opinion, they are excluding the possibility of an adequate appreciation of what it is that makes that religion a living experience for the practitioner.

Bibliographical Conclusions

The problem for implementing the proposed change of focus is that there are so few sources available to facilitate courses. Of course there are individual books or projects and it may be helpful to note some of them. The list cannot conceivably be comprehensive, but identifies simply some books which, in part at least, pick up some of the issues in this essay. Balance is impossible in so short a space, so I have simply noted books which have made me think, not always in agreement with the author! The most obvious work to refer to is A. C. Moore, *The Iconography of Religions*, (London 1977) which pursues some of these issues seriously, but suffers, perhaps, from attempting to include too many religions and therefore 'spreads the academic jam' a little thinly at time. Some recent American publications have raised some of the theoretical issues in the study of religion and the arts. Two examples are D. Adams and D. Apostolos-Cappadona, *Art as Religious Studies*, New York, 1987, and J. Dillenberger, *A Theology of Artistic Sensibilities: The Visual Arts and the Church*, New York, 1986.

Inevitably there is more material published on Christianity. One of the major sources of reference is G. Schiller, *Iconography of Christian Art*, 2 vols, E.T. London, 1972, but this has something of an art historical approach. Small though it is, and intended for schools as it was, in my opinion a very perceptive book is P. Moore, *The Arts and*

Practices of Christianity, London, 1982. There is a companion volume
on Judaism by Alan Unterman, also published in 1982. Unfortunately
the abject failure of the publishers, Ward Lock Educational, to
publicise these books makes them hard to consult. Two classic works
on western art are E. H. Gombrich, *The Story of Art*, first published
in 1951 and reprinted numerous times by Phaidon. The other is by
K. Clark, *The Nude*, first published in London in 1956, then
republished by Penguin. Art histories commonly neglect the role of
the icon in Orthodox Art (Peter Moore's book is an exception) and
that is a loss of an appreciation of the powerful spirit of a major
dimension of Christianity. Among the many books one might perhaps
pick out L. Ouspensky, *The Theology of the Icon*, New York, 1978.

It is obviously impossible in so short a space to list books for each
religion. All that can be done is to note those which pursue some at
least of the points made above, notably D. Snellgrove, *The Image of
the Buddha*, London, 1978; G. Michell, *The Hindu Temple*, London,
1977 (a more comprehensive study is by S. Kramrisch with a two
volumed work on the temple and a wide ranging one-volume work,
The Art of India, London, 1954). A major, if sometimes idiosyncratic,
writer on Indian religious art is A. Coomaraswamy (e.g. *History of
Indian and Indonesian Art*, London, 1927). Exhibition catalogues may
provide useful information; one that I find helpful is G. Michell, C.
Lampert and T. Holland, *In the Image of Man*, London, 1982, helpful
because it includes material on the use of objects in the religion.
There is a useful overview in J. V. C. Harle, *The Art and Architecture
of the Indian Subcontinent*, Penguin, 1986. But here we are getting
close to straight art history rather than what is needed, namely a
book which approaches the religion as a powerful living force for the
adherents. Speaking personally, I find this best approached, for
teaching purposes, through the use of video or 16mm film material,
notably a series produced by Syracuse University (Film rental library,
1455 East Colvin St., Syracuse, New York 13210) by H. Daniel
Smith and 15 videos entitled 'Exploring the religions of South Asia'
produced by David M. Knipe of the South Asian Studies department
of Wisconsin University (Video Distribution, Dept. of South Asian
Studies, 1244 Van Hise Hall, University of Wisconsin, 53706). The
significant point about these resources is that they show the art
actually in use.

A rich field, almost by definition, are the non-literate traditions of
'primal societies' (e.g. D. Williams, *Icon and Image*, a *Study of Sacred and
Secular Form of African Classical Art*, London, 1974). It is interesting

1974). It is interesting to note that with his appreciation of religion in western Africa, Geoffrey Parrinder himself, many years ago, stressed the importance of the study of the arts, and it is, therefore, hoped that this essay is an appropriate tribute to him, following a thematic path he has trodden before. Whether the peoples be in the Pacific, Australasia, Africa or North American Indians, the dance, music and visual arts have been a primary means of communicating the tradition so that they provide outstanding examples of the theme of religion and the arts. An insightful study of a 'popular' art form in Pacific religions, A. & M. Strathern, *Self-decoration in Mount Hagen*, London, 1977, highlights two points (a) the crucial nature of art in 'primal' societies (b) the diverse nature of the arts.

The richness of Islamic art is far too often mentioned only in passing; two classic works are O. Grabar, *The Formation of Islamic Art*, London, 1973, and B. Gray, *Persian Painting*, London, 1977. Beyond these it is important to notice the local, popular expressions of Islamic art, but here it is very difficult to obtain material without chasing through exhibition catalogues of 'folk art', such as rugs, tents, clothing, the decoration of vehicles and music.

The only major effort, thus far, to effect a study of religion through art is the Iconography of Religions series produced by the Institute of Religious Iconography, the State University of Groningen. These are generally in the form of monographs on aspects of the religious art of the traditions. The series includes some notable studies usually on these single dimensions (for example calligraphy in Islam). But if a teacher in the Comparative Study of Religions wishes to introduce a course where the experiential dimension of a religion is seen through its various art forms, the books simply do not exist. A major difficulty is that there are few specialist equipped to write such books on the spread of the arts in any one tradition. I am currently starting a series on 'Religion and the Arts' with Pinter books, but find that individuals cannot deal alone with the many aspects of the subject and I assume that commonly one will have to find a team of authors. The books will not only deal with 'isms' but also some cross-cultural studies, for example 'The image of women in religious arts'. There is here, it seems to me, a whole new area opening up for an appreciation of the spirit, the ecstasy, the popular, the unarticulated, emotional and the living, daily forms of religion experienced by the people rather than as elaborated by the theologians.

SUGGESTED READING

D. Adams and D. Apostolos-Cappadona, *Art as Religious Studies*, New York: Crossroad, 1987.

J. Dillenberger, *A Theology of Artistic Sensibilities: The Visual Arts and the Church*, New York: Crossroad, 1986, London: SCM, 1987.

A. Gaston, *Śiva in Dance, Myth and Iconography*, London: Oxford University Press, 1985.

O. Grabar, *The Formation of Islamic Art*, London and New Haven: Yale University Press, 1973.

G. Michell, *The Hindu Temple: An Introduction to its Meaning and Forms*, London: Elek, 1977; Chicago: Chicago University Press, 1988.

P. Moore, *The Arts and Practices of Christianity*, London: Ward Lock Educational, 1982.

D. Snellgrove, *The Image of the Buddha*, London: Serindia Publications, 1978.

D. Williams, *Icon and Image, a Study of Sacred and Secular Form of African Classical Art*, London: Allen Lane, 1974.

18. RELIGION AND GENDER

Ursula King

During the 1970s and 1980s feminist thought has had a deep impact on several academic disciplines. It has led to critical questioning and a careful re-examination of what has until now been taken for well established and generally accepted knowledge. In the area of Religious Studies this impact has only been felt slowly, and much less so in Britain and the rest of Europe than in North America. The American Academy of Religion, the largest body of scholars in Religious Studies, has had a 'Women and Religion' section at its annual conference since 1974, and many North American colleges and universities have a regular 'Women and Religion' programme, often organised and funded on an interdisciplinary basis.

Such programmes are much rarer in Britain, if not to say non-existent, and few are the Religious Studies courses which give particular attention to the variable of gender in the study of religion. It is equally true, however, that it is rare to find any reference to religion in any of the numerous Women's Studies courses in British universities and institutions of further and higher education. And yet many current issues in the debate about women, their self-understanding, image, status and role, are still influenced by or directly related to religious teachings and worldviews, even where these are sharply criticised and rejected. For centuries religion has been the matrix of culture; it has shaped people's thoughts and actions and affected their lives, not least the lives of women. Today an increasing number of scholars, especially women scholars, have come to realise the importance of paying special attention to gender in the study of religion. I consider this a significant turning point, or what other scholars have described as a paradigm shift, in the contemporary study of religion. It was given scholarly recognition in Britain when the British Association for the Study of Religions (formerly the British Association for the History of Religions) chose 'Religion and Gender' as its annual conference theme for 1989 with contributions by both female and male scholars.

Some Clarifications

To avoid confusion in the reader's mind, it may be helpful to introduce a few basic distinctions here. Whilst 'sex' refers to the biologically given differences between women and men, the notion of 'gender' points to the historically and culturally constructed understanding of what it means to be a man or a woman, i.e. how sexual differences are interpreted in terms of images, roles and relationships, an interpretation which can differ widely in different religions and cultures. But it is quite obvious that many religious teachings, especially scriptural statements and theological doctrines, are closely related to such interpretations.

In principle the attention to gender analysis relates to data about women as well as men, but given the overwhelmingly male-oriented framework of all knowledge and the urgent need for a critique of this fundamental imbalance, in practice the attention to religion and gender is at present primarily directed towards women. Contemporary feminist theory and gender analysis are affecting both the practice and the study of religion, and it is the latter in particular which concerns us here.

The invisibility or, at best, marginality of women in religious thought and institutions, both past and present, is a very striking phenomenon. One's attention is drawn to this with increased frequency as soon as one's consciousness has become more critical and special attention is paid to gender differences. To set the matter right, to correct this imbalance is not simply a matter of adding the study of women as yet another new theme to Religious Studies. On the contrary, looking at women in different world religions requires a new perspective and raises new questions which affect the whole of Religious Studies. Traditional religious teachings, as well as the scholarship about them, are set in a patriarchal and androcentric framework; they are almost exclusively the creation of men who have taken their experience as normative and universal without taking into account the experiences and thoughts of women. To make a comparison here, this exclusive, self-sufficient male stance is not so unlike the exclusive religious attitude of some people towards 'other' religions. To enter into dialogue requires a new attitude – one has to listen and accord to the other person's position equal recognition and respect (the more one enters this path and the deeper the dialogue grows, the more one receives and gives, the more humble one grows about one's own position). This 'dialogical approach' is not only needed among religions, but also between men and women if we want to transcend an exclusive, patriarchal stance.

The existence of patriarchy has been a major focus of women's critique in contemporary feminism. The wider meaning of patriarchy relates to theories of history and society and even of religion which need not retain us here, but the word patriarchy is often simply used to refer to an all-male power structure – a situation which exists in most religions we know. Whilst the word patriarchy is mostly used in relation to institutions and attitudes, the term androcentric is more applicable to thought structures and language. It refers to a situation where the male experience is without question taken as the universally valid human norm. This is true of many religious teachings, just as many religious institutions are guilty of what some women theologians have called 'the sin of sexism', i.e. the exclusion and subordination of women by not recognising their contribution or marginalising their existence.

Historical and Institutional Perspectives

The feminist critique is by no means an exclusively contemporary phenomenon of very recent origin; on the contrary, it has its beginnings in earlier developments, not only in the Enlightenment, but also in certain religious ideas of the Judaeo-Christian tradition. One cannot fully understand the rise of the women's movement in the early nineteenth century without looking at its religious roots. The vision of universal equality, justice, love and peace which inspired the early feminists was not only based on ideas of the Englightenment, but was often nourished by biblical teachings and by a strong religious commitment. The American women who, in the early nineteenth century, worked with great fervour for the abolition of slavery realised that their conscience called them to strive with equal zest for the abolition of the subordination and oppression of women, present in society and church alike. Christian and Jewish women, and black women too, worked together as 'sisters of the spirit' to bring about a better life for all women.

These historical roots of contemporary feminism and the religious motivation of many early feminists are often not sufficiently recognised. Nor are western people always aware of the global and cross-cultural ramifications of contemporary feminism which, far from being only an urban, western, white, middle-class phenomenon, has developed truly international dimensions and is affecting the consciousness of people everywhere. Many young women and girls growing up now have already internalised the ideas, choices and changes of consciousness stemming from the women's movement without necessarily belonging to an organised women's group or wanting to be called a 'feminist'. Religiously committed women are raising voices of challenge regarding many traditional religious teachings, but they are also rediscovering the female side of their religious heritage which can be a source of affirmation and strength.

But it is not only religious beliefs which inspired some of the pioneering work of women in the nineteenth century; many women working in the churches helped to bring about reforms and became active in teaching and preaching. Women's involvement with and contribution to religious activities in the United States is well documented in the several volumes of documentation on *Women and Religion in America* (eds R. Radford Ruether and R. Skinner Keller, San Francisco, 1981, 1983). The Congregational Church in New York undertook the revolutionary step of ordaining the first woman minister, the Reverend Antoinette Brown, in September 1853. Oberlin College in the USA allowed a few women to attend its theological school in the 1840s, whereas Methodist and Congregational seminaries admitted a few students by the late nineteenth century. Women's admission to theological studies has been the most important contributory factor in making women theologically literate, thus enabling them to contribute to theological debates on their own terms. However, Harvard Divinity School did not admit women students until 1955 and the same is probably true of most other mainstream theological faculties.

The great American pioneer Elizabeth Cady Stanton realised only towards the end of her life, when she had spent decades campaigning for women's political and legal equality, that women's subordinate position was ultimately due to biblical teaching whose antifeminist passages had to be excised. With an indomitable spirit and great courage she proceeded with a committee of women to create an amended version called *The Woman's Bible* (1895–98), considered outrageous at the time, but hailed today as a pioneering publication, even though it no longer meets contemporary women's expectation of what is needed in terms of a more differentiated critique of the androcentric language and thought world of the Bible.

Feminist biblical interpretation and feminist theology have taken off in a big way since the 1970s, as is evident from many recent publications and conferences although in Britain, in contrast to the USA, the subject has found far less institutional anchorage and is sometimes more developed outside than inside universities and colleges. So far, the University of Nijmegen (Netherlands) is unique in Europe in having created a professorship in the area of 'Feminism and Christianity'.

To some extent this is also true of the wider topic of women in world religions. During the late eighteenth, nineteenth and even twentieth century several outstanding women scholars studied and wrote on world religions but, again, they mostly did not hold official positions and their contribution to scholarship has so far been little acknowledged and remains to be charted.

In the past male scholars have sometimes paid attention to gender differences by enquiring into the image and role of women in different religions or by investigating understandings of and attitudes to sexuality. Mention may be made of the German scholar Friedrich Heiler who, from the 1920s onwards, lectured on women in world religions (see his posthumously published work *Die Frau in den Religionen der Menschheit*, Berlin, 1977); Geoffrey Parrinder's *Sex in the World's Religions* (London, 1980) also belongs here. Judged from a contemporary perspective these works are rich in descriptive material, but they do not critically analyse the framework and assumptions about women inherent in different religions. A turning point in the study of women, religion and gender occurred with the impact of feminist critical theory on Religious Studies (see Constance Buchanan, 'Women's Studies' in M. Eliade, ed., *The Encyclopaedia of Religion*, Chicago, 1987, vol. 15: 433–40). Now women are no longer primarily an object of study for male authors, but women themselves have become the subject and object of their own study through women scholars investigating the religious lives, experiences, rites and beliefs of women, including a critique of what men had formerly written about them from a onesided perspective.

As mentioned earlier, the 'Women and Religion' section of the American Academy of Religion came into existence in 1974 and has attracted numerous distinguished contributions, as is evident from several volumes published since then. The women students of Harvard Divinity School founded a Women's Caucus in 1970 which laid the foundation for a regular 'Women's Studies in Religion' programme begun in 1973 with its own lectures, seminars and conferences and now the publications of 'The Harvard Women Studies in Religion Series'.

By comparison the International Association for the History of Religions (IAHR) has been less innovative and enterprising by giving much less sustained support to women scholars. A considerable number of women scholars took part in the early Congresses (for example, at the 1908 Oxford Congress out of a total of 599 participants 253 were women, of whom 183 attended independently, i.e. they were not accompanying a male scholar). In more recent years the participation of women seems to have decreased rather than increased, and it is difficult to find an explanation for this. At the XIVth IAHR Congress in Winnipeg (1980) a new section on women and religion was created, oddly enough entitled 'Femininity and Religion', but unfortunately it was not even recorded in the published Proceedings. The section disappeared again at the following Congress in Sydney (1985) and has not been reintroduced at the Rome Congress (1990). However, after considerable efforts the organisers agreed to a panel on Religion and Gender where nineteen women scholars presented papers on different topics relating to women, religion and gender issues.

Several British universities and colleges now offer some teaching, or sometimes a whole course, on feminist theology, women and religion, or women and spirituality, within their BA programme. Lancaster University introduced an MA in 'Women and Religion' in 1989 and Bristol University offers an MA on 'Religion and Gender' as from 1990. Teachers in Religious Education, an area once described as guilty of 'sexism by omission', grouped themselves together in 1989 to form WIRE or 'Women in Religious Education' which has a particular interest in promoting the topic of women in RE teaching and educational materials. The Shap Working Party on World Religions in Education devoted its annual publication of 1988 to 'Women in Religion'. This covers many different religions and contains much useful information and material for teachers.

At the European level women scholars from different parts of Europe founded in 1986 the 'European Society of Women for Theological Research' which holds bi-annual, multi-lingual conferences. So far these have taken place in Switzerland, the Netherlands, and Germany; the next one, in 1991, will be held in England, at the University of Bristol. Until now the focus has mainly been on various aspects of Christian and Jewish feminist theology, but different workshops have also explored a number of other themes, including mysticism and spirituality, and there is some intention to invite to the conference women from other faiths than Judaism and Christianity.

As this brief description indicates, the topic 'religion and gender' points to a wide range of questions and possible scholarly investigations – from specific theological issues to historical and comparative studies, and also to methodological questions about the nature of Religious Studies and the paradigm shift created by the change in consciousness brought about by specific attention to gender in the study of religion.

Theoretical and Practical Perspectives

So far, the feminist challenge to religion has been primarily addressed to the Judaeo-Christian tradition as most women writers are more familiar with either Christian or Jewish beliefs, but there is now also a growing body of publications on women in Hinduism, Buddhism, and Islam. Feminist theology, both Christian and Jewish, has produced a large body of literature dealing with all aspects of theology in a new, critical perspective. This is very refreshing and often offers new insights. The central debate turns around the question whether traditional symbols and teachings can be reformed or reconstructed or whether, on the contrary, they must be replaced by completely new ones. This applies also to practical matters, such as the celebration of the liturgy, the use of hymns, the celebration of different rites, and the most appropriate way of worship. A dominant theme, on which much valuable work has been done, is the enquiry into the image and concept of God, or to put it more neutrally, into our constructs of Ultimate Reality. How far have these images been linked to anthropomorphous forms which have been predominantly male rather than female? What are the female dimensions of the sacred in the Judaeo-Christian tradition, and how far is it appropriate to speak also of the motherhood, in addition to the fatherhood, of God?

Feminist theologians have written widely on our understanding of God, the nature of religious language, and on women in the churches; much exciting and substantial work has also been done on biblical translation and reinterpretation from the perspective of women and on the decisive contribution of early Christian women to the rise and development of Christianity.

But it is not only in theology that attention has been given to gender; scholars in the comparative study of religion have also increasingly focussed their work on this issue. If one looks at women in world religions systematically and comparatively rather than historically, three different perspectives can be singled out. These concern both external and internal aspects of religion and imply a progressive level of depth and interiority. There is first the question of what is women's role and status in different religious traditions and their institutions? What are the patterns of participation or exclusion from ritual and liturgy? What religious authority can women wield? Are women given equal status in the religious life, i.e. in priesthood, monasticism or religious leadership? Have women formed their own religious communities or created rites of their own? It has been shown that in general women hold higher positions in archaic, tribal and relatively non-institutionalised religions than in highly differentiated religious traditions which have evolved complex structures and hierarchical organisations over a long time. In both primal and ancient religions we find the widespread presence of women magicians, shamans, healers, visionaries, prophetesses and priestesses. Also, during the formative period of a religion women often play a leading role or are closely associated with the work of the founder whilst later they are relegated to the background (see, for example, the women associated with the work of the Buddha, Jesus or Mohammad).

Another, second perspective concerns the question of how women are presented in religious language and thought. What do the different sacred scriptures teach about women? Do they project images of women which are strong and powerful, or debilitating? Does their language remain exclusive and androcentric, emphasising the subordination of women, or does it express equality and partnership? Are feminine symbols and imagery used, especially in relation to an ultimate, transcendent focus or in speaking about the experience of God or the disclosure of the Spirit? In the Judaeo-Christian tradition the whole theological 'sexology' underpinning the traditional exegesis of Genesis 1 and 2 and the teaching about being created in the image of God have come under much scrutiny by feminist theologians. In contrast to Christianity, where the father model of God has been dominant, Hinduism provides us with one of the richest traditions regarding feminine perceptions and embodiments of the Divine, whether in terms of the power of *shakti*, or its numerous, widely celebrated goddesses or its Great Goddess, the *Mahadevi*. The Hindu tradition can provide inspiring symbolic resources for women, but the wealth of female religious symbolism in Hinduism perhaps more than any other raises the difficult, if not unanswerable, question of what is the relationship between the realm of the symbolic and real women in day-to-day life? A religion may have many goddesses, but that does not necessarily mean they enhance the actual lives and status of women.

The most important issue, however, is not what world religions teach *about* women, defining them extraneously in a way women do not necessarily understand and define themselves. The greatest problem lies in the fundamentally patriarchal and androcentric framework of the theological and religious writings of the past where women have been written about and defined by others, without having a voice themselves. In most religions women are marginalised, often to the point of invisibility, and women have largely been defined in terms of their social function as wife and mother rather than a being in their own right.

To recognise that women have a voice of their own and the determination and power to define themselves, leads to a third and most important question, namely, what is women's own religious experience and how far has this been articulated in a way which may well be different from that of men? Yet has women's own experience ever been officially reflected upon? Has it been integrated into or given its place in the intellectual articulations of religious doctrine and spiritual teachings? What is the pattern of women's religious lives, i.e. their experience in the ordinary sense of day-to-day religious practice, but also their extraordinary experiences as expressed in a rich tradition of mystical and devotional literature? In an informal and largely non-institutionalised way women saints and mystics have provided much spiritual counsel, guidance and leadership through the ages, and remarkable examples of this can be found in all religious traditions. It comes as no surprise that 'women of spirit', women of spiritual power or the 'power of holiness', exercise much fascination on contemporary women, as these women of the past provide strong role models in terms of female identity, autonomy and strength. So far, the many studies on religious experience have hardly paid any attention to gender differences, but the comparative study of the writings of female and male mystics, which is only in its infancy, raises some new and challenging questions, not least for religious practice.

Over the last few years women scholars, and sometimes male scholars too, have gathered an impressive body of data on women in world religions. But published work still remains frequently at a factual-descriptive level without sufficient theoretical analysis to advance our insight and understanding. Of course, the number of women scholars in Religious Studies is still comparatively small, and many have considerable difficulties in establishing themselves in academic institutions and in gaining recognition. Like in other disciplines, the paradigm shift in Religious Studies is not an easy one. Religious Studies has been for too long simply 'men's studies' rather than a fully inclusive enquiry into both women's and men's religious experiences, beliefs and practices. One only has to look at the historiographies and reference works of the discipline widely used today to see how much this unbalanced presentation is still prevalent.

A particularly striking example is *The Encyclopaedia of Religion* (ed. Mircea Eliade, New York and London, 1987) where there are only about 175 women among the 1357 international contributors. Worse, however, is the fact that among the 142 significant 'scholars of religion' to whom the *Encyclopaedia* devotes a separate article, only four women scholars in the whole world were deemed important enough to be included – two of them American, and two British. This also says something about the anglocentric bias of this international publication!

It is important to give women more space in Religious Studies by directing more attention – that is to say, more teaching and research – to the interaction between women and religion. One can look at this in two ways, for the investigation of women's religious lives and experiences can be done from two different directions. On the one hand, we can ask what active contribution women make to religion, how they influence and shape it in their own way. On the other hand, we must also analyse the different and complex ways in which women are influenced and shaped, oppressed and liberated by religion. This twofold perspective indicates that the relationship between religion and gender is not a static one, but dynamic. Both terms must not be conceived of as a reification, but as an interactive process which concerns people and their transformative growth.

For this reason, I call the study of religion and gender a self-reflexive process which leads to a new, more differentiated consciousness on the part of the person(s) undertaking it and implies, of necessity, a self-critical examination of one's own beliefs, attitudes and experiences. I have observed this transformation not only in myself, but also in my class where both female and male students have responded in a very personal and individual way to the study of religion and gender topics, and have drawn conclusions from and for their own lives from their study. In that sense no Religion and Gender course is a neutral, 'value-free' undertaking where cool analysis and traditional academic distancing in the name of objectivity and detachment reign supreme. No, such a course has existential implications, for it requires what has been called a 'participatory hermeneutic', and elicits personal decisions and commitment which may affect not only one's outlook, but one's life.

Looking at the direction which Religious Studies is currently taking, attention to gender is on the increase, and is likely to be given more room in the future. In some institutions it may still be difficult at present to get a course on Religion and Gender off the ground, and if such a course is seen as being exclusively concerned with women in world religions, there may be a danger to consider it merely as a separate 'women's ghetto subject', of interest to women only, but of no consequence for Religious Studies as a whole. However in my view, and that of many others, the topic has to be an integral one, concerned with both women and men, and a study to be undertaken by both sexes jointly. This will lead to a profound shift in orientation. Gender is an issue that affects all other topics; it has historical, philosophical, theological and existential dimensions and is ultimately concerned with the meaning of sexual differentiation, that is to say, what it means to be a person with a gendered self in relationship with other such persons.

If critical attention to gender becomes a really integral part of Religious Studies, this will have significant implications for the concept of religion used in both empirical research and theoretical analysis. However, it will not only influence and enrich the study of religion, but also bring about deep changes in religious practice. Nowhere can this be seen more clearly than in the area of spirituality and religious ritual where women today are experimenting with a fresh creativity and inventiveness unthinkable before. These experiments, and the new questions arising from them, may have consequences as yet difficult to foresee, but as far as one can judge at present, attention to gender in the study of religion signals an important turning point which indicates a promising new direction for Religious Studies.

SUGGESTED READING

Eck, Diana L. and Jain, Devaki, eds, *Speaking of Faith: Cross-Cultural Perspectives on Women, Religion and Social Change*, London: The Women's Press, 1986.

Eliade, Mircea, ed. *The Encyclopaedia of Religion*, New York and London: Collier Macmillan, 1987; see for 'Androcentrism', vol. 1: pp. 272–6; 'Goddess Worship: Theoretical Perspectives', vol. 6: pp. 53–9; 'Women's Studies', vol. 15: pp. 433–40.

King, Ursula, *Women and Spirituality. Voices of Protest and Promise*, London: Macmillan, 1989.

Loades, Ann, *Feminist Theology—A Reader*, London: SPCK and Louisville: Westminster, John Knox, 1990.

Plaskow, Judith and Christ, Carol, P., eds, *Weaving the Visions. New Patterns in Feminist Spirituality*, San Francisco: Harper and Row, 1989.

Ruether, Rosemary, *Sexism and God-Talk. Towards a Feminist Theology*, London: SCM Press, 1983.

Shap Working Party/CRE, *World Religions in Education: Women in Religion*, London: Commission for Racial Equality, 1988.

Sharma, Arvind, ed., *Women in World Religions*, Albany: State University of New York Press, 1987.

9. RELIGION AND INFORMATION TECHNOLOGY

Kim Knott

At first glance this title might suggest a discussion about the way in which contemporary religions have or have not risen to the challenge of the technological revolution. This would indeed be an interesting subject, exploring as it might televangelism, the use of satellite communication in overseas mission, the computerisation of mailing lists and credit facilities and their impact on the expansion of evangelical organizations. The specific concern here, however, is the study of religion and religions. How has this venture been informed and changed by information technology?

Strictly speaking, the term information technology refers to any technology which focuses on the management and distribution of information. In teaching and research in the humanities this would include tape recorders, slide and overhead projectors, TV and video, as well as computers of all kinds. All of these, with the exception of computers, are extensively used at all levels of Religious Studies education. The potential uses of computing, however, have not yet been realised by Religious Studies teachers and researchers, in Britain or elsewhere. This short article, of necessity, tends toward an exploration of the possibilities rather than a recording of the achievements of the Religious Studies' utilisation of information technology.

It was not long ago that humanities scholars and educators kept a distance from the world of computing, seeing it as largely irrelevant to their interests. Understandably, we were also somewhat afraid of it and debilitated by its demands. Computing was seen as numeracy-related, and the use of computers to perform tasks involving 'number-crunching' discouraged a view of computing as either creative or useful for those who worked with words. Now, a great many people engaged in the study of religion own or use either a 'dedicated wordprocessor' (a machine of which the sole or prime function is wordprocessing) or a computer with wordprocessing software. These are used for any task from copy typing through to the entire production of a text from the first uncertain words to the camera-ready copy.

This has become possible because certain skilled people – computer specialists, 'humanists' willing to learn programming and try out prototypes, and business people with an eye for what will sell – have investigated our needs and limitations, and have hidden the difficult bits (the engineering, maths and logic) behind a friendly interface which enables us to utilise and instruct machines and programmes that we have no time to understand. So, while it is true that computer programming is at its heart about numbers, it is not the case that all tasks involving computers demand a knowledge of numbers or require their manipulation. Wordprocessing is an example of this and there are others as I will show.

Computing need not be uncreative either. Computers can certainly perform repetitive tasks with accuracy and speed, tasks which save researchers as well as organisations time and effort. Bibliographical searches by computer are of this nature. However, computers can also be harnessed in more spontaneous, intuitive and playful capacities. We can keep all our thoughts and notes on disc if we want to, and build these later into more considered literary productions. With the right technology, we can send immediately a memo describing a new idea to a colleague across the world, without waiting for the airmail to arrive.

For any computer user there will be issues to be considered, of time and energy, finance, ethics, personal predilection. Some people just prefer pen and paper. Some tasks involve a considerable investment of time in terms of learning or data-input which might outweigh their eventual use. Some machines and some items of software are extremely expensive: our opportunities may be severely limited by this fact alone. In teaching tasks, human interaction may in most cases be preferable to students working alone at a VDU. Nevertheless, Religious Studies specialists at all levels could make more use of information technology if they had the time, support, resources and inclination. It is accepted that, most of the time, most of us, regrettably, do not.

The potential applications of computing in Religious Studies are many, though, while conceivable, they are as yet largely unrealised. The remainder of this article will explore these applications in relation to the three areas of research, writing and publication, and teaching in our subject area.

A Preliminary Note

As a field of enquiry, Religious Studies involves the use of many methods (e.g. historical, textual-linguistic and sociological) which also have relevance to other areas of interest – to other kinds of social groups, ideological orientations or types of behaviour. As a result of this, information technology has no special relation to Religious Studies that it does not also have to historical studies, critical analysis and sociological studies as conducted by historians, English literature specialists or sociologists. The field of relevance to us as teachers and researchers of Religious Studies is computing in the humanities and to a lesser extent the social sciences. Naturally, this is an interdisciplinary field in which those involved learn from one another about potential applications in their own areas of interest. Many of the examples given below relate to past or existing projects, primarily British, in which computers are used to enhance the study or teaching of religion; some are ideas derived from comparable projects in history, classics, literature etc. Undoubtedly, there will be many people, of whom I am currently unaware, whose work in Religious Studies involves the imaginative use of information technology.

Research

Few researchers in Religious Studies or theology make use of a computer for tasks other than wordprocessing. I make this assertion on the basis of having scanned both the biographical section of 'Humanist' (an on-line information service run on the academic computer network) and the programme of the joint American Academy of Religion/Society for Biblical Literature (AAR/SBL) conference held in Chicago in 1988.

The first of these showed a number of people engaged in biblical studies using computers, including amongst others John Hughes of Stanford whose recent publication, *Bits, Bytes and Biblical Studies: A Resource Guide for the Use of Computers in Biblical and Classical Studies* (Zondervan, 1987) reveals the extent of ground-breaking work in that area. Several others in the US were involved in entering texts in non-roman alphabets, e.g. Sanskrit and Chinese, for analysis. Two people were working in a preliminary way on topics in the sociology of religion, one mentioned textual work in Jewish mysticism, computer use in RE in schools was cited by an English researcher, and the ethics of health care were also mentioned.

The conference guide of the AAR/SBL was also revealing. In the SBL programme, a special section was held by the 'Computer Assisted Research Group' and computer applications were mentioned in other contributions. In the AAR programme, computer analysis was not mentioned in the titles of any papers given. It must be said of course that, when used in research, computers are part of our methodological apparatus – not something we necessarily mention in a paper title. Nevertheless, one might expect computerisation to have made sufficient methodological impact to warrant some focused attention in such an academic programme.

Oddly enough, what is generally recognised to be the first humanistic enquiry using modern data-processing equipment involved research on a religious subject. In 1949, a Jesuit, Father Roberto Busa, who was researching 'presence' in the work of St Thomas Aquinas, began the lengthy task of producing a detailed concordance of the Corpus Thomisticum. This, as I hope to show, is one example of the kind of computer work which has liberated academics from certain time-consuming and tedious tasks. In other cases, the computer has enabled researchers to speed up or undertake operations which otherwise would have been difficult or labour intensive. Many, though not all, of these tasks involve the management of large amounts of data.

In order to explore the potential of computing in Religious Studies research, I have divided the remainder of this section into four parts: *information retrieval*, including some of the many uses of databases, *work with texts*, *statistical work*, and *personal information management*.

(a) *Information Retrieval*

Computers are extremely useful for sorting and searching information, tasks which might consume time that individuals could spend in more creative pursuits. Considerable amounts of information, whether numeric or alphabetic, can be held in computer files which, if formatted correctly, can be used in these processes. For large computers with many users (mainframes) or for personal, micro computers, software is available which enables users to input, store, sort and search data, and produce reports of searches. This software allows users to create 'databases'.

Many Religious Studies scholars and students already make use of databases in their work, often unwittingly, by requesting computer searches of on-line bibliographies for references of, for example, all publications whose titles refer to the 'Ramayana', the 'hajj' or the 'Shakers'. The major database for Religious Studies users is the *Religion Index* with some 400,000 references. Other databases utilised in such searches are the *Arts and Humanities Search* and *Social SciSearch* (which correspond to the Arts and Humanities and Social Science Citation Indexes), *Humanities and Social Sciences* (corresponding to British Library catalogues in these areas), *British Books in Print and the Bookseller*, *CNRS-SHS* (Centre National de la Recherche Scientifique: Science de l'homme et de la societé), and *FRANCIS* (French Retrieval Automated Network for Current Information in Social Science). Each of these includes in excess of 800,000 citations.

Individual users or groups of users can also produce their own bibliographies on mainframe computers or micros. The Community Religions Project in the Department of Theology and Religious Studies at the University of Leeds has its own bibliography on the University Amdahl computer of works on religions in Britain which can be searched by author, title, date or keyword (e.g. Islam, Coventry, Dialogue, Punjabi, Expository etc.). Similarly, thesis writers might find a database useful for storing bibliographical references with short abstracts.

Databases also have many non-bibliographical uses. Technically, they are of several different kinds, some suited to coping only with multiple items of a regular shape and size housed in a single file, others – relational databases – able to store, search, compare and match information in different formats. Historians use databases for many mundane operations involving the sorting and linkage of historical materials such as parish and government records, census information and court papers. Religious Studies researchers using archival sources might employ similar techniques.

Any single text or collection of texts, from very small items like citations to large items such as books themselves, can form a database. I have catalogued media references to religious themes which I have then searched and sorted, and have computerised interview data for content analysis. One interesting project currently in progress in Britain is a computer-assisted study of accounts of religious experience which is being undertaken at the Alister Hardy Research Centre, Oxford, and which has involved the production of a coding system suitable for the categorisation and analysis of features of transcendent experience. A major difficulty in work of this kind is the need to isolate and classify meanings rather than words alone: not all those who have experiences of a religious nature use the same words to describe them.

Perhaps the most exciting current use of the database is what is called 'hypertexts'. These are software packages, such as 'Guide',

'Hyperties' and 'Intermedia', which allow for the initial inputting and collation of different 'texts' which can then be used interactively by others for various learning and information-gathering tasks. Like other types of database they provide opportunities for items of information or texts to be linked but, unlike others, they allow the user more freedom to move around the material, to make connections and to add his or her own thoughts and ideas. In addition to passages of the written word – literary, biographical, historical, sociological, critical – tables, maps, diagrams and pictures can be incorporated which might enhance a user's understanding and appreciation of the historical, social or cultural context of the textual material. These might be included in separate sections or on different levels through which a user might browse as they would through a pile of different books, articles, and visual materials on the same topic. There might also be room in the programme for the user to make notes.

Hypertexts are better demonstrated than described. What is more, I know of no examples of their use in Religious Studies at present though several scholars in the USA and UK have ideas for their development.

Hypertexts are clearly not solely research-related; nor are they limited to information retrieval. Their use could make us rethink the way we write up and distribute our research, and their application in teaching is already having an impact in other disciplines. It goes without saying that, like all computer initiatives they could be used to dull or to stimulate the creative task.

(b) *Work with Texts*

I have already begun the discussion of this area by introducing hypertexts, in which religious texts may be used alongside 'texts' of other kinds. In this section, however, I want to mention some of the work done already and the possibilities for further work in the area of machine-readable texts and their analysis.

The main task of Roberto Busa in his work on Aquinas mentioned earlier was the production of both a 'database' in which the Corpus Thomisticum was able to be stored and tools whereby it might be analysed morphologically. Similarly, institutions in the US and Europe have produced machine-readable versions of many important religious texts in recent years. In the vast majority of cases this has involved someone sitting at a keyboard typing them in, though the development of optical recognition systems or scanners (most notably

Kurzweil and Octopus) promises to reduce the human effort involved in this (scanners still have difficulty with non-standard type faces and most handwritten documents). The other issue has been the 'mark-up' or encoding of texts to enable the computer to recognise and 'read' them. Many different systems have been used in the past though the one now generally in use is the 'Standard Generalized Markup Language'.

In Britain, the Oxford Text Archive at the University of Oxford Computing Service holds a large number of computer-readable texts (for which a list is available) including such items as the Rig Veda and the Bhagavad Gita. These, and the Heart Sutra (in Sanskrit and Tibetan), are also to be found – with many others in different languages and alphabets – on a new set of two discs produced for 'CD Rom'. Most of us are accustomed to using either floppy discs or hard discs in association with micro computers, or magnetic tape for information storage in mainframes. Forms of storage from audio-visual technology are being used increasingly in computing. The compact disc (CD) enables large amounts of information to be stored and accessed by micro users. The two discs mentioned above have been produced at Irvine, California where, since 1972, the Thesaurus Linguae Graecae (TLG) has been developed which is a vast collection of texts in Classical Greek in machine-readable form.

Further examples with some potential interest for Religious Studies are the databases currently being built up at the University of Bombay. These include a textbase on Kalidasa, India's national poet, called DOKAL. This is planned to include his writings, as well as translations and critical accounts of his work in various languages including Sanskrit, Hindi, Kannada and Marathi.

Once available in machine-readable form, texts like those above become suitable for computer-assisted analysis. This is a field which has received much attention in the last two decades, with software written to search and recognise linguistic elements in many languages and alphabets. In Britain, the Oxford Concordance Programme, developed in the late 1970s and now available for micros, can create wordlists, indexes and concordances from a text in any alphabetic language. It can be used in stylistic analysis, morphology, dictionary-making and content analysis. Elsewhere, initiatives in this area include CATSS (Computer Assisted Tools for Septuagint Study) devised jointly in Philadelphia and Jerusalem, which not only makes available the entire texts of the Hebrew and Greek Bibles but has the means to produce bilingual concordances with full vocalisation and accenting.

(c) *Statistical Work*

In addition to sorting and listing words, the software described in the last two sections also enables simple quantitative analysis to take place, for example, counting citations or occurrences or particular words. More sophisticated numerical work can be achieved with statistical packages, used most commonly by social scientists but also by historians and others.

One obvious use of such software is in the analysis of questionnaire data. Recent projects of this kind undertaken in Britain have included a study of the worldwide Zoroastrian community (University of Manchester) and research on conventional and common religion in Leeds (University of Leeds). This type of analysis requires the coding of answers to questions and the inputting of these data into files which can be read and analysed using a programme such as SAS (Statistical Analysis System) or SPSS (Statistical Package for the Social Sciences). These programmes are able to calculate and display frequencies, cross tabulations, correlations, variance, regressions and so on. Like many other computer tools, they are extremely powerful and sophisticated if used well, but they require considerable knowledge and commitment to produce useful results. These and other packages can also be used for work with archival materials. For example, research is currently being undertaken at Leeds on the accuracy of the 1851 census of religious worship of England and Wales.

(d) *Personal Information Management*

Most of the applications I have described above concern the analysis of research data. Collection and analysis are obviously central to the research task. However, it is also composed of less lofty activities such as note-taking, the jotting down of thoughts for future use, the compilation of a bibliography and writing up. The number and scale of operations conducted at a computer terminal or workstation will depend on the individual. Similarly, the range of software used will vary. In addition to a wordprocessor and any tools used in data analysis, one might consider the use of a simple database for references, even the use of hypertexts for the organisation and writing up of book notes, thoughts, interviews, fieldwork notes, drafts of chapters or articles, footnotes and appendices. Computerising all aspects of the research task in this way will appeal to some researchers and not to others.

Research and writing are inextricably interwoven for all students and scholars, particularly those in the humanities. Having discussed some of the ways in which computers can help us to analyse and organise data, we must now reflect in brief on their use in the preparation and presentation of manuscripts.

Writing and Publication

The main contribution in the area, and one I need say little about, is wordprocessing. Like the photocopier, wordprocessing software has had a dramatic impact on the production of manuscripts and teaching materials. The period between composing the first draft and running off the perfect copy has been reduced by the use of wordprocessing facilities for tasks such as editing, laying out and pagination of text. Cutting and pasting continue, but these no longer require scissors and glue. The manufacture and marketing of cheap and reliable dedicated wordprocessors with printers have enabled and encouraged large numbers of staff and students to learn wordprocessing skills.

Of the software currently available perhaps the most exciting for Religious Studies users – and the most expensive – is 'Nota Bene', developed for professional writers and researchers. It can process words in a number of languages and alphabets, with vocalisation and accenting. It includes spelling checker, thesaurus and special formatting and editing features. As well as wordprocessing, it also operates as a textbase with space for thousands of pages of unstructured notes which can be accessed for use in manuscript writing. Additionally, it contains a bibliographic utility. Nota Bene brings together the wordprocessor with several of the other useful features described in earlier sections.

A related function of computing for scholars is 'desk-top publishing'. In reality, major aspects of the business of publishing are mass-manufacture and marketing, neither of which, as far as I know, can be undertaken at the desk (though databases can help in the production of standard letters, mailing lists and address labels). Essentially, the term 'desk-top publishing' refers to the preparation of camera-ready copy, complete with inclusive graphics, headings, end notes and computer-aided indexing. Additionally, with the help of laser printing, high quality copy can be produced.

Teaching

A great deal has been written already about the use of computers in teaching (e.g. *Information Technology and Education: The Changing School* edited by R. Ennals, R. Gwyn and L. Zdravchev, Chichester, 1986). The aim here is to draw on examples of initiatives with implications for Religious Studies.

One breakthrough which will have a major impact in years to come on computer use at all levels of education is the advanced interactive system which uses compact discs and video cassettes for the creation of an attractive learning environment. They store text and images through which users can browse and with which they can enter into dialogue. Some readers will have seen the 'Domesday Project' discs which contain an immense amount of information collected around the country by schools and other institutions on British national and community life in the 1980s. Additionally, a project at the University of Southampton called HIDES (Historic Document Expert System) is currently developing interactive videodiscs for the teaching of history.

In British schools at present, less sophisticated but nevertheless exciting interactive methods are used. In Religious Studies, story boards are available (which enable students to overlay a keyboard with a picture, ask for relevant information and key in responses), for example, a multi-level introduction to a Sikh gurdwara.

In higher education, the most common use of computers in teaching at present is in language learning, and this has been a feature in several departments of religion, principally at the University of Durham where the CALIBAL programme has been developed. 'Computer Assisted Learning in Biblical and Ancient Languages', which like some of the other projects mentioned here was funded by the Computers in Teaching Initiative, enables students to learn a text-based language, New Testament Greek, with the aid of a computer. Non-language orientated CAL programmes (Computer Assisted Learning) in British universities include Project Pallas at the University of Exeter, the aim of which was to introduce both humanities staff and students to wordprocessing and information retrieval, and DISH (Design and Implementation of Software in History) at Glasgow.

Those involved in the development of software for teaching at all levels are acutely aware of the need to avoid using new technology to teach with archaic methods. Schemes involving rote learning and unsophisticated question and answer sessions, though easy to design, are not seen as the right way forward. There is an awareness of the need to use computers to develop critical skills, the ability to compare and evaluate, and the opportunity to explore new interpretations as well as for the provision of information.

Some Resources for RS Users of IT

As the sections above have shown, apart from proprietary products (wordprocessors, databases, statistical packages etc.), there is little software available or currently in development specifically for Religious Studies scholars and students. Unfortunately, this situation can only be changed if those in the area have the will to do so, either by applying the computing skills they already have or by learning new ones. We cannot expect that software specialists outside the subject will fill the vacuum; we do not constitute an adequate market.

Anyone interested in pursuing computer-aided research or teaching will find that a support network exists to put humanities users in touch with one another. Internationally, there are a number of relevant associations, including the Association for Computers and the Humanities (ACH), the Association for Literary and Linguistic Computing (ALLC), the Association for History and Computing, the Computer Assisted Language Learning and Instruction Consortium and the Association for the Development of Computer-based Instructional Systems. In Britain, there is a further body, the Computers in Teaching Initiative Support Service. Several journals are published, including *Computing in the Humanities*, *Literary and Linguistic Computing* and the *Journal of Computer-Based Instruction*.

Through the academic computer network (within Britain, this is the Joint Academic Network (JANet); internationally, it is BitNet/NetNorth/Earn), individuals can communicate electronically with users elsewhere, working in teams or just exchanging information and ideas. A list of electronic mail addresses of Religious Studies scholars linked to this network is currently being compiled within the International Association for the History of Religions. A comparable list, circulated in the form of an electronic newsletter, is produced by the International Association for Biblical Literature (AIBI). This is also helped by the information facilities available on the network: HUMBUL, the Humanities Online Bulletin Board on

JANet run from the University of Leicester; and HUMANIST, a group-mail-forwarding facility sponsored by the ACH and ALLC, and run from the University of Toronto. These enable users to be aware of work in progress elsewhere.

There are also regular conferences run by the major associations and often supported by the information technology industry. In 1989 in Toronto a joint ACH/ALLC conference was held under the title of 'The Dynamic Text'. Sessions were held on many aspects of humanities computing, from teaching to the use of databases, from literary analysis to editing and indexing. During the conference a fair was held, 'Tools for Humanists', at which participants could examine software and hardware with potential for their work.

Information on the whole range of agencies and facilities, available software and bibliographic references to humanities computing can be found in a single volume published in 1988, *The Humanities Computing Yearbook 1988*, edited by Ian Lancashire and Willard McCarty (Oxford). One item to which the editors refer in their excellent book is a collection of articles on arts computing in Britain, *Information Technology in the Humanities: Tools, Techniques and Applications*, edited by Sebastian Rahtz (Chichester, 1987). This provides a historical survey, information about teaching, databases, the processing of words and the art of programming, and articles about the use of computers in the studies of history, art and design, literature, music, biblical studies and archaeology.

Information technology is like religion in two respects: everchanging and manifesting itself in new forms, but also open to abuse. With regard to both of these it provides a challenge, first, that we harness the fruits of technical innovation for the production of imaginative research and teaching, and secondly, that we resist the urge to become slaves to the machine.

SUGGESTED READING

R. Ennals, R. Gwyn and L. Zdravchev, eds, *Information Technology and Education: The Changing School*, Chichester: Ellis Horwood, 1986.

I. Lancashire and W. McCarty, eds, *The Humanities Computing Yearbook 1988*, Oxford: Clarendon Press, 1988.

S. Rahtz, ed., *Information Technology in the Humanities: Tools, Techniques and Applications*, Chichester: Ellis Horwood, 1987.

CONCLUDING REFLECTIONS: RELIGIOUS STUDIES IN GLOBAL PERSPECTIVE

Ninian Smart

An Age of Opportunity

We are, of course, entering on a new global civilisation. This presents us with a great opportunity for enhancing the ideals enshrined in the modern study of religion and religions. Those ideals I would define as follows: the treatment of religions in a crosscultural or plural context, as distinguished from the more limited (though in its own context valid) theological or buddhological study of religion from within a tradition, aimed at articulating its doctrines or philosophy; the attempt to gain a sensitive understanding of religions and of religious history; the treatment of religions as traditionally understood in the context of other symbol systems and ideologies (that is, other worldviews); and the process of reflection about religious values in a plural or as some might say dialogical context.

The modern study of religion, because it is warmly dispassionate, and has both scientific and humanistic aspects, already contains within its logic the seeds of an ethos which is important for today's world. Its recognition of differing religious and other traditions implies that the comparative study of religions can never go back to a phase where sometimes it was suspected of masking a sense of western and Christian cultural and spiritual superiority. On the other hand, it is most important for us not to abandon the liberal framework within which the modern study of religion now occurs, namely a framework in which various points of view are encouraged and in which scholars are free to carry on with scientific and impartial delineation of the subject-matter. There is a danger that the ethos of the modern university will be identified as merely western (as sometimes wrongly science is thought of as western), and in a post-colonial backlash Religious Studies will be reduced to various theologies (Islamic, Hindu and so forth).

Unfortunately, though this is a period of great global opportunity, many of the institutions devoted to the study of religion retain a conservative stance, in effect going back to the time of church-state solidarity. Thus so much of the study of religion in Germany and

Britain – to take two prominent European examples – is predicated on earlier arrangements for training ordinands in officially recognized faiths. It was only during the 1960s that the United States embarked seriously on programmes of Religious Studies in publicly supported universities. The situation has been worse in Marxist countries where the old church–state solidarity has largely remained in force – only it is the Communist Party which functions as the church. Not dissimilar arrangements regarding Buddhist studies can be found in Sri Lanka, and regarding Islamic studies in Malaysia, Saudi Arabia and many other Islamic countries.

Now of course it does not follow from this that committed studies have nothing to offer the wider field of the study of religion. They are something which indeed we can build upon. But they can represent a problem in getting the true recognition of the pluralistic ethos in today's world.

There are, of course, reasons why intellectually and for social reasons the crosscultural study of worldviews is important. First, in today's world there are so many migrations and so many places where cultures live together that it is vital that some understanding of diverse values should be generated. If the typical inhabitant of Birmingham, England, wears a shamrock in his turban, so too do the citizens of many other places (or at least some differing combination of headgear), such as Singapore, Melbourne, Karachi, Tashkent, Munich, Los Angeles, Lagos, Fiji and so on. There is a decreasing number of societies which are at all ethnically monolithic. Second, we are now heirs not just of British or American history, but of world history. The study of religions is a vital ingredient in understanding the character of the various civilisations. Most of them are build upon religious foundations. Third, we have an increased awareness of the vital role of the symbolic aspect of human existence, alongside economic and other factors.

As well as these three there is a fourth factor. Many people are searchers, realising that the truth is not monolithically laid down, as Sunday School might lead us to think. We emerge into the adult world realising that there are varieties of living worldviews: and these increasingly have become living options. This has been especially obvious since the 60s. In fact this is the chief contribution of the 60s to modern awareness. In searching we may also be looking for a global outlook to go with the emerging global civilization. Is there some overarching worldview which we all share and within whose framework the varying religious and ideological traditions can operate? I do not advocate here Religious Studies mysteriously turning into a new religion. But I do say that the deeper are the ways in which we come to understand human religious diversity, the more urgently we are liable to reflect upon the mode in which that diversity can express itself within the overall context of a global civilisation.

Some might think that so far I have made too much of contemporary issues. There are those fine scholars patiently working among the Hittites or ancient Zoroastrians, or piecing together the data on the Indus Valley civilisation, working out the conclusions to be drawn from the great new archaeological discoveries in China or deciphering the iconography of the Toltecs. Actually, in my view, the study of religion must always retain balance: it must be both ancient and modern. Moreover, ancient studies will likely increase in interest and influence in the coming decades. The reason is that public interest will greatly grow. This will be not only because many more folk from all over the world will, through the tourist industry, see ancient ruins and dreamily speculate about values long ago: but also perhaps more importantly because as the globe shrinks, our claustrophobia will demand new outlets, and one of them is the past. People will go in for the best of all time-travel – into the past. This will greatly enhance the value of history.

In short, this is a period of great opportunity for Religious Studies. If we consider the time since the second world war, we can detect three periods, the third of which we are now entering upon. The first was one of struggle, especially in Britain – struggle to keep the comparative study of religion alive. In this Geoffrey Parrinder played an altogether notable role, together with older stalwarts, including E. O. James and A. C. Bouquet. He also played a striking part throughout the second period, which was one of wonderful expansion and consolidation, especially in the United States and Canada, and to a lesser degree in Europe, Japan, Africa and Australasia. The second period has put the subject on the map. At the American Academy of Religion conventions some four or five thousand scholars come together, a number of them from Europe and Japan and elsewhere. Now we have a period for reaching further forward. This may be helped in some places by demography. We are due for a new expansion of higher education in many areas in the middle of the 1990s, and because many professors will retire, there will be much fresh blood in the profession. But there remain severe weaknesses and problems.

Remaining Problems and Weaknesses in the Religious Studies Scene

The first main problem is to do with institutional recognition of Religious Studies. In the University of California, for instance, there is only one doctoral prgramme and fully-fledged Department of Religious Studies, at Santa Barbara. Three other campuses have programmes. But elsewhere, in the other four main campuses there is very little. We can compare the situation in history or English or philosophy, which occur at all campuses. Now this is in a university which is relatively benign in its attitude to the study of religion. There are quite a few big state universities where the picture is much worse. In Britain we have the complication of many universities which teach theology rather than, or alongside, Religious Studies: but there are also plenty of universities where the field, if taught at all, occurs within sociology, as sociology of religion, or anthropology. These are just two examples of the way in which the modern study of religion is struggling to find its place in the world of academe. People fear that it is really a place for preachers, and do not understand the academic shape of the discipline.

A second problem has to do with the ghettoisation of traditional studies. For instance, nearly all Christian history is studied and written by Christians. Notoriously Jewish studies are a virtually unique preserve for Jewish scholars. Increasingly in the West students of Buddhism are Buddhists. Now it is of course natural enough that many of those who deal with a religion belong to it. But it is a much healthier position if there were a reasonably balanced mixture of people researching a faith. For one thing, adherents can be over-sensitive. Or they may be too inclined to emphasize one dimension of religion over against others: much Christian history has concentrated on the development of doctrine, for instance. An outsider can have a fresher view. The dialectic between insider and outsider will be fruitful in our studies.

Moreover, the ghettoisation of studies may mean that otherwise insightful people do not venture into wider studies and wider explorations. Too many Jewish and Christian scholars keep very much to their specialisations. This gives these studies often a high technical standard. But all this does not help the wider appreciation of religious forces. St Francis Xavier is said to have remarked when he got to Japan and encountered true Pure Land Buddhism that Luther had arrived in Japan before him. There is a question here, is there not? Are devotional piety and the idea of grace something which we find in a number of civilisations and do they arise from some main type of religious experience? If so, what does this say about human nature? And, by the way, what does it tell Barth? (Kraemer tried to brush away this question with a theory of the organic character of religions, so that apparent likenesses are differences in the wider organic context.)

There are institutional reinforcements of the ghettoisation of traditions. Naturally, many university chairs are tied to churches, and many to state-sponsored faiths. They are in turn often divided into ideologically loaded definitions, like Old Testament, New Testament, church history and so on. Fortunately of course many forward-looking scholars do not worry too much about such appellations. Even so, these arrangements do help to keep scholars in their compartments, somewhat unnaturally.

Another problem is the lack of agreement about exploring secular ideologies as part of the study of religions. It is of course notorious that many scholars profess to be unable to define religion. Yet on the other hand they often shy away from treating parallel symbolic systems. This leads in my view to a lot of unclarity about church-state relations and such matters. But more importantly it neglects the fact that secular ideologies and religions are often competitors for humans' allegiance; and it neglects ways too in which ideologies combine with religions – for instance in liberation theology, liberal Protestantism, Buddhist socialism and so forth. It is, I think, necessary from a modern perspective to treat all symbolic systems or worldviews together. It does not matter whether we decide to treat philosophical Confucianism as religious or not: the fact is it can be explored as belonging within the same wider basket. In my view the study of religions is more broadly conceived as worldview studies, and its more descriptive part can be thought of as worldview analysis. From this perspective we could conceive a field in which Taoism, Maoism, nationalisms, Buddhism, Christianity, humanism and Judaism, etc., would all be part.

A third problem is that often the study of religions, which ought to be polymethodic or multidisciplinary, does not integrate into itself very well sociological and anthropological approaches. Or perhaps I should put this more broadly and say that Religious Studies does not see its place among the social sciences, as well as the humanities. So we often have freakish divisions – between new religious movements, generally western, and new African religions and other 'third world' movements. Even the division between anthropology and sociology is artificial, by the way. All this shows the force of institutional arrangements upon thought processes. The sometimes irrational history of academic organisations gets to be reflected in patterns of study. This is being reinforced by the global character of today's world. International societies for this and that are growing more influential, and the definition of the this or that is often that of traditionalist western universities. Globalism helps to cement rather than to loosen up categories.

Another general problem is the rather uneven development of the subject. Its most flourishing state is in North America, as I have indicated, followed by Europe. But in the Islamic countries, the Marxist regimes and in Catholic regions such as Latin America it is still for largely ideological reasons much less developed. Even in India, traditionally favourable to pluralist attitudes to religions, it is surprisingly underdeveloped.

Also, the subject is unevenly developed in another sense. Hardly any textbooks for instance deal with certain parts of the world, particularly in South Pacific, Latin America, Central Asia and the USSR. I have tried to remedy this problem in my recent *The World's Religions* (Cambridge: Cambridge Unversity Press, 1989). But clearly much work needs to be done on various global areas. As regards modern studies, there are surprising lacunae even in apparently well-covered areas – e.g. religion in modern Italy and its relationship to nationalism, contemporary Irish Christianity, Hindu diaspora populations, etc.

Are there Solutions to these Problems?

The above problems need to be worked at piecemeal and on the ground, though I have one global proposal which might go a long way to deal with them. I should not, incidentally, give the impression that there has not been progress in recent years. In fact during the period from about 1955 till now (let us date it by the two Rome Congresses of the International Association for the History of Religions, [IAHR], 1955 to 1990), there has been fabulous progress in many areas. It was once hard to find anyone working on Chinese religions, and now a whole cohort of younger scholars has done fine work, and one could point to many fields where there has been a like flowering of scholarship, itself facilitated by the development of departments during the 60s – in Tibetan studies, Indian regional religions, Tantrism, Shi'a studies, Polynesian religions, and so on. But though all this is good, the problems I cited earlier do remain.

Some of the above problems can be met by ad hoc arrangements. For instance I would encourage the formation of groups of concerned scholars from different traditions to meet together to discuss the histories of the ghettoised traditions. To some extent working parties in the underdeveloped areas I have cited could be created. There are plenty of good regional historians and sociologists who could be brought together with history-of-religions scholars and religious scholars. Also such working parties and study groups could as far as possible be international. Existing organisations such as the IAHR could work on these matters.

But it may be that the time has come to form a new umbrella organisation – a World Academy of Religion. Existing global institutions like the IAHR have done noble and effective things. But you need a more embracing organisation with not too much attention to purism. What I mean is that though the overall aim of a World Academy of Religion would be the crosscultural, multidisciplinary and reflective study of religion, it has, to make real progress, to embrace all kinds of committed and non-committed scholarly organisations – it has to embrace Jewish exegetes and Christian theologians, Islamic historians and editors of Vaishnava texts, Marxists historians of atheism and Catholic jurisprudents, liberal New Testament scholars and Sikh professors, and so forth. It has to embrace as much as possible of the scholarship of all sorts going on in the world. This is more or less the attitude of the American Academy of Religion, which has certain areas of chaos by consequence and could easily slide into some kind of theological debating society if it is not careful. But the embracing strategy is, I am sure, a sound one. Such a World Academy of Religion could also contain powerful elements which would enhance the field, particular crosscultural Women's Studies, already having a strong impact especially in North America. It could be genuinely crosscultural, which would be much easier if it is not tied to the rightly and strictly scholarly and scientific stance of the IAHR.

For I believe that in the long run the plural and crosscultural approach to Religious Studies is bound to triumph. Further, the World Academy of Religion could be a force for permitting deeper conversations between religions, without reverting into a simple exchange of pieties.

So it seems to me that in entering on this third phase of the study of religions we might be ambitious in order to set up an organisation which would loosely preside over the multitudinous studies which now represent our field. By being relatively non-purist it could attract associations of committed religious scholars who have much to offer, but who do not as yet have much sympathy for or grasp of what I have called the modern study of religion. Such an organisation could have as affiliates many of the learned societies in the world which deal with religions (and ideologies). It could be something which could stimulate further the fine developments which have occurred during the second phase of the post world war II period.

In brief, we have now entered on a new era of opportunities in our field. In moving into it, we should also be grateful to those who, like Geoffrey Parrinder, have kept the subject going in hard times and have contributed mightily to its expansion in lusher times.

APPENDIX

BIBLIOGRAPHY OF GEOFFREY PARRINDER'S PUBLICATIONS

(*NOTE*: Special gratitude is recorded here for the great help given by Professor Parrinder in compiling this bibliography. Valuable assistance in checking publication details was provided by Mr Robert Gleave. This bibliography is as complete as possible but does not include book reviews.)

I. BOOKS BY GEOFFREY PARRINDER

1949   *West African Religion*: A Study of the Beliefs and Practices of the Akan, Ewe, Yoruba, Ibo and Kindred Peoples, London: Epworth Press. Revised 1961. French tr. *La religion en Afrique Occidentale*, Paris: Payot, 1950.

1949   *Learning to Pray*: A Method of Spiritual Life, London: Epworth Press.

1950   *The Bible and Polygamy*: A Study of Hebrew and Christian Teaching, London: SPCK. 2nd edition 1958.

1951   *West African Psychology*: A Comparative Study of Psychological and Religious Thought, London: Lutterworth Press.

1953   *Religion in an African City*, London: Oxford University Press. Reprinted Westport/Conn.: Negro Universities, 1972.

1954   *African Traditional Religion*, London: Hutchinson's University Library. Revised 1962; 3rd edition, London: Sheldon Press, 1974. Spanish tr. 1956.

1956   *The Story of Ketu*: An Ancient Yoruba Kingdom, Ibadan: University Press. Revised 1967.

1957   *An Introduction to Asian Religions*, London: SPCK. Reprinted 1958; republished as *Asian Religions*, London: Sheldon Press, 1975.

1958   *Witchcraft*, Harmondsworth: Penguin. Spanish tr. 1963. Revised 1963 and 1965 as *Witchcraft, European and African*, London: Faber & Faber.

1960   *The Christian Approach to the Animist*, with Rev. W. T. Harris, London: Edinburgh House Press.

1960   *A Daily Bible and Prayer Book*, London: SPCK.

1961   *Worship in the World's Religions*, London: Faber & Faber, 2nd edition, London: Sheldon Press, 1974.

1961   *The Way to Worship*, United Society for Christian Literature, London: Lutterworth Press.

1962   *Comparative Religion*, London: George Allen & Unwin and
       New York: Greenwood.
1962   *Upanishads, Gītā and Bible*: A Comparative Study of Hindu
       and Christian Scriptures, London: Faber & Faber; 2nd edition,
       London: Sheldon Press, 1975. Spanish tr. *Hinduismo y
       Cristianismo*, Buenos Aires: Lidiun, 1982. Italian tr. 1964.
1963   *What World Religions Teach*, London: George Harrap & Co.;
       enlarged edition Bombay: Oxford University Press, 1968.
1964   *The Christian Debate: Light from the East*, London: Victor
       Gollancz Ltd. and New York: Doubleday.
1964   *The World's Living Religions*, London: Pan Books. Revised
       edition *The Handbook of Living Religions*, London: Arthur
       Barker, 1967. Revised edition 1974, reprinted as *The Faiths
       of Mankind*, New York: Crowell, 1965. Swedish tr. 1964;
       Norwegian tr. 1965; Finnish tr. 1969.
1965   *Jesus in the Qur'ān*, London: Faber & Faber. Reprinted 1976,
       Italian tr. Turin, 1977; Dutch tr. Baarn, 1966, 1978.
1965   *A Book of World Religions*, London: Hulton Educational
       Publications. Revised edition 1982; Italian tr. Turin 1977.
1967   *African Mythology*, London: Paul Hamlyn. Revised edition
       1982; Paris: Payot 1969.
1968   *The Significance of the Bhagavad Gītā for Christian Theology*, Dr
       Williams's Library – Friends of Dr Williams's Library.
1969   *Religion in Africa*, London: Penguin. Republished as *Africa's
       Three Religions*, London: Sheldon Press, 1976.
1970   *Avatar and Incarnation*: The Wilde Lectures in Natural and
       Comparative Religion, London: Faber & Faber; New York:
       Oxford University Press, 1982.
1971   *A Dictionary of Non-Christian Religions*, London: Hulton
       Educational Publications and Philadelphia: Westminster Press.
       Revised edition 1981.
1973   *The Indestructible Soul*, London: George Allen & Unwin.
1973   *Themes for Living*: A Source Book Selected from Religious
       and Ethical Writings of the World, London: Hulton
       Educational Press.
1974   *The Bhagavad Gita*: A Verse Translation, London: Sheldon Press.
1974   *Something after Death?* London: Denholm House Press and
       Illinois: Argus, 1975.
1975   *The Wisdom of the Forest*: The Sages of the Indian Upanishads,
       tr. by G.P., London: Sheldon Press; New York: New
       Directions, 1976.

1976 *Mysticism in the World's Religions*, London: Sheldon Press; New York: Oxford University Press, 1976.
1977 *The Wisdom of the Early Buddhists*, compiled by G.P., London, Sheldon Press; New York: New Directions, 1978.
1980 *Sex in the World Religions*, London: Sheldon Press; New York: Oxford University Press, 1980; French tr. *Le sexe dans les religions du monde*, Paris: Le Centurion, 1986.
1984 *Storia Universale delle Religioni*, published in Italian, Milan: Mondadori.
1986 *The Bhagavad Gita and World Scriptures Today*, Canterbury University: Centre for the Study of Religion and Society.
1987 *Encountering World Religions*: Questions of Religious Truth, Edinburgh: T & T Clark.
1990 *A Dictionary of Religious and Spiritual Quotations*, London: Routledge; New York: Simon and Schuster.

II.   BOOKS EDITED BY GEOFFREY PARRINDER

(a)   *With Articles*

1970 *Teaching about Religions*, Inter-European Commission on Church and School, Canterbury, London: Harrap & Co., 1971. 'Introduction' (pp. 11–18); 'The meeting of religions in the world today – a new situation' (pp. 19–37).
1971 *Man and his Gods*, London: Hamlyn; 2nd revised edition as *An Illustrated History of the World's Religions*, Newnes, 1983. 'Foreword' (p. 7); 'Introduction' (pp. 9–21); 'Traditional Africa' (pp. 54–61); 'Conclusion' (pp. 425–31).

(b)   *Without Articles*

1971 *Religions of the World*: From the Primitive Believers to Modern Faiths, New York: Madison Square Press.
1985 *Illustrated Who's Who of Mythology*, ed. M. Senior, Consultative ed. G.P., London: Orbit.

(c)   *Joint Editorship*

1968 *Swami Vivekananda in the East and West*, ed. Swami Ghanananda and G. P., London: Vedanta Centre.

(d)   Books with Forewords or Introductions by Geoffrey Parrinder

1947 'Foreword' (p. 4) in *Devotions to the Passion* by C. Wesley, London: SPCK.

1954 'Foreword' (pp. 9–15) in *My Life in the Bush of Ghosts* by Amos Tutuola, London: Faber & Faber, 1954, revised 1978.

1971 'Preface' (pp. v–vi) in *African Civilisations in the New World* by Roger Bastide, London: C. Hurst.

1972 'Introduction' (pp. xiii–xv) in *The Way of All the Earth*: An Encounter with Eastern Religions, by John S. Dunne, London: Sheldon Press.

1976 'Foreword' (pp. ix–x) in *The Way of the Mystics* by Margaret Smith, London: Sheldon Press, originally published as *Studies in Early Mysticism in the Near and Middle East*, London: Sheldon Press, 1931.

1976 'Foreword' (pp. i–ii) in *Papuan Belief and Ritual* by John Parratt, New York: Vantage Press.

1976 'Foreword' (pp. 11–12) in *Pears Encyclopaedia of Myths and Legends*, vols. 1–4, eds M. Barker and C. Cook, London: Pelham Books.

1979 'Foreword' (pp. xi–xii) in *Yoruba Beliefs and Sacrificial Rites* by J. Omosade Awolalu, London: Longman.

1980 'Foreword' (pp. vii–viii) in *The Rise of the Religious Significance of Rama* by F. Whaling, Delhi: Motilal Banarsidass.

1986 'Introduction' (pp. 1–18) in *Festivals in World Religions*, ed. A. Brown, London: Longman.

III.   BOOKS WITH ARTICLES BY GEOFFREY PARRINDER

1950 'Theistic Beliefs of the Yoruba and Ewe peoples of West Africa' in *African Ideas of God: A Symposium*, ed. E. W. Smith, 2nd edition ed. G. Parrinder, London: Edinburgh House: 224–40.

1956 'The possibility of Egyptian Influence on West African Religion', *Proceedings of the Third International West African Conference*, Ibadan, Nigerian Museum. Lagos: 61–7.

1961 'The Immanent Creator', *Proceedings of the Tenth International Congress of the IAHR, 1960*, Leiden: E. J. Brill: 81.

1961 'Religions of the World' in *Reader's Digest Great World Atlas*, ed. F. Debenham, 132–33.

1963 'An African Saviour' in *The Saviour God: Comparative Studies in the Concept of Salvation Presented to E.O. James*, ed. S. G. F. Brandon, Manchester: Manchester University Press: 117–28.

1965   'Le mysticisme des médiums en Afrique Occidentale' in *Réincarnation et vie mystique en Afrique noire*, ed. D. Zahan, Paris: Presses Universitaires de France: 131–42.

1968   'The Place of Jesus Christ in World Religions' in *Christ for us Today*, Fiftieth Annual Conference of Modern Churchmen, Oxford, 1967, ed. N. Pittenger, London: SCM: 13–28.

1968   'Traditional Religions and Modern Culture, Africa', *Proceedings of the Eleventh International Congress of the IAHR, 1965*, Leiden: E. J. Brill: 99–113.

1969   'Islam in West Africa' in *Religion in the Middle East*, ed. A. J. Arberry, London: Cambridge University Press, vol. 2: 220–35.

1969   'The Idea of Providence in Other Religions' in *Providence*, ed. M. Wiles, London: SPCK: 34–49.

1969   'African Traditional Religion' in *Africa Handbook*, revised edition, ed. C. Legum, Harmondsworth: Penguin: 583–606.

1969   'God in African Mythology' in *Myths and Symbols: Studies in Honor of Mircea Eliade*, eds J. Kitagawa and C. Long, Chicago: University of Chicago Press: 111–25.

1970   'The Ethics and Customs of the Main Immigrant Peoples' in *Comparative Religion in Education: A Collection of Studies*, ed. J. Hinnells, Newcastle: Oriel Press: 72–91.

1971   'Religions of Illiterate People','Africa'; 'The Present Religious Situation' in *Historia Religionum: Handbook of the History of Religion*, eds C. Bleeker and G. Widengren, Leiden: E. J. Brill: 550–5; 556–72; 629–41.

1971   'Revelation in Other Scriptures' in *Revelation, Studia Missionalia* 20, ed. M. Dhavamony, Rome: Gregoriana: 101–13.

1972   'Introduction to the Middle Period'; 'Orthodox philosophy I–III'; 'The Goddess and Other Deities'; 'Vaishnavism'; 'Shaivism'; 'Tantra'; 'Yoga'; 'Teaching Hinduism in the University' in *Hinduism*, eds E. J. Sharpe and J. R. Hinnells, Newcastle: Oriel Press: 41–60; 64–9; 189–96. Reprinted 1973.

1972   'Hindu Worship'; 'Buddhist Worship' in *A Dictionary of Liturgy and Worship*, ed. J. G. Davies, London: SCM Press: 192–3; 95–6.

1972   'Christian Theology and Two Asian Faiths' in *Comparative Religion: The Charles Strong Lectures 1961–70*, ed. J. Bowman, Leiden: E. J. Brill: 35–52.

1972 'Definitions of Mysticism' in *Ex Orbe Religionum, Studia Geo Widengren*, Leiden: E. J. Brill: 307–17.

1973 'The Salvation of Other Men' in *Man and his Salvation*: Studies in Memory of S. G. F. Brandon, eds E. J. Sharpe and J. Hinnells, Manchester: Manchester Univerisity Press: 189–203.

1973 'The Witch as Victim' in *The Witch Figure*: Folklore Essays by a Group of Scholars in England Honouring the 75th Birthday of K. M. Briggs, ed. V. Newall, London: Routledge and Kegan Paul: 125–38.

1974 'Is the Bhagavad-Gītā the Word of God?, in *Truth and Dialogue: The Relationship between World Religions*, ed. J.Hick, London: Sheldon Press: 111–25.

1974 'The Place of Religion in the History of Mankind' in *Religion in School History Textbooks*: Proceedings of the Symposium in Louvain, 18–20 September 1972, ed. L. Genicot, Strasbourg: Council of Europe: 43–62.

1974 'The Nature of God (Sikhism)', seminar paper in *Perspectives on Guru Nanak*, ed. H. Singh, Patiala: Punjabi University: 83–92.

1975 'Religions of the East' in *Life after Death*, A. Toynbee, A. Koestler and others, London: Weidenfeld and Nicholson: 80–96.

1975 'Bhagavadgita' in *The Encyclopaedia of Sikhism*, ed. H. Singh, Patiala: Punjabi University.

1976 'Mysticism in African Religion' in *Religion in a Pluralistic Society*: Essays presented to C. G. Baeta, Leiden : E. J. Brill: 48–59.

1976 'The Nature of Mysticism' in *Philosophy East and West*: Essays in honour of T. M. P. Mahadevan, ed. H. D. Lewis, Bombay: Blackie: 155–65.

1976 'The Beginnings of Religion' in *Reader's Digest Encyclopaedia*, London.

1977 'Mystery and Mysticism' in *Prajñāpāramitā and Related Systems*: Studies in Honour of Edward Conze, ed. L. Lancaster, Berkeley: University of California, Institute for Buddhist Studies: 395–402.

1977 'The Great World Religions: Similarities and Differences' in *The Search for Absolute Values*, New York: International Cultural Foundation: 29–39.

1977 'Recent Trends in the British Association for the History of Religions' published in Japanese by the International Christian University, Tokyo: Mitaka: 1–13.

1979 'The Vitality of Life' in *The Vitality of Death*, Tokyo: International Christian University: 1–15.

1980 'The African Spiritual Universe' in *Afro-Caribbean Religions*, ed. B. Gates, London: Ward Lock Educational: 16–25.

1980 'Death in the World Faiths' in *Death*: Standing Conference in Inter-Faith Dialogue in Education 1977, ed. J. Prickett, Guildford: Lutterworth Press: 3–20.

1981 'Religion and Socio-Cultural Transformations in Modern Asia' in *Asian Cultural Studies 12*, Tokyo: International Christian University: 5–17.

1981 'Religion and Social Change in Africa' in *Asian Cultural Studies 12*, Tokyo: International Christian University: 73–8.

1981 'Religious Foundations at Ibadan' in *Ibadan Voices*, ed. T. N. Tamuno, Nigeria: Ibadan University Press: 102–8.

1983 'Theistischer Yoga' in *Sehnsucht nach dem Ursprung*, ed. H. P. Duerr, Frankfurt: Syndikat: 422–32.

1983 'Buddhism' ; 'Hinduism' ; 'Islam' ; 'Koran' ; 'Sufism' in *A Dictionary of Christian Spirituality*, ed. G. S. Wakefield, London: SCM: 60–2; 191–4; 217–19; 241–3; 364–5.

1984 'Thematic Comparison' in *The World's Religious Traditions*: Current Perspectives in Religious Studies, Essays in Honour of Wilfred Cantwell Smith, ed. F. Whaling, Edinburgh: T & T Clark: 240–56.

1985 'Solomon'; 'Akhenaton'; 'Asoka'; 'Zoroaster'; 'Lao Tzu'; 'Confucius'; 'Buddha'; 'Plato'; 'Aristotle'; 'Mani'; 'Augustine' in *100 Great Lives of Antiquity*, ed. J. Canning, London: Methuen: 83–7; 350–4; 359–63; 481–6; 486–90; 490–5; 501–5; 505–10; 510–14; 519–24; 524–7.

1986 'Theological Attitudes towards Sexuality' in *Heaven and Earth*, eds A. A. Linzey and P. Wexler, Worthing: Churchman Publishing: 87–103.

1987 'A Theological Approach' in *Theories of Human Sexuality* eds J. H. Geer and W. T. O'Donohue, New York: Plenum: 21–48.

1987 'Charisma'; 'Exorcism'; 'Ghosts'; 'Peace'; 'Touching'; 'Triads' in *The Enclyclopaedia of Religion*, ed. M. Eliade, London and New York: Macmillan: 3:218–22; 5:225–33; 5:547–50; 11:221–24; 14:578–83; 15:39–44.

1989 'Buddhism'; 'Christianity'; 'Confucianism'; 'Daoism'; 'Islam'; 'Mahayana Buddhism'; 'Religion'; 'Shinto'; 'Theravada Buddhism' in *Political and Economic Encyclopaedia of the Pacific*, ed. G. Segal, London: Longman: 20–1; 45–8; 52; 56; 97; 145–6; 198–201; 204; 243–4.

IV. JOURNAL ARTICLES BY GEOFFREY PARRINDER

1939   'The Christian Attitude to non-Christian Religions', *The Expository Times* 50/9: 390–3
1942   'A Reasoned Approach to Religion', *The Expository Times* 54/5: 124–7
1946   'Worship in Protestant Missions', *International Review of Missions* 35: 187–93
1947   'Yoruba-Speaking Peoples in Dahomey', *Africa* 17: 122–9.
1947   'Christian Marriage in French West Africa', *Africa* 17: 260–8.
1948   'Totem and Taboo: A Revaluation', *International Review of Missions* 37: 307–12.
1948   'Furrows of Death', *West African Review*.
1949   'King for the Day', *African World*, London: 17.
1951   'Ibadan Annual Festival', *Africa* 21: 54–8.
1951   'Dahomey', *University Herald*, Ibadan: 6–7.
1952   'The Importance of Ancestral Religion', *West Africa*: 1117 and 1139.
1952   'Separatist Sects in West Africa', *World Dominion*, London: 343–6.
1955   'Moslem Revival in Nigeria', *West Africa*: 698.
1956   'Divine Kingship in West Africa', *Numen* 3: 111–21.
1956   'Music in West African Churches', *African Music* 1/3: 37–8.
1956   'African Ideas of Witchcraft', *Folk-Lore* 67: 142–50.
1956   'The Prevalence of Witches', *West Africa*, London: p. 320.
1957   'Varieties of Belief in Re-incarnation', *The Hibbert Journal* 55: 260–7.
1958   'Les Sociétés Religieuses en Afrique Occidentale', *Présence Africaine* 17/18: 17–23.
1958   'Academic Subtopia', *Ibadan*, Ibadan University Press: 3: 30.
1959   'Islam and West African Indigenous Religion', *Numen* 6: 130–41.
1959   'Immortality in the non-Christian Religions', *The Modern Churchman* 3/1: 12–20.
1960   'Christianity and Other Faiths', *The Modern Churchman* 4/2: 116–21.
1960   'The Religious Situation in West Africa', *African Affairs* 59/234: 38–42.

1960 'Progress in Church Autonomy', *West Africa*: 973.
1960 'Islam in West Africa', *West African Review*, London: December: 13–15.
1960 'Indigenous Churches in Nigeria', *West African Review*, London: September: 87–93.
1961 'Early Buddhist Dates', *The Hibbert Journal* 60: 61–6.
1962 'Omar Khayyam – Cynic or Mystic?', *London Quarterly and Holborn Review*: 222–6.
1962 'Africa's Churches Advance', *West African Review*, London: January: 4–9.
1963 'Is the World Council in Heresy?', *The Hibbert Journal* 61/243: 161–71.
1964 'Srī Aurobindo on Incarnation and the Love of God', *Numen* 11: 147–60.
1965 'Islam', *The Listener* 83/1867: 17–19.
1965 'Recent Views of Indian Religion and Philosophy', *Religious Studies* 1: 109–18.
1966 'Myths for Moderns', *Times Literary Supplement* 10.2.1966: 102.
1966 'The Origins of Religion', *Religious Studies* 1: 257–61'
1967 'On the Wickedness of Witch Hunting', *Encounter* 29: 91.
1968 'Scriptures in African Art', *Orita* 11/1: 3–11.
1969 'Religions of Asia', *Far East and Australasia*: 36–44.
1970 'Teaching about Indian Religion', *Learning for Living* 10/5: 5–10.
1970 'Monotheism and Pantheism in Africa', *Journal of Religion in Africa* 3/2: 81–8.
1971 'Indian Studies', *Religious Studies* 7: 169–74.
1971 'Learning from Other Religions IV: African Religion', *The Expository Times* 88/3: 324–8.
1971 'Islamic Doctrine', *Learning for Living* 11/3: 19–26.
1971 'Religions of Africa', *Africa South of the Sahara*: 90–4.
1971 'The Hindu Avatars', *Hemisphere*, Sydney.
1972 'And Is It True?' Inaugural Lecture for the Chair in the Comparative Study of Religions, University of London, *Religious Studies* 8: 15–27.
1973 'Ethical Standards in African Religion', *The Expository Times* 85/6: 167–71.
1973 'La place de la religion dans l'histoire de l'humanité', *Humanités Chrétiennes*, Bruxelles: 224–43.
1974 'Letters to the Editor: Rabindranath Tagore', *Times Literary Supplement* 11.10.1974: 1126.

1975   'Religious Studies in Great Britain', *Religion* 5: 1–11.
1976   'Robert Charles Zaehner, 1913–1974', *History of Religions* 16: 66–74.
1977   'The Religious Nature of Scientology', Church of Scientology, East Grinstead: 1–9.
1979   'Data Sheet on World Religions', *Epworth Review*, September: 26–8.
1980   'A Pastoral Problem: On What Premises? Comment 2', *Epworth Review*, September: 14–15.
1988   'Wet Magic or Real Miracles', *The Guardian* 21.11.1988.
1989   'Myths of the Virgin Birth that Obscure Jesus's Family Life', *The Sunday Correspondent* 24.12.1989: 18.
1989   'Dahomey Half a Century Ago', *Journal of Religion in Africa* 19/3: 264–73.
1990   'Eternal Dilemma of Free Will', *The Sunday Correspondent* 13.5.1990: 18.
1990   'Theological Assessments of Other Faiths', *Epworth Review*, May: 59–67.

Articles on 'Religion' in *The Annual Register of World Events* (London: Longman). [This *Register* has been compiled annually since 1759, with political, economic and general articles. There was no article on religion, but before the 200th publication in 1959 Geoffrey Parrinder was asked to contribute the article on religion in 1958 and he has done so every year since, the only writer to have covered this subject.]

The page numbers of the articles are:

1958: 363–71;	1959: 373–81;	1960: 377–84;	1961: 366–73;
1962: 370–78;	1963: 380–87;	1964: 366–73;	1965: 369–76;
1966: 382–89;	1967: 376–82;	1968: 368–74;	1969: 367–74;
1970: 367–73;	1971: 375–80;	1972: 375–81;	1973: 382–88;
1974: 383–88;	1975: 344–49;	1976: 357–61;	1977: 356–61;
1978: 358–62;	1979: 376–81;	1980: 376–81;	1981: 375–81;
1982: 379–83;	1983: 368–73;	1984: 387–92;	1985: 378–84;
1986: 388–94;	1987: 418–23;	1988: 435–41;	1989, 425–31.

NOTES ON CONTRIBUTORS

MARCUS BRAYBROOKE is well known for his interfaith activities. He was for many years Secretary and then Chairman of the World Congress of Faiths. He is editor of the journal *World Faiths Insight* and was until recently Executive Director of the Council of Christians and Jews.

PETER B. CLARKE is Lecturer in the History and Sociology of Religion, Department of Theology and Religious Studies, King's College, University of London.

W. OWEN COLE is a free lance lecturer and writer. He was until recently Head of Religious Studies at the West Sussex Institute of Higher Education, Chichester, where he still lectures part-time.

MICHAEL COMBERMERE is Senior Lecturer in Biblical and Religious Studies at the Centre for Extramural Studies, Birkbeck College, University of London. He was Chairman of the World Congress of Faiths from 1983–88.

ADRIAN CUNNINGHAM is Head of the Department of Religious Studies, University of Lancaster and editor of the journal *Religion*.

JOHN FERGUSON (+1989) was Dean and Director of Studies of the Faculty of Arts at the Open University (1969–79) and President of the Selly Oak Colleges (1979–87).

BRIAN E. GATES is Principal Lecturer and Head of Religious Studies and Social Ethics at St Martin's College, Lancaster. He is Chairman of the Religious Education Council of England and Wales.

ROSALIND I. J. HACKETT is Assistant Professor in the Department of Religious Studies, University of Tennessee, Knoxville, USA.

FRIEDHELM HARDY is Reader in Indian Religions in the Department of Theology and Religious Studies, King's College, University of London.

ADRIAN HASTINGS is Professor and Head of the Department of Theology and Religious Studies, University of Leeds, and editor of the *Journal of Religion in Africa.*

DAVID HAY is Director of the Religious Experience and Education Project, Nottingham University, and was until recently Director of the Alister Hardy Research Centre, Oxford.

JOHN R. HINNELLS is Professor of Comparative Religion at the University of Manchester. His original training, teaching and practical work was in the visual arts, especially painting.

ROBERT JACKSON is Reader in the Department of Arts Education, University of Warwick, and currently Chairman of the Shap Working Party on World Religions in Education and a member of the Religious Education Council of England and Wales.

URSULA KING is Professor and Head of the Department of Theology and Religious Studies, University of Bristol, and was Honorary Secretary of the British Association for the Study of Religions from 1981–87.

KIM KNOTT is Lecturer in the Department of Theology and Religious Studies, University of Leeds, and Bulletin Editor of the British Association for the Study of Religions.

STUART MEWS is Lecturer in the Department of Religious Studies, University of Lancaster, and was editor of the journal *Religion* from 1983–89.

PETER MOORE is Lecturer in Theology and Religious Studies at the University of Kent, Canterbury.

ELEANOR NESBITT is part-time Lecturer in the Department of Arts Education, University of Warwick.

GLYN RICHARDS is former Head of the Department of Religious Studies at the University of Stirling.

ROSALIND SHAW is Assistant Professor in the Department of Sociology and Anthropology, Tufts University, Medford/MA, USA.

NINIAN SMART is Professor of Comparative Religions at the University of California, Santa Barbara, and was from 1967–89 Professor of Religious Studies at the University of Lancaster.

STEWART R. SUTHERLAND is Vice-Chancellor of the University of London and was formerly Principal of King's College, London. He was editor of the journal *Religious Studies* from 1984–90.

TERENCE THOMAS is Senior Lecturer in Religious Studies at the Open University and currently Honorary Secretary of the British Association for the Study of Religions.

DESMOND TUTU is Anglican Archbishop of Cape Town, South Africa.

KEITH WARD is Professor of the History and Philosophy of Religion in the Department of Theology and Religious Studies, King's College, University of London. He is also Chairman of the World Congress of Faiths and co-editor of *Religious Studies*.

ANDREW WALLS was formerly Professor and Head of the Department of Religious Studies, University of Aberdeen, and editor of the *Journal of Religion in Africa* until 1985. He is now Director of the Centre for the Study of Christianity in the Non-Western World at New College, University of Edinburgh.

MAURICE WILES is Regius Professor of Divinity, Christ Church, Oxford.

CYRIL G. WILLIAMS is Professor Emeritus at St David's University College, University of Wales, Lampeter.

PAUL WILLIAMS is Lecturer in Indo-Tibetan Studies in the Department of Theology and Religious Studies, University of Bristol.

INDEX

Abbott, J., 151
Adams, D., 271, 274
African religions,
    Christianity, 201–210
    Islam in sub-Saharan Africa, 211–220
    new religious movements, 192–200
    'Traditional', 181–191
Agbebi, Mojola, 203
Agreed Syllabus Conferences, 103, 104
Agreed Syllabuses, 104, 105, 107, 108
Ajayi, Jacob, 203
Akwaowo, A. O., 197
al-Hajj, Muhammad, 213
Al-Maghili, A. K., 215
Ali, Sheikh Anas Al-Sheikh, 52
Alistair Hardy Research Centre, 238–239, *see also* Religious Experience Research Unit
Allsop, Bruce, 72, 73
Ally, Mashuq, 52
American Academy of Religion, 275, 279, 301
Andrezejewski, B. W., 216
Apostolos-Cappadona, D., 271, 274
Aquinas, Thomas, St, 290
Ardener, Edwin, 191
Ardener, Shirley, 191
Aristotle, 227–228
art, role of, in religion, 261–265
Arthur, C., 52
arts, the,
    and Buddhism, 258, 261, 262
    and Christianity, 259, 260, 262, 264, 267–268, 271–272
    and Hinduism, 259, 262, 265, 266–267
    and Islam, 269–271, 273
    and the nude, 267–269
    and primal religions, 266, 273
    and symbolism, 260–261
    and Zoroastrianism, 262
Asad, Talal, 186
Ashoka, Emperor, 158
Askari, Hasan, 141
Aurora, G. S., 177
Austin, Jack, 136
Avalon, A., 152
Ayandele, Emmanuel, 203
Ayer, A. J., 223, 225, 227, 230

Babalola, 193
Badawi, Zaki, 96, 138
Badham, Paul, 52

Baeta, Christian, 203
Bajaj, S. K., 179
Bakker, Jim and Tammy, 197
Ballard, Roger and Catherine, 177
Bareau, A., 159–160, 167
Barrett, D. B., 193, 199, 205, 210
Barrier, N. Gerald, 173, 179
Barth, K., 35, 87, 132, 222, 303
Bastow, David, 44
Baum, Robert, 190
Bechert, H., 158, 159, 167
Bediako, Kwame, 42
Bell, Peter, 135
Bell, Richard, 34
Bennett, Clinton, 135
Bertocci, Peter, 233
Bhattacharya, D., 151
Bivar, A. D., 213
Bleeker, C. J., 133
Bloom, Alfred, 164
Blythin, I., 48, 50, 51, 54
Bocking, Brian, 44
Boin-Webb, Sara, 156
Boulaga, F. Eboussi, 209
Boulay, Shirley de, 11
Bouquet, A. C., 301
Bowker, John, 63, 65
Boyd, J., 219, 220
Braithwaite, R. B., 224
Brandon, G. S. F., 5
Braybrooke, M., 132–141, 136, 141
Brenner, L., 218
British Association for the Study of Religions, 275
Brockington, J. L., 43, 149, 155
Brown, Alan, 113
Brown, Antoinette, 278
Brown, Peter, 31
Brubaker, R., 153
Bruner, Jerome, 106
Brunner, E., 222
Buchanan, Constance, 279
Buchignani, Norman, 177, 179
Buddhism, 156–167
    and the arts, 258, 261, 262
    in China and Japan, 163–164
    early history, 159–160
    and Mahasamghikas, 159
    Mahayana, 161–163
    Theravada, 160–161
Buddhist philosophy,
    Madhyamaka, 164–165, 166

Walker, Joan Hazelden, 63
Walls, A. F., 5, 32–45, 42, 43, 70, 183
Ward, Keith, 221–231, 231
Watkinson, Anthony, 74
Watson, Brenda, 120
Watson, James L., 179
Watt, J., 53
Watt, W. Montgomery, 34, 43
Weber, Max, 236
Webster, D., 116
Webster, James, 203
Weightman, Simon, 61
Welbourn, F. W., 195, 199, 204, 205
Welch, Holmes, 163
Welch, James, 10
Weller, John, 206
Weller, Paul, 141
Werblowsky, Zwi, 133
Westerlund, David, 209
Westphal-Hellbusch, S., 153
Whaling, F., 43, 66, 149
Wiles, Maurice F., 7–9, 10
Wilks, Ivor, 212
Williams, Cyril G., 46–56, 49, 51, 55
Williams, D., 272, 274
Williams of Pantycelyn, William, 55
Williams, Paul, 156–167, 167
Williams, R. B., 155
Williams, Roger, 234, 235

Williams, Rowland, 51
Wilshire, B., 235, 241
Wilson, John, 73
Wittgenstein, L. J. J., 225
women and religion *see* gender studies
Woman in Religious Education, 280
Wood, A., 113
Wood, H. G., 24
Woods, Richard, 253
World Academy of Religion, 17, 305
World Conference on Religion and Peace, 134, 135, 137
World Congress of Faiths, 132, 133, 137
worship, school, and the Education Reform Act (1988), 117–131
Wyatt, Nicholas, 41, 42

Xavier, Francis, St, 302

Zaehner, R. C., 23, 61, 149, 151, 155, 174, 245, 246, 248, 250, 251, 253
Zaki, Yakub, 141
Zaleski, Carol, 249
Zdravchev, L., 296, 298
Zoroastrianism, and the arts, 262
Zürcher, Erich, 163
Zvelebil, K., 151

KING ALFRED'S COLLEGE
LIBRARY